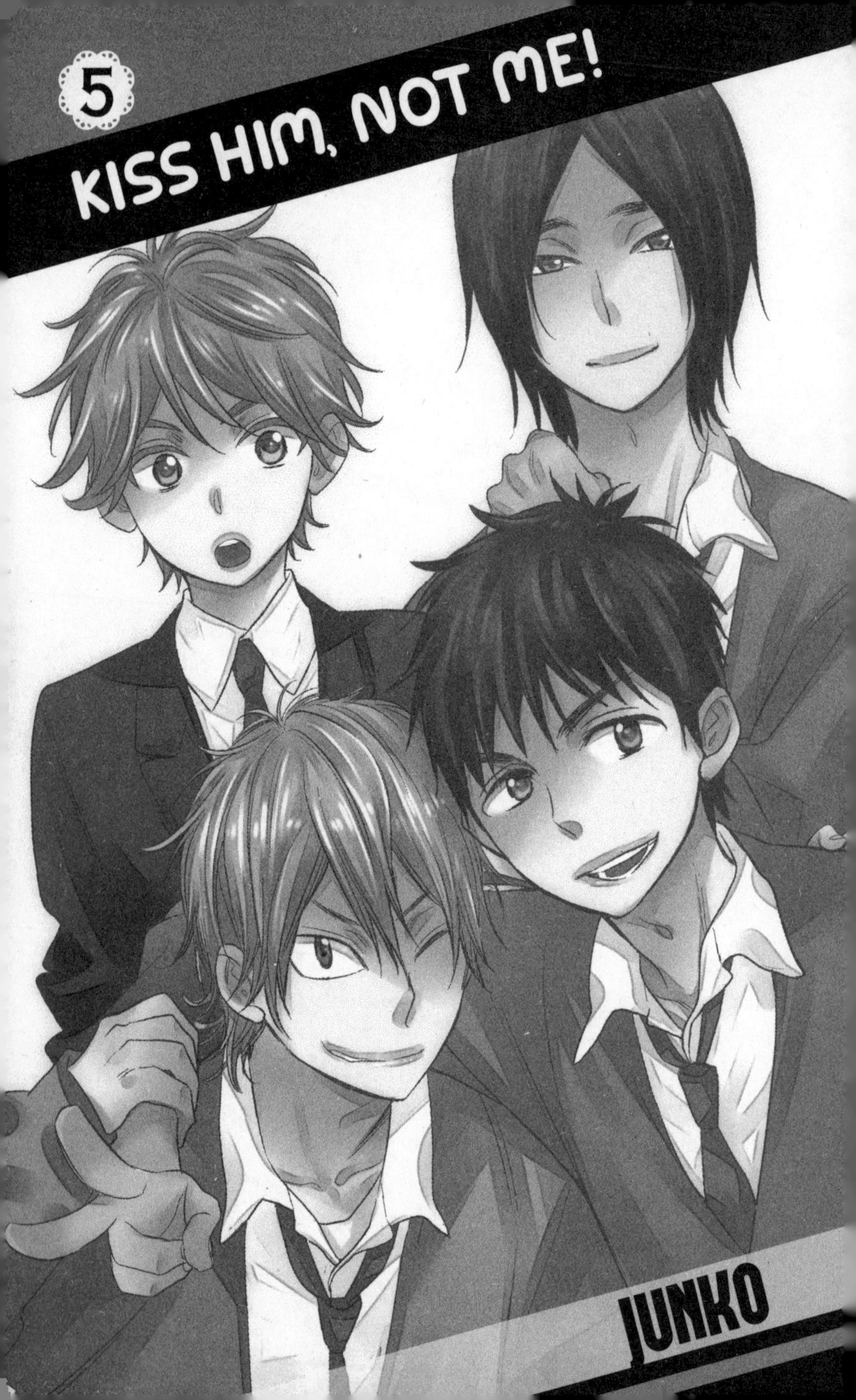
5
KISS HIM, NOT ME!
JUNKO

CONTENTS

#16 4
#17 TREASURE MAP 43
#18 BROTHER, ATTACK 79
#19 BROTHER, UNRIVALED 115
#20 DUEL BETWEEN BROTHERS 151
THE "KISS HIM, NOT ME" POST-RECORDING ·· 151

STORY

DURING THE SUMMER BREAK, **KAE** AND THE GANG END UP **STAYING** AT **SHIMA'S** COTTAGE.

SHINOMIYA, WHO WANTS TO SHOW **KAE** HIS MASCULINE SIDE, GETS PUMPED UP ABOUT SURFING AND BBQ PREP, BUT HE **FAILS MISERABLY**! MORTIFIED, HE RUNS OFF INTO THE FOREST. **KAE** FINDS **SHINOMIYA**, AND TOGETHER, THEY TRY TO RETURN TO THE COTTAGE, ONLY TO BE STUCK IN A SUDDEN DOWNPOUR! THEY TAKE SHELTER IN AN ABANDONED BUILD-ING, BUT THEY MEET THE TWO PUNKS WHO HAD PICKED FIGHTS WITH THEM AT THE BEACH! ALTHOUGH **SHINOMIYA** TRIES HIS BEST TO PROTECT **KAE**, IT'S THEIR FOUR FRIENDS WHO COME TO THE **RESCUE**...! BUT DESPITE ALL THIS, THE KLUTZY **SHINOMIYA** THOUGHT TO HIMSELF, "I'M NOT AS STRONG AS THE OTHER THREE, BUT **I DON'T WANT TO GIVE UP KAE TO ANYONE!**"

I ♥ BL

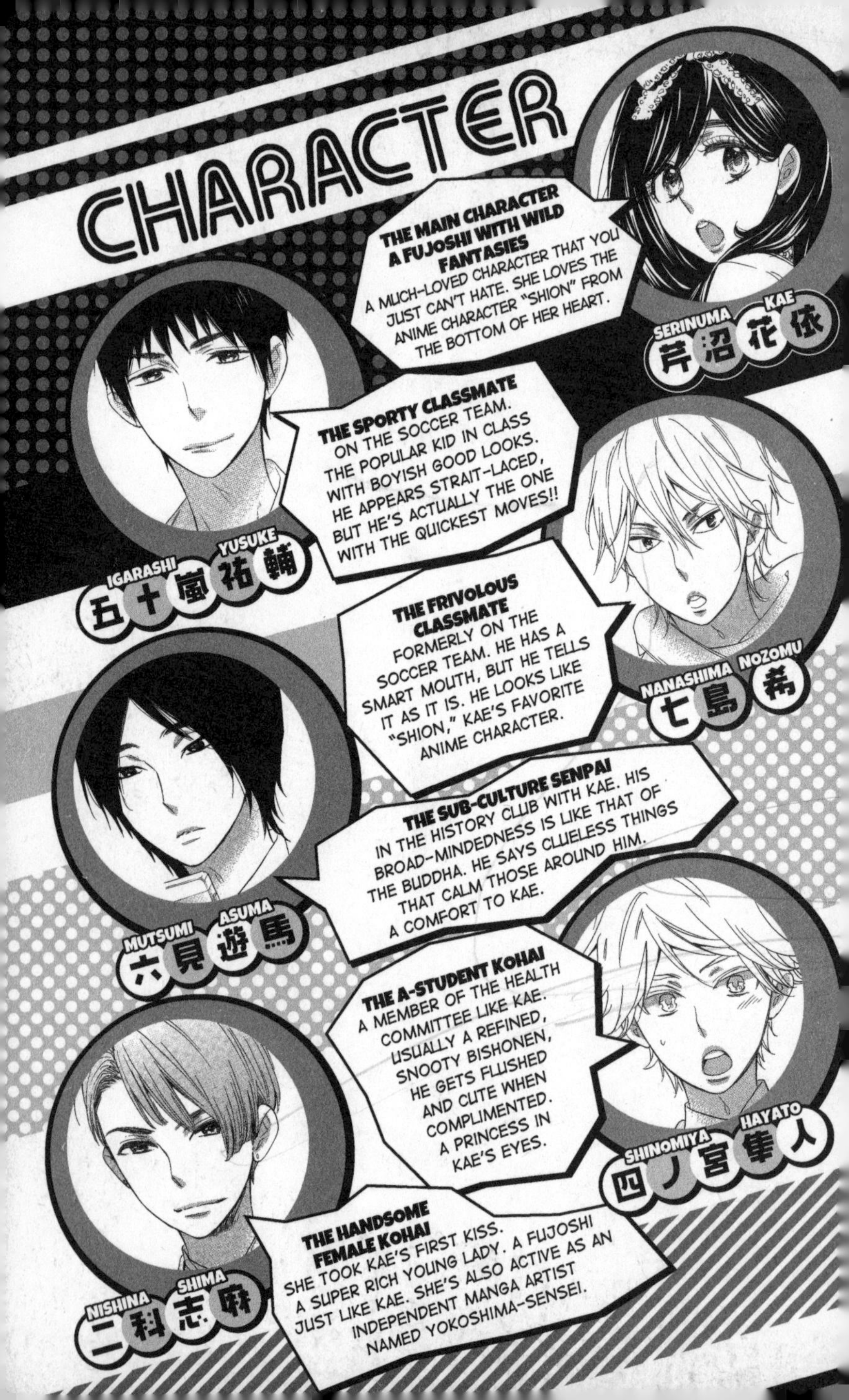
CHARACTER
THE MAIN CHARACTER A FUJOSHI WITH WILD FANTASIES
A MUCH-LOVED CHARACTER THAT YOU JUST CAN'T HATE. SHE LOVES THE ANIME CHARACTER "SHION" FROM THE BOTTOM OF HER HEART.
SERINUMA KAE
芹沼花依
THE SPORTY CLASSMATE
ON THE SOCCER TEAM. THE POPULAR KID IN CLASS WITH BOYISH GOOD LOOKS. HE APPEARS STRAIT-LACED, BUT HE'S ACTUALLY THE ONE WITH THE QUICKEST MOVES!!
IGARASHI YUSUKE
五十嵐祐輔
THE FRIVOLOUS CLASSMATE
FORMERLY ON THE SOCCER TEAM. HE HAS A SMART MOUTH, BUT HE TELLS IT AS IT IS. HE LOOKS LIKE "SHION," KAE'S FAVORITE ANIME CHARACTER.
NANASHIMA NOZOMU
七島希
THE SUB-CULTURE SENPAI
IN THE HISTORY CLUB WITH KAE. HIS BROAD-MINDEDNESS IS LIKE THAT OF THE BUDDHA. HE SAYS CLUELESS THINGS THAT CALM THOSE AROUND HIM. A COMFORT TO KAE.
MUTSUMI ASUMA
六見遊馬
THE A-STUDENT KOHAI
A MEMBER OF THE HEALTH COMMITTEE LIKE KAE. USUALLY A REFINED, SNOOTY BISHONEN, HE GETS FLUSHED AND CUTE WHEN COMPLIMENTED. A PRINCESS IN KAE'S EYES.
SHINOMIYA HAYATO
四ノ宮隼人
THE HANDSOME FEMALE KOHAI
SHE TOOK KAE'S FIRST KISS. A SUPER RICH YOUNG LADY. A FUJOSHI JUST LIKE KAE. SHE'S ALSO ACTIVE AS AN INDEPENDENT MANGA ARTIST NAMED YOKOSHIMA-SENSEI.
NISHINA SHIMA
二科志麻

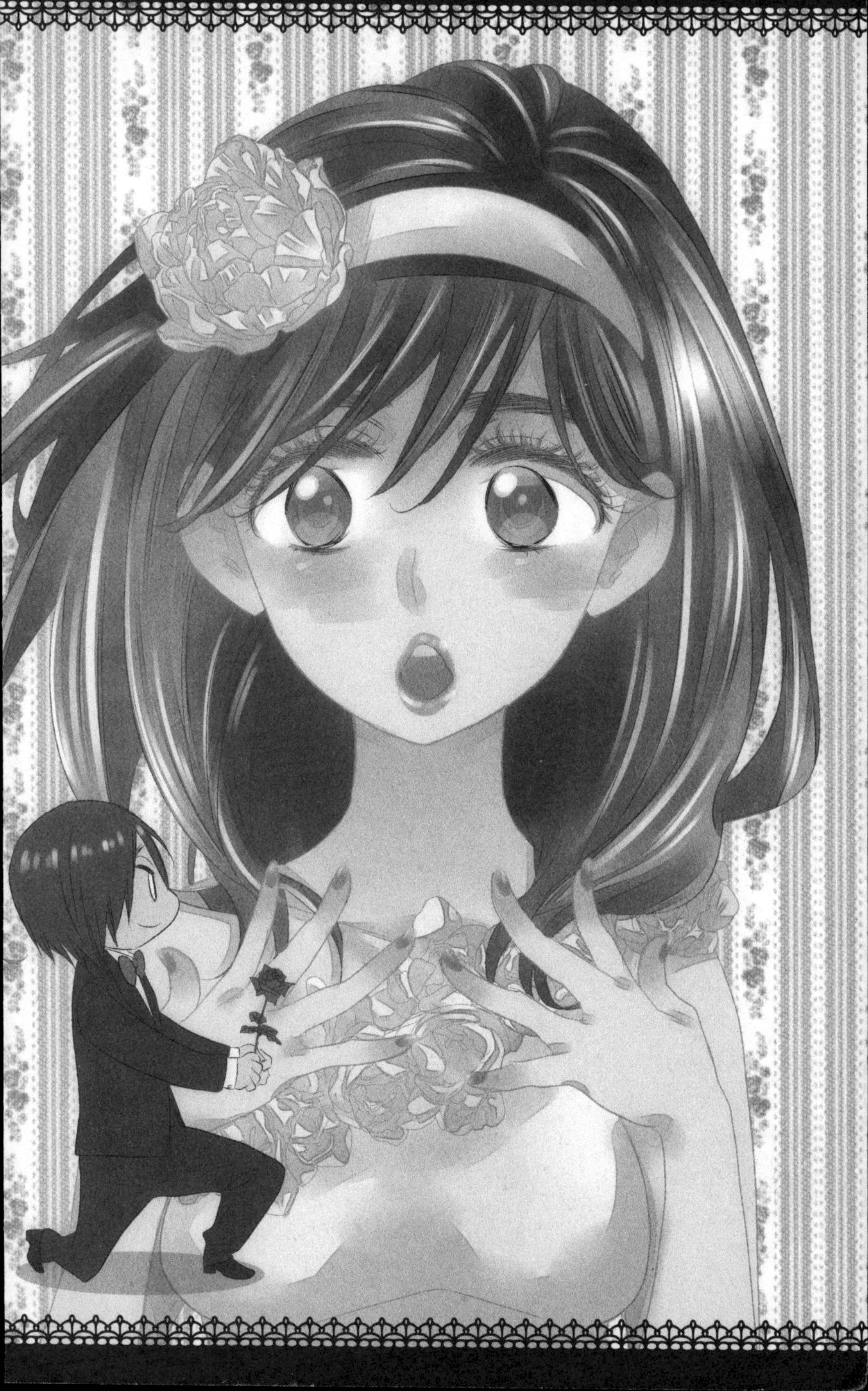

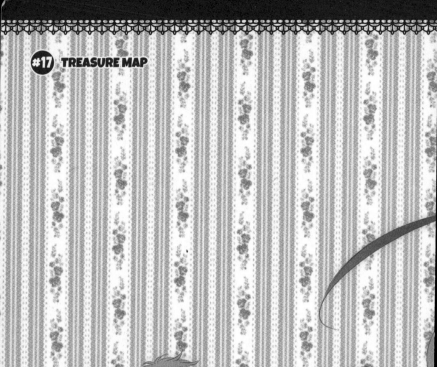

#17 TREASURE MAP

KiSS HiM, NOT ME!

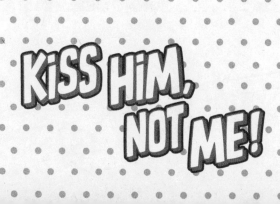

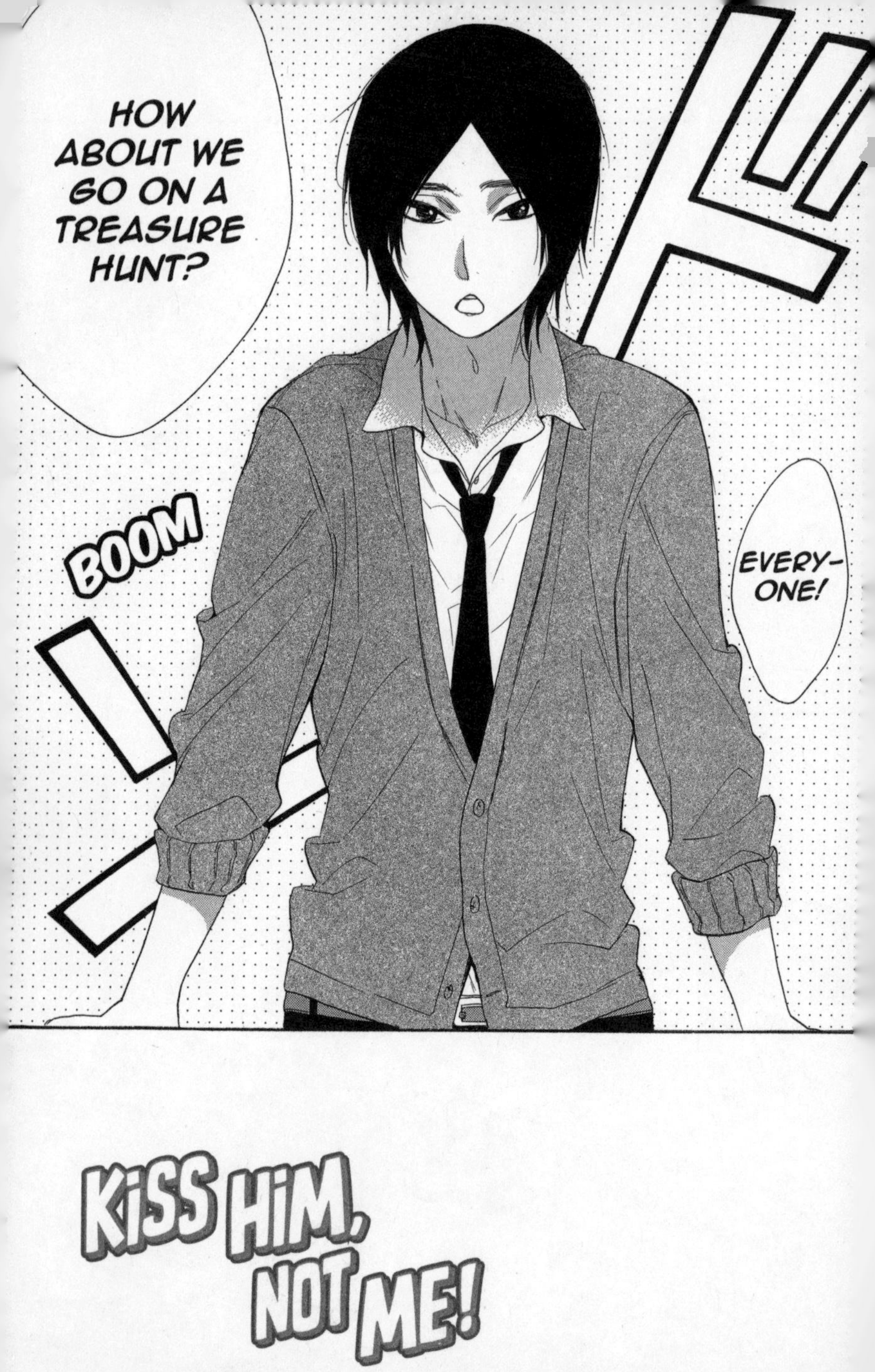
EVERY-ONE!
HOW ABOUT WE GO ON A TREASURE HUNT?
BOOM

KiSS HiM, NOT ME!

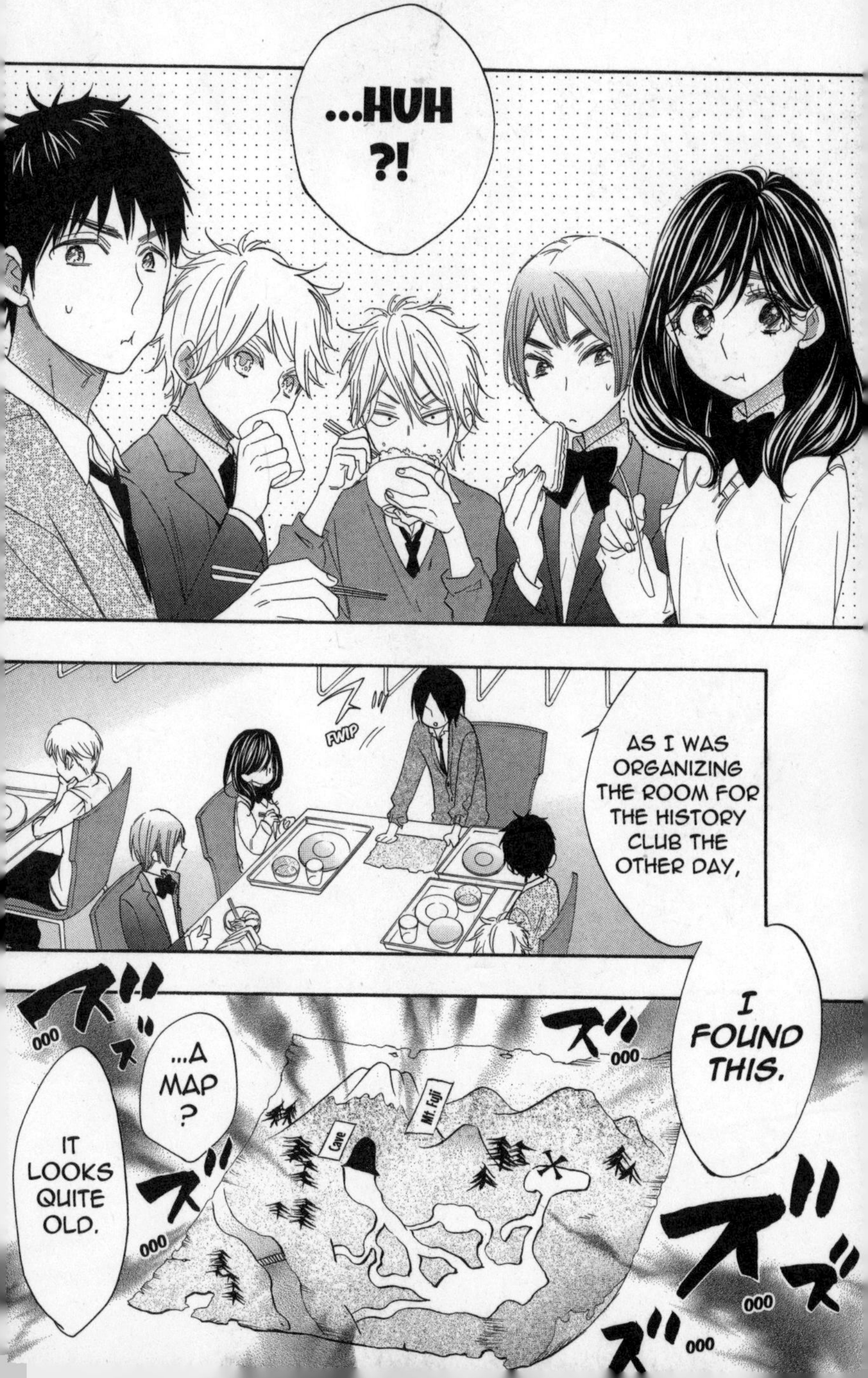
...HUH ?!
FWIP
AS I WAS ORGANIZING THE ROOM FOR THE HISTORY CLUB THE OTHER DAY,
I FOUND THIS.
...A MAP ?
IT LOOKS QUITE OLD.
Mt. Fuji
Cave

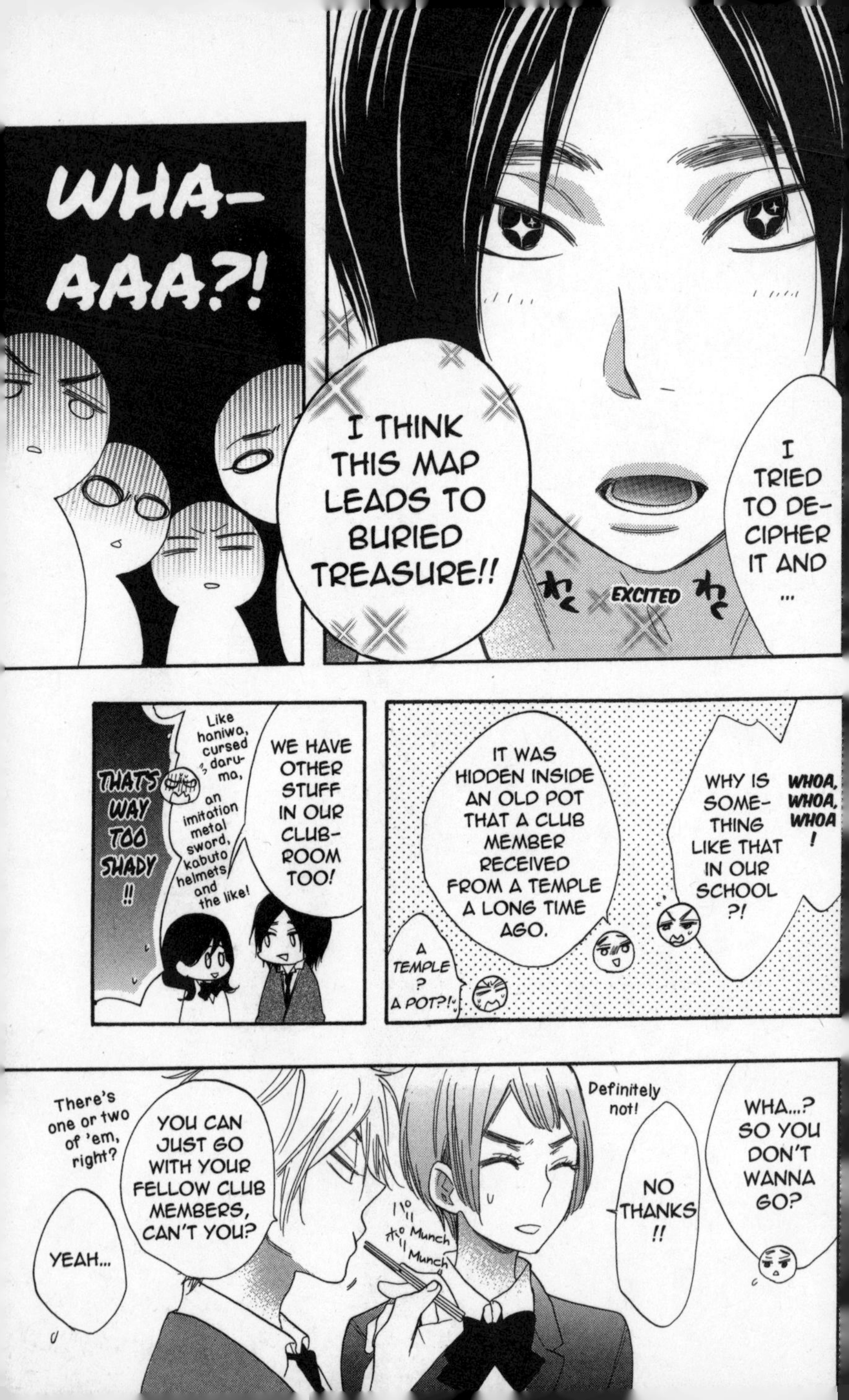
I TRIED TO DE-CIPHER IT AND ...
I THINK THIS MAP LEADS TO BURIED TREASURE!!
わく EXCITED わく
WHA-AAA?!
WHOA, WHOA, WHOA!
WHY IS SOME-THING LIKE THAT IN OUR SCHOOL ?!
IT WAS HIDDEN INSIDE AN OLD POT THAT A CLUB MEMBER RECEIVED FROM A TEMPLE A LONG TIME AGO.
A TEMPLE? A POT?!
WE HAVE OTHER STUFF IN OUR CLUB-ROOM TOO!
Like haniwa, cursed daru-ma, an imitation metal sword, kabuto helmets and the like!
THAT'S WAY TOO SHADY!!
WHA...? SO YOU DON'T WANNA GO?
Definitely not!
NO THANKS!!
パク Munch パク Munch
YOU CAN JUST GO WITH YOUR FELLOW CLUB MEMBERS, CAN'T YOU?
There's one or two of 'em, right?
YEAH...

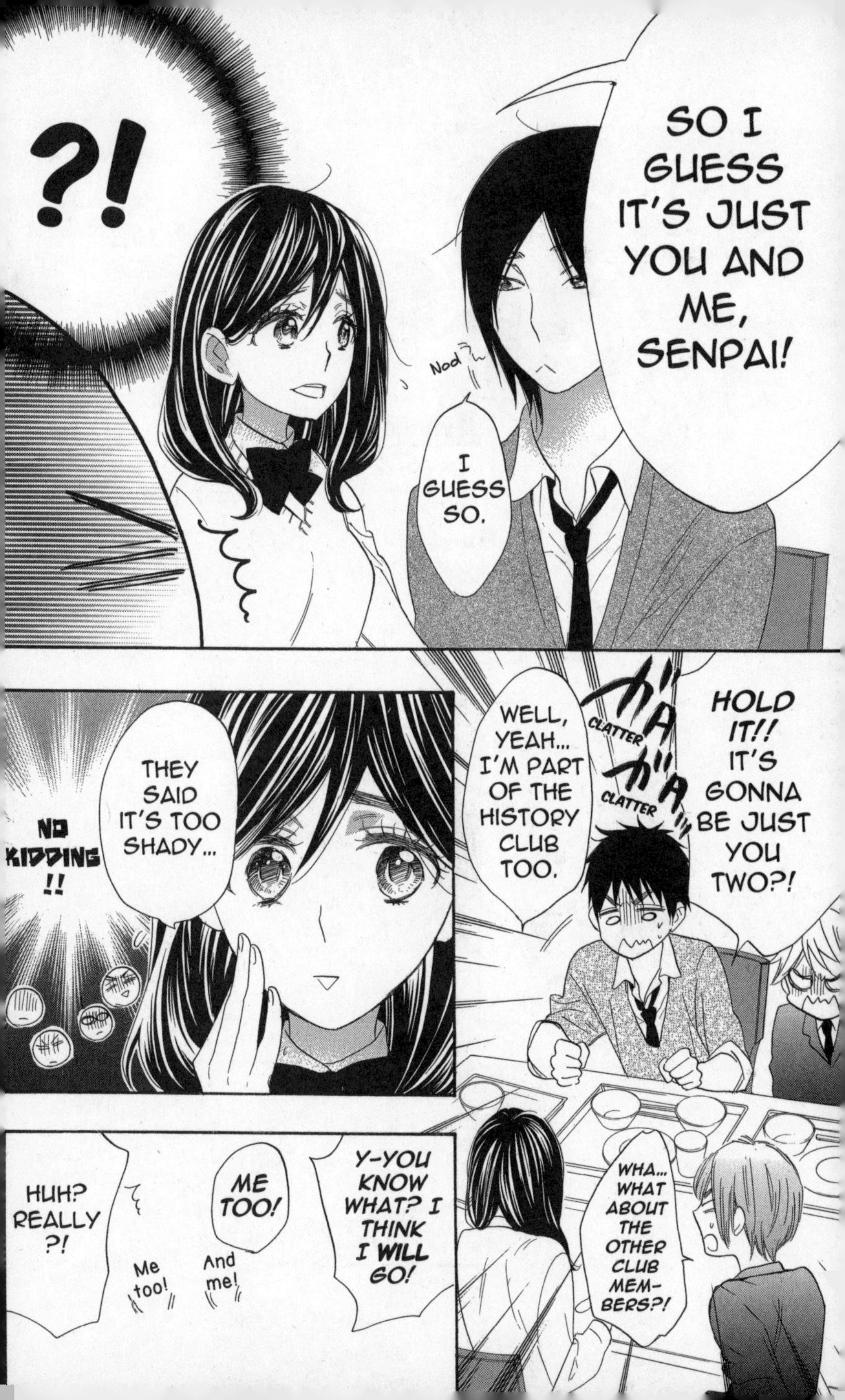
SO I GUESS IT'S JUST YOU AND ME, SENPAI!
Nod
I GUESS SO.
?!
HOLD IT!! IT'S GONNA BE JUST YOU TWO?!
CLATTER
CLATTER
WELL, YEAH... I'M PART OF THE HISTORY CLUB TOO.
THEY SAID IT'S TOO SHADY...
NO KIDDING!!
WHA... WHAT ABOUT THE OTHER CLUB MEM-BERS?!
Y-YOU KNOW WHAT? I THINK I WILL GO!
ME TOO!
And me!
Me too!
HUH? REALLY?!

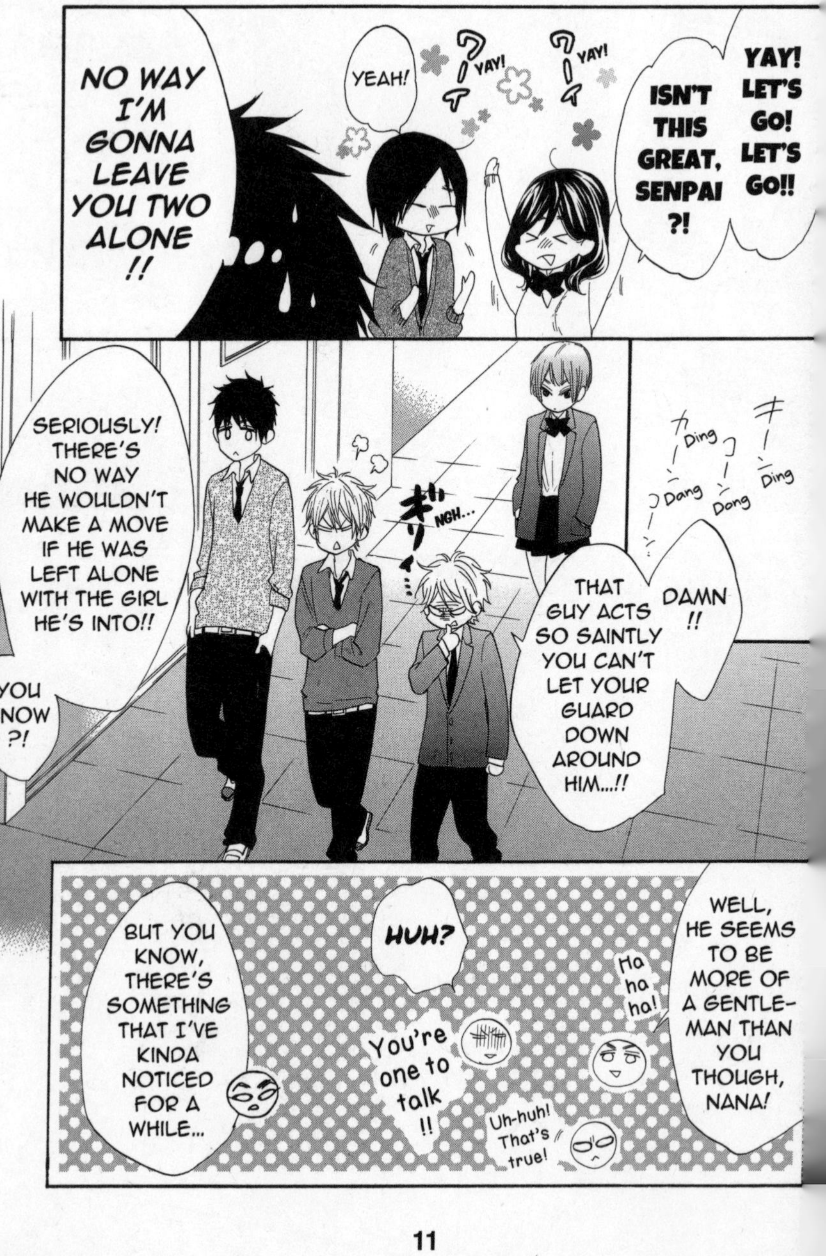
YAY! LET'S GO! LET'S GO!!
ISN'T THIS GREAT, SENPAI?!
YAY!
YAY!
YEAH!
NO WAY I'M GONNA LEAVE YOU TWO ALONE!!
Ding
Dong
Ding
Dang
DAMN!!
THAT GUY ACTS SO SAINTLY YOU CAN'T LET YOUR GUARD DOWN AROUND HIM...!!
NGH...
SERIOUSLY! THERE'S NO WAY HE WOULDN'T MAKE A MOVE IF HE WAS LEFT ALONE WITH THE GIRL HE'S INTO!!
YOU KNOW?!
WELL, HE SEEMS TO BE MORE OF A GENTLE-MAN THAN YOU THOUGH, NANA!
Ha ha ha!
HUH?
You're one to talk!!
Uh-huh! That's true!
BUT YOU KNOW, THERE'S SOMETHING THAT I'VE KINDA NOTICED FOR A WHILE...

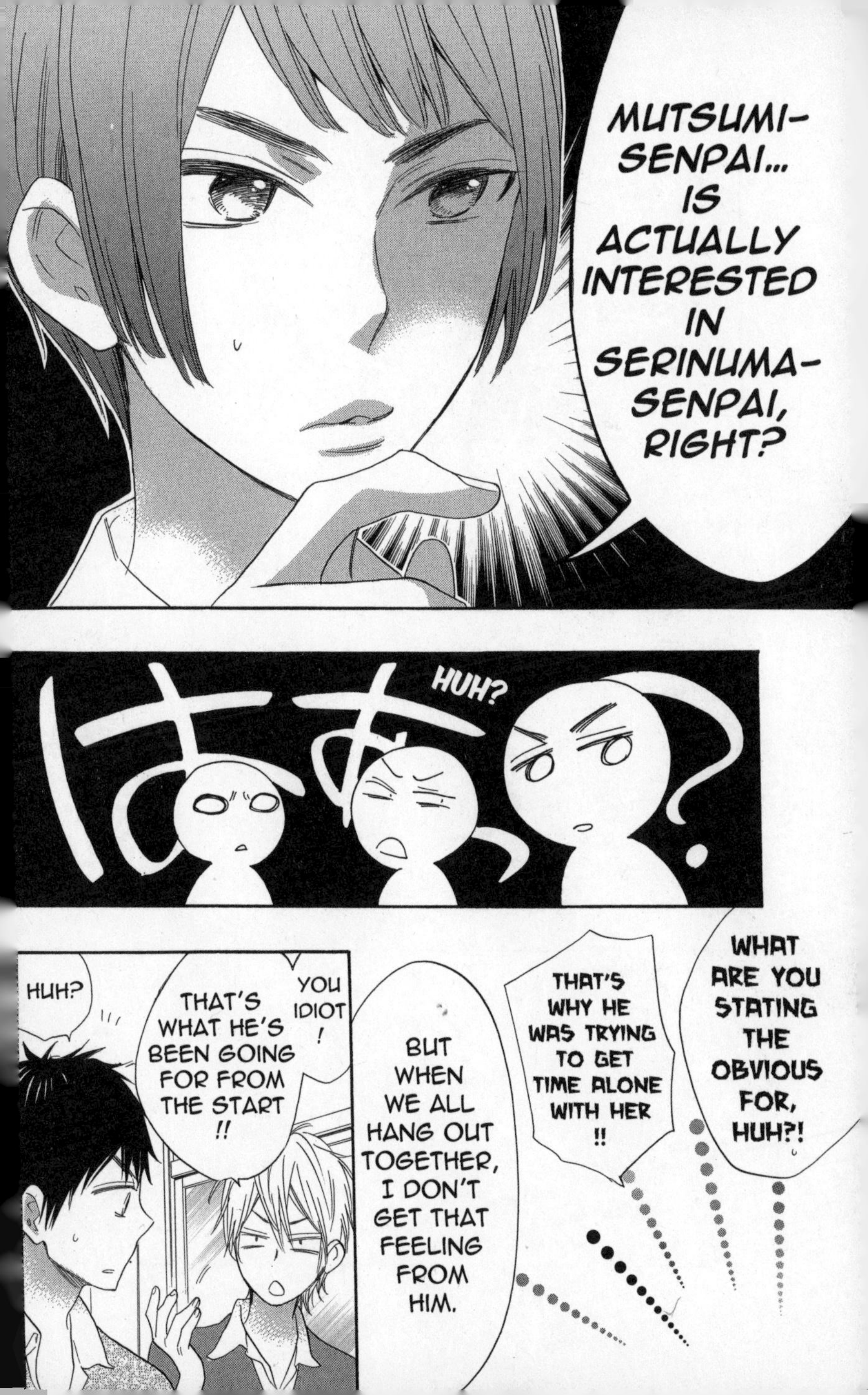
MUTSUMI-SENPAI... IS ACTUALLY INTERESTED IN SERINUMA-SENPAI, RIGHT?
はあっ?
HUH?
WHAT ARE YOU STATING THE OBVIOUS FOR, HUH?!
THAT'S WHY HE WAS TRYING TO GET TIME ALONE WITH HER!!
BUT WHEN WE ALL HANG OUT TOGETHER, I DON'T GET THAT FEELING FROM HIM.
YOU IDIOT!
THAT'S WHAT HE'S BEEN GOING FOR FROM THE START!!
HUH?

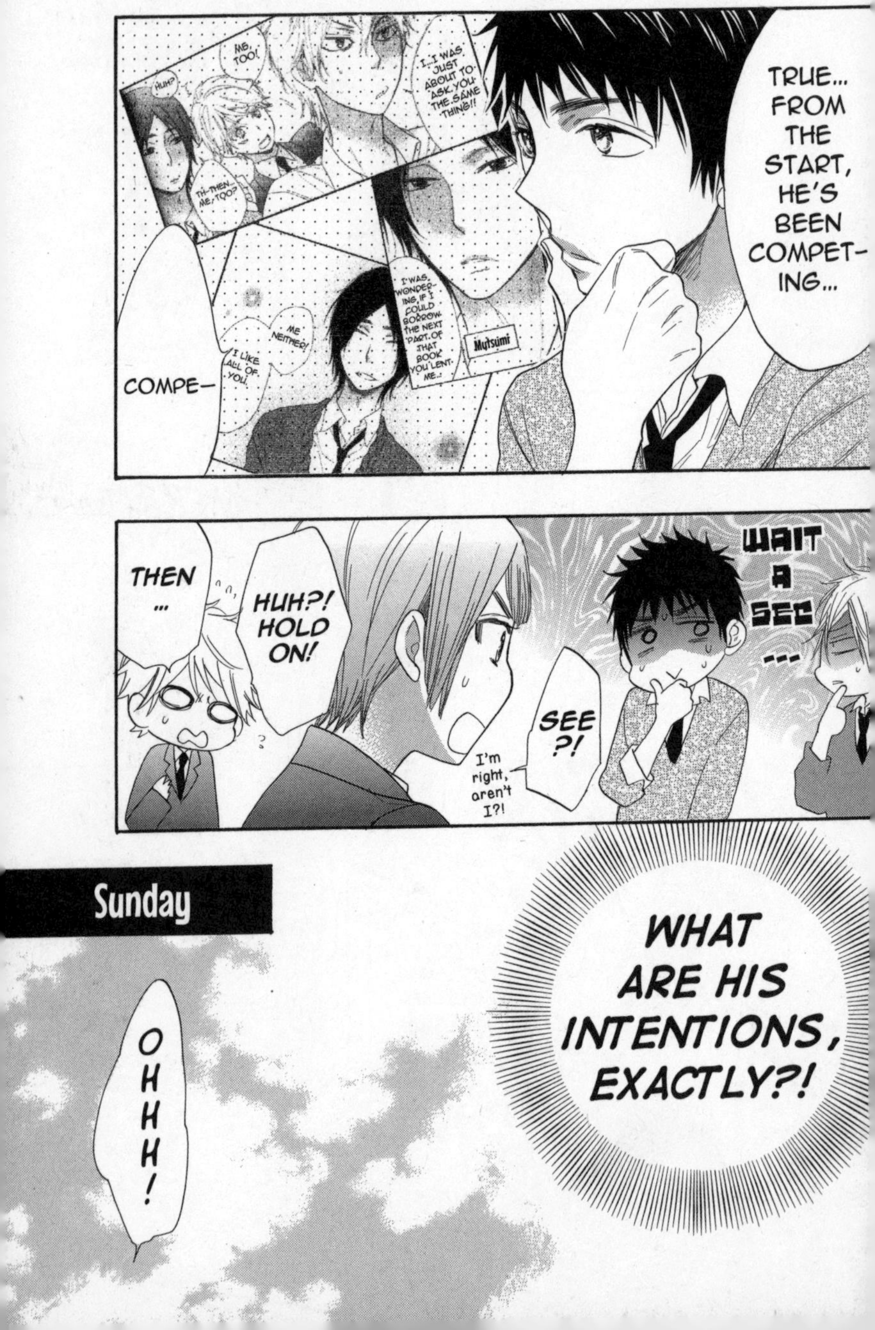
TRUE... FROM THE START, HE'S BEEN COMPETING...
I...I WAS JUST ABOUT TO ASK YOU THE SAME THING!!
ME, TOO!
HUH?
TH-THEN... ME, TOO?
I WAS WONDERING IF I COULD BORROW THE NEXT PART OF THAT BOOK YOU LENT ME...
Mutsumi
ME NEITHER!
I LIKE ALL OF YOU.
COMPE—
WAIT A SEC ---
SEE?!
I'm right, aren't I?!
HUH?! HOLD ON!
THEN ...
WHAT ARE HIS INTENTIONS, EXACTLY?!
Sunday
OHHH!

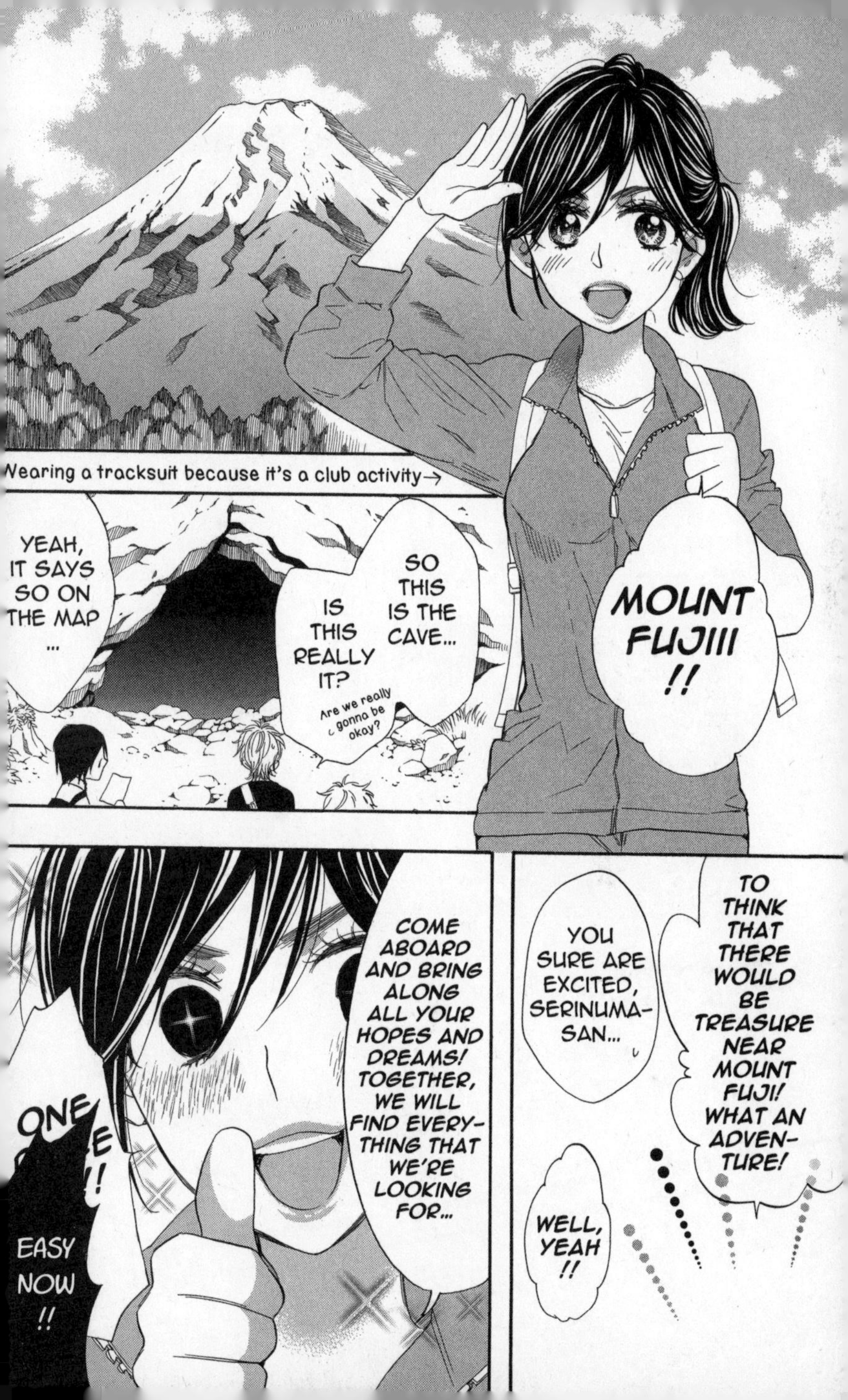
MOUNT FUJIII !!
Wearing a tracksuit because it's a club activity→
SO THIS IS THE CAVE...
IS THIS REALLY IT?
Are we really gonna be okay?
YEAH, IT SAYS SO ON THE MAP ...
TO THINK THAT THERE WOULD BE TREASURE NEAR MOUNT FUJI! WHAT AN ADVEN-TURE!
YOU SURE ARE EXCITED, SERINUMA-SAN...
WELL, YEAH !!
COME ABOARD AND BRING ALONG ALL YOUR HOPES AND DREAMS! TOGETHER, WE WILL FIND EVERY-THING THAT WE'RE LOOKING FOR...
EASY NOW !!

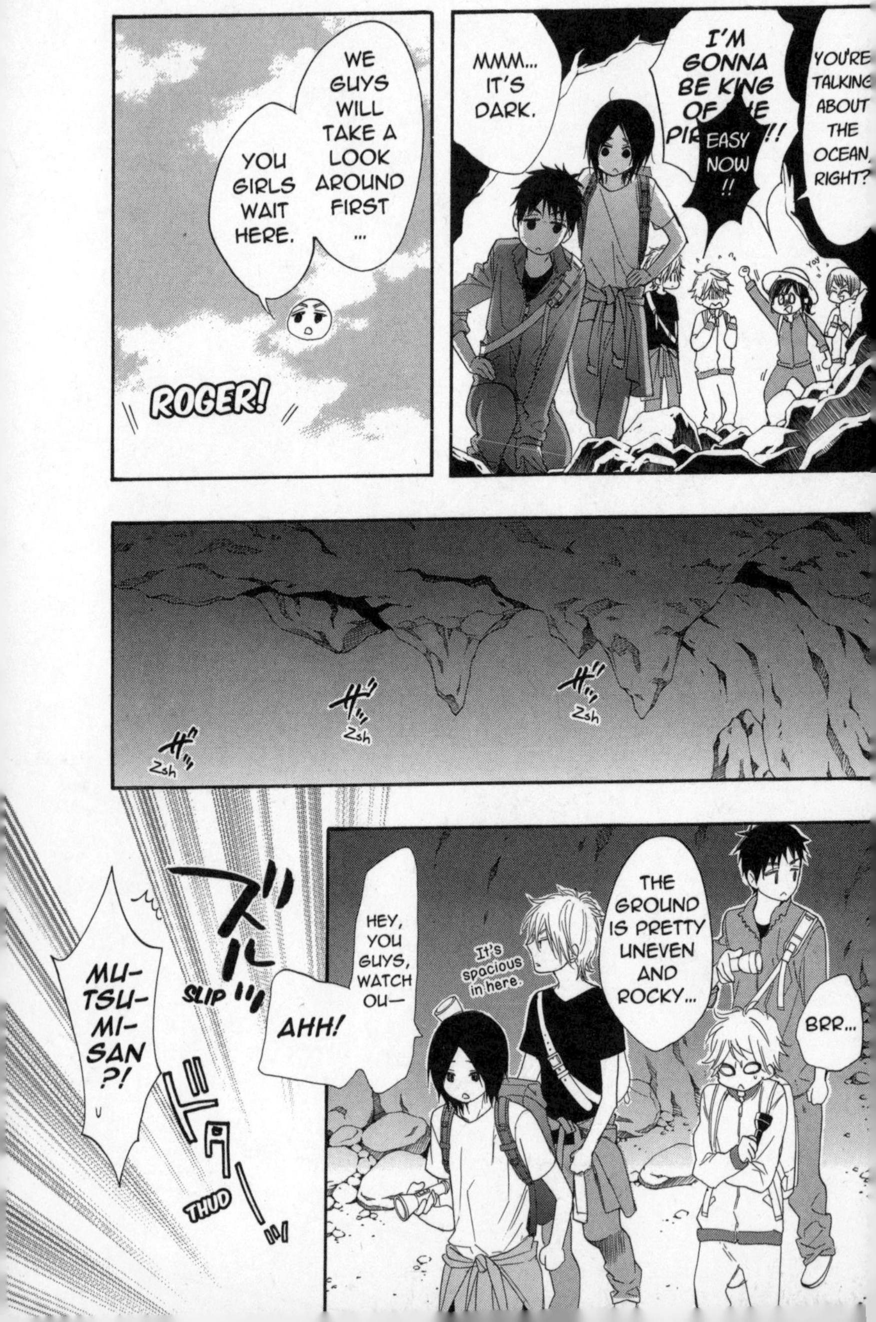
YOU'RE TALKING ABOUT THE OCEAN, RIGHT?
I'M GONNA BE KING OF PI !!
EASY NOW !!
Yay
MMM... IT'S DARK.
WE GUYS WILL TAKE A LOOK AROUND FIRST ...
YOU GIRLS WAIT HERE.
ROGER!
Zsh
Zsh
Zsh
BRR...
THE GROUND IS PRETTY UNEVEN AND ROCKY...
It's spacious in here.
HEY, YOU GUYS, WATCH OU—
AHH!
SLIP
THUD
MU-TSU-MI-SAN ?!

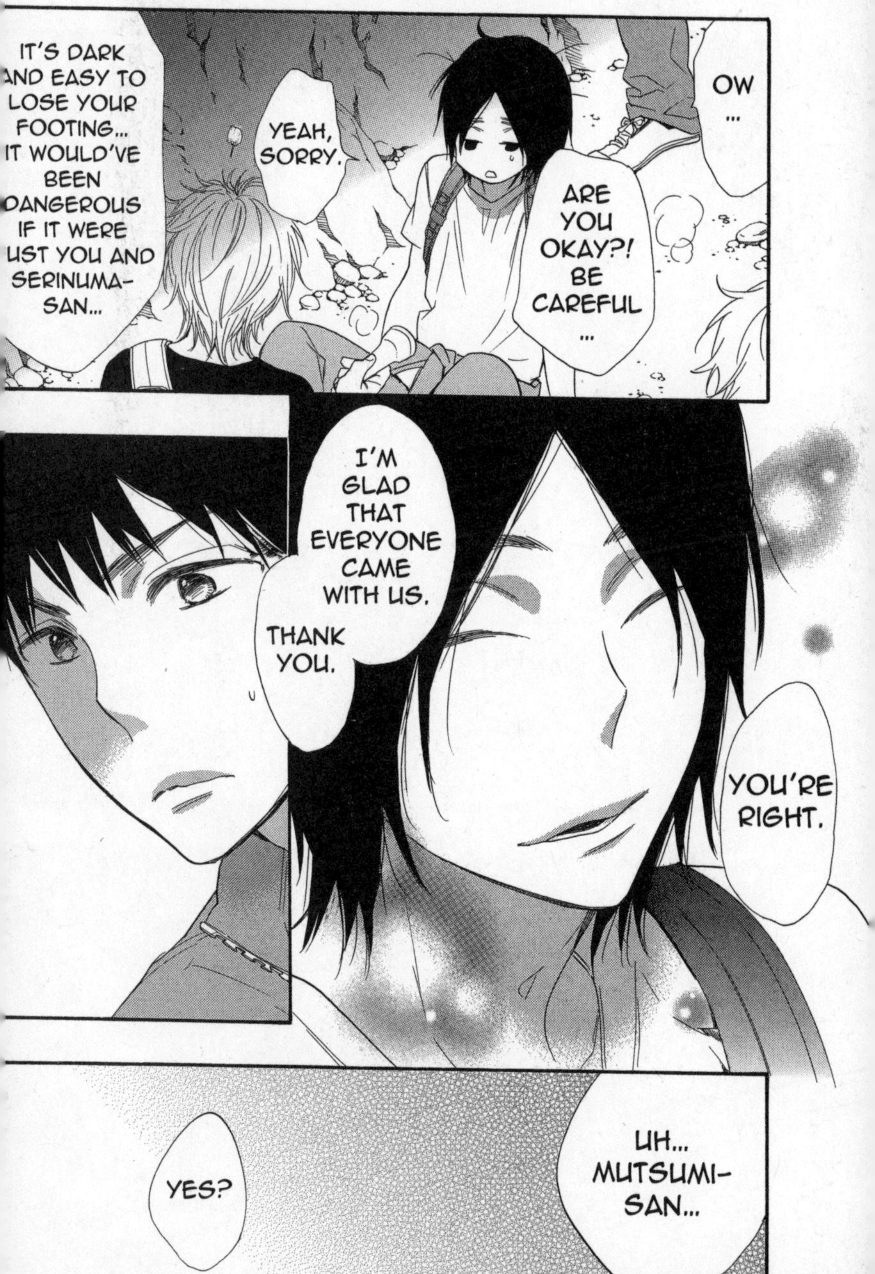
OW ...
ARE YOU OKAY?! BE CAREFUL ...
YEAH, SORRY.
IT'S DARK AND EASY TO LOSE YOUR FOOTING... IT WOULD'VE BEEN DANGEROUS IF IT WERE JUST YOU AND SERINUMA-SAN...
YOU'RE RIGHT.
I'M GLAD THAT EVERYONE CAME WITH US.
THANK YOU.
UH... MUTSUMI-SAN...
YES?

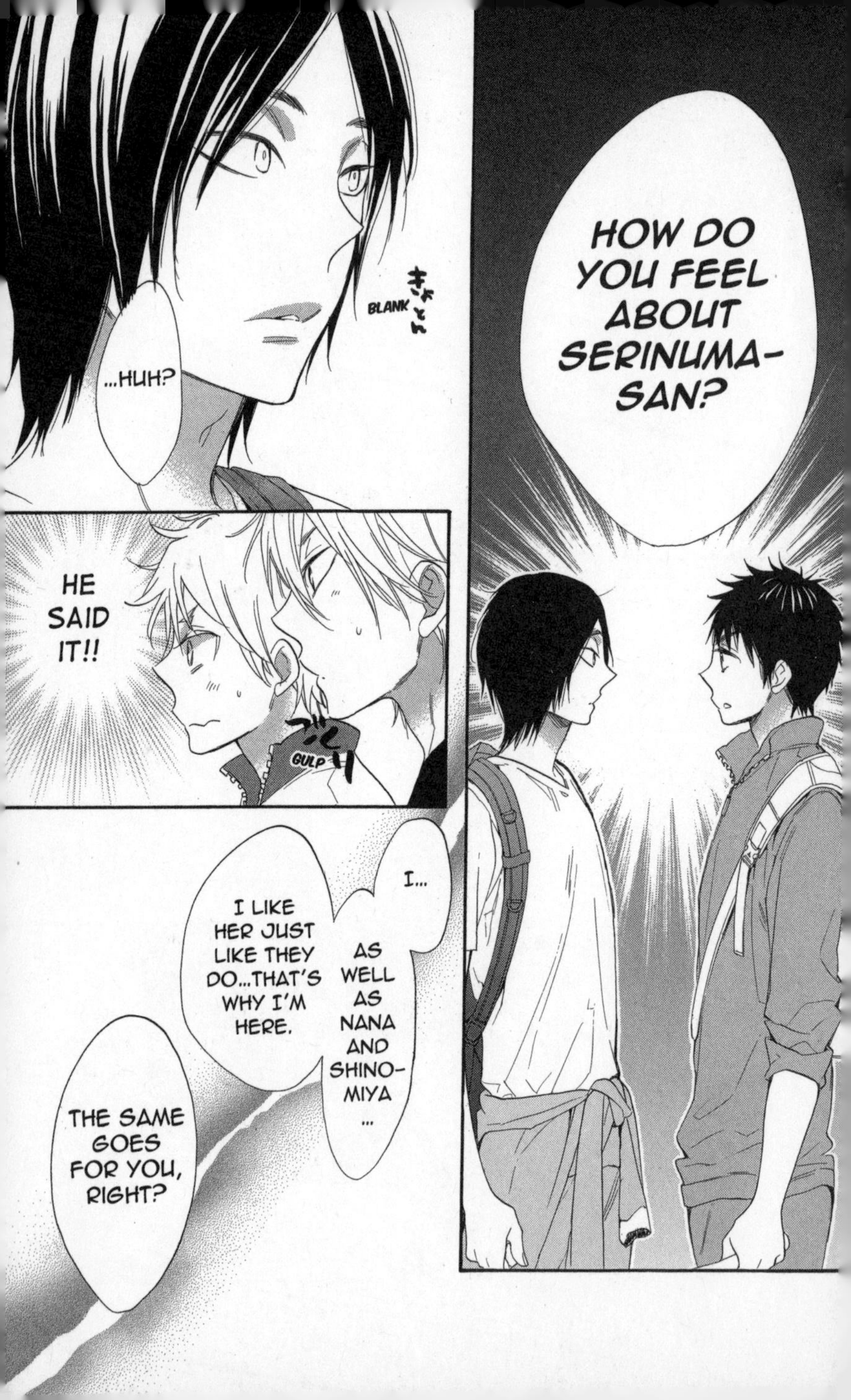
HOW DO YOU FEEL ABOUT SERINUMA-SAN?
BLANK
...HUH?
HE SAID IT!!
GULP
I...
AS WELL AS NANA AND SHINOMIYA...
I LIKE HER JUST LIKE THEY DO...THAT'S WHY I'M HERE.
THE SAME GOES FOR YOU, RIGHT?

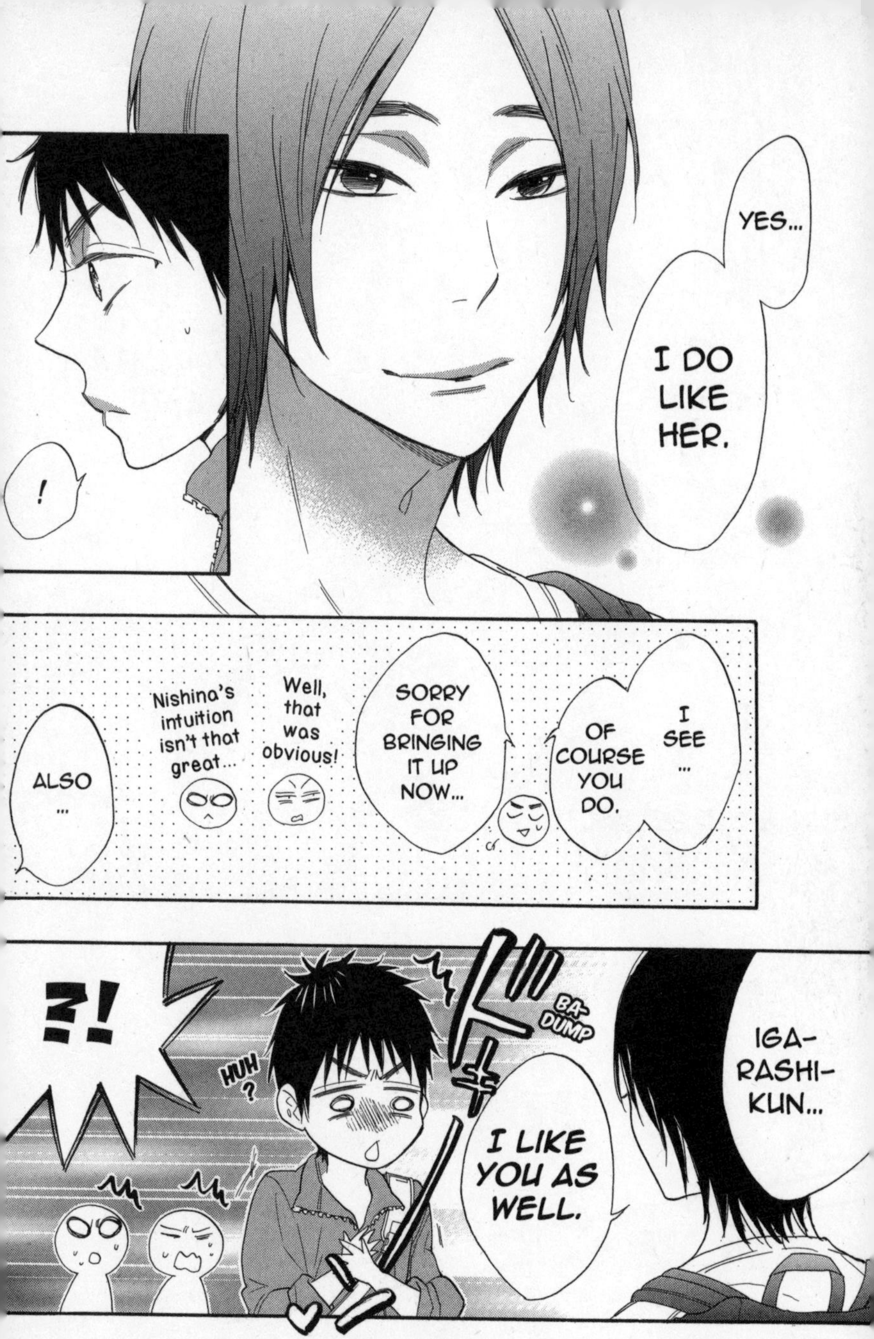
YES...
I DO LIKE HER.
!
I SEE ...
OF COURSE YOU DO.
SORRY FOR BRINGING IT UP NOW...
Well, that was obvious!
Nishina's intuition isn't that great...
ALSO ...
IGA-RASHI-KUN...
I LIKE YOU AS WELL.
BA-DUMP
HUH ?
?!

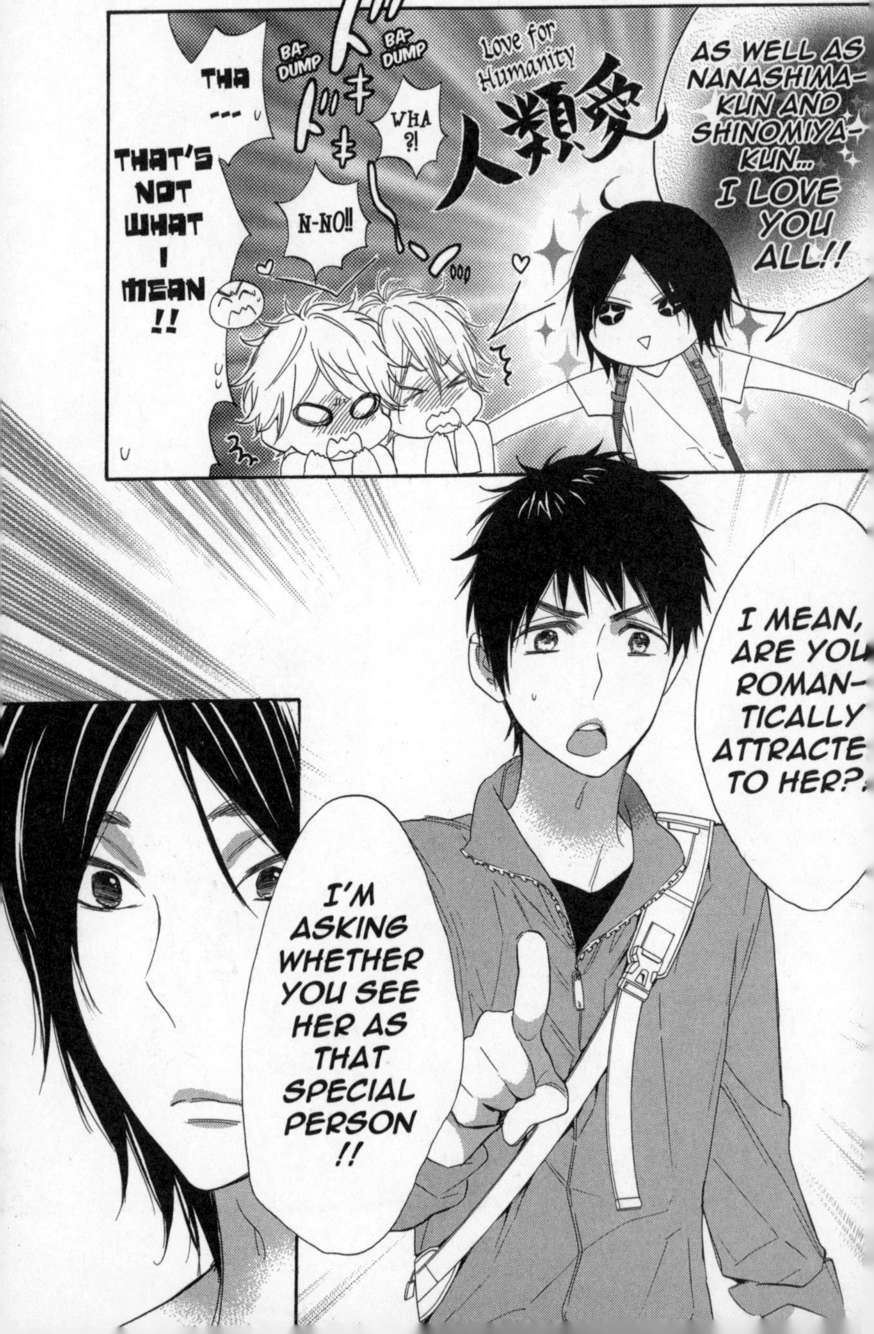
AS WELL AS NANASHIMA-KUN AND SHINOMIYA-KUN... I LOVE YOU ALL!!
Love for Humanity
人類愛
BA-DUMP
BA-DUMP
WHA ?!
N-NO!!
THA--- THAT'S NOT WHAT I MEAN!!
I MEAN, ARE YOU ROMAN-TICALLY ATTRACTE TO HER?
I'M ASKING WHETHER YOU SEE HER AS THAT SPECIAL PERSON!!

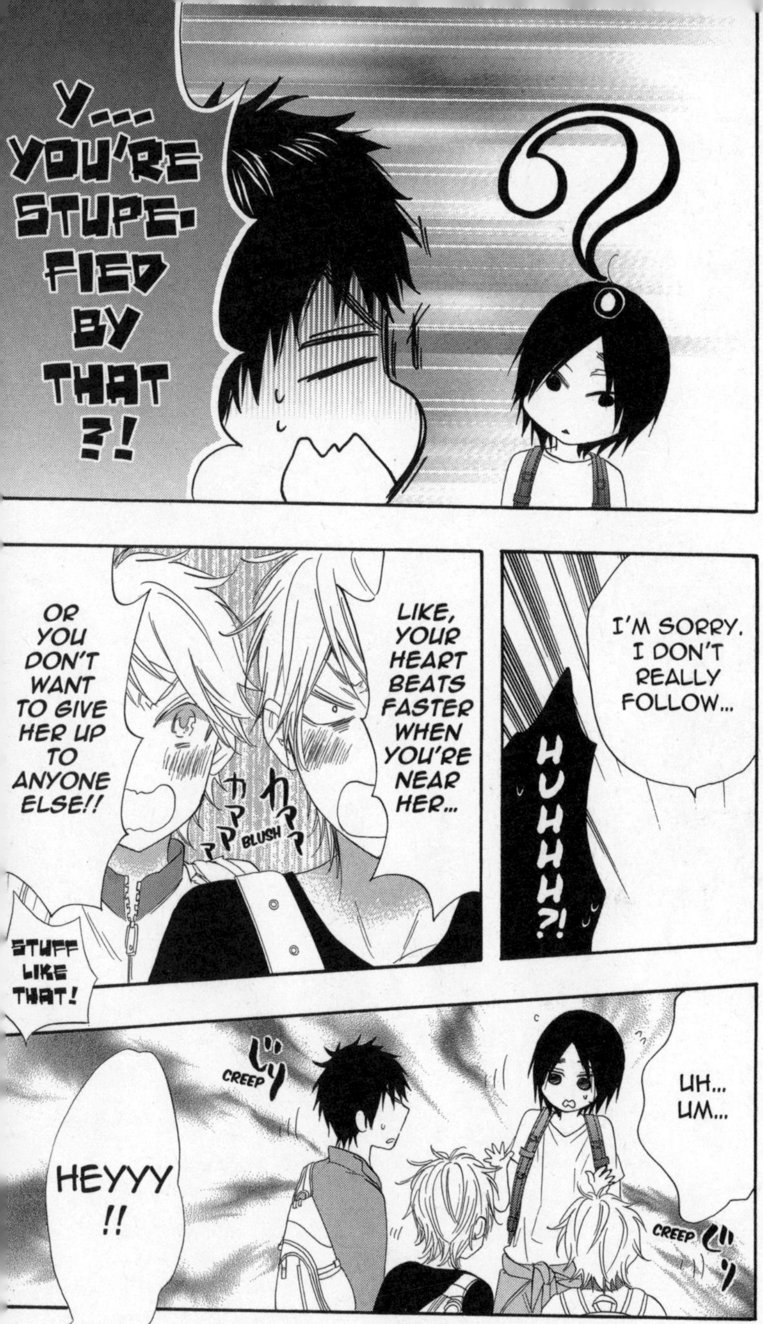
Y.... YOU'RE STUPE-FIED BY THAT?!
I'M SORRY. I DON'T REALLY FOLLOW...
HUHHHH?!
LIKE, YOUR HEART BEATS FASTER WHEN YOU'RE NEAR HER...
OR YOU DON'T WANT TO GIVE HER UP TO ANYONE ELSE!!
BLUSH
STUFF LIKE THAT!
UH... UM...
CREEP
CREEP
HEYYY!!

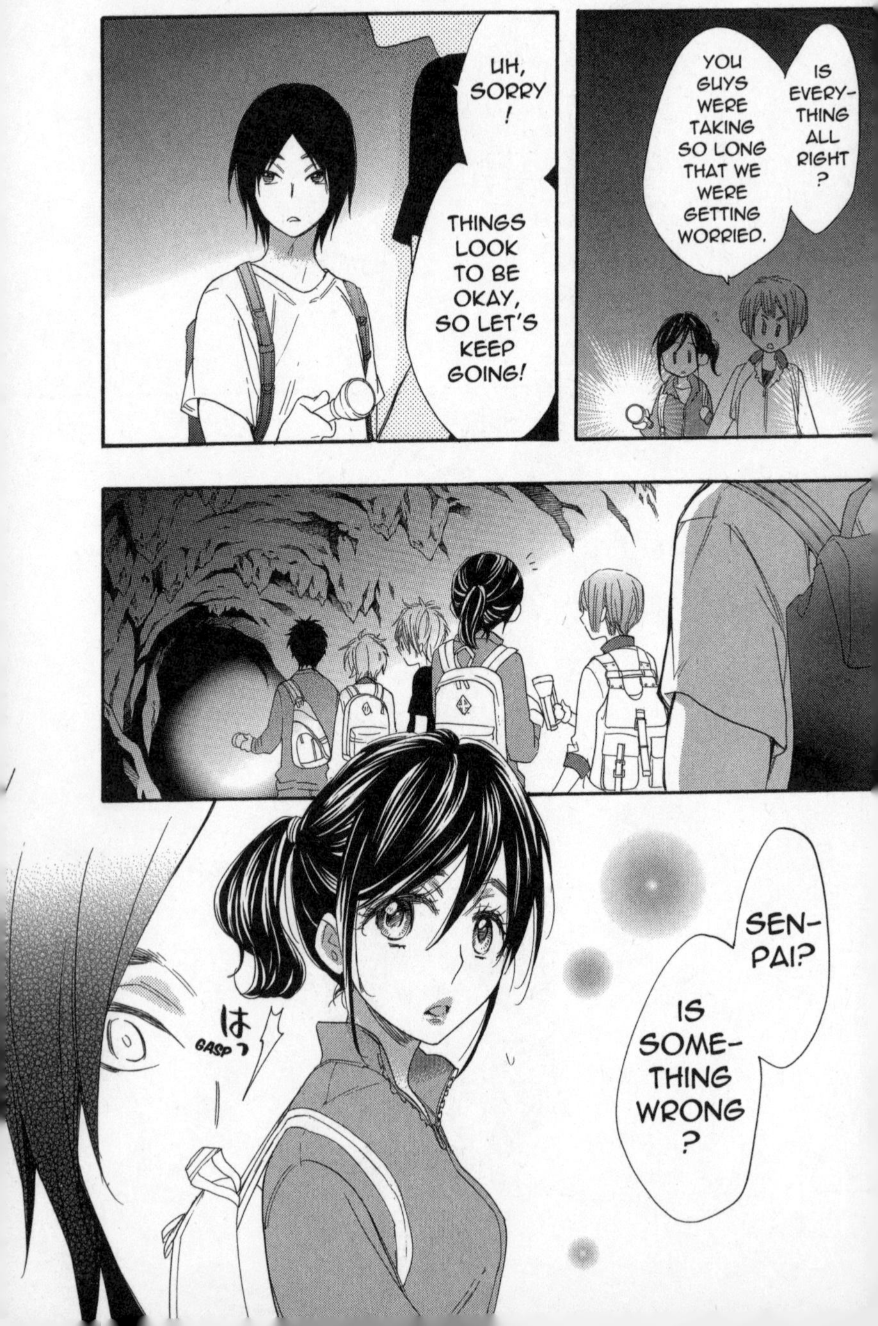
IS EVERYTHING ALL RIGHT?
YOU GUYS WERE TAKING SO LONG THAT WE WERE GETTING WORRIED.
UH, SORRY!
THINGS LOOK TO BE OKAY, SO LET'S KEEP GOING!
SEN-PAI?
IS SOME-THING WRONG?
は GASP

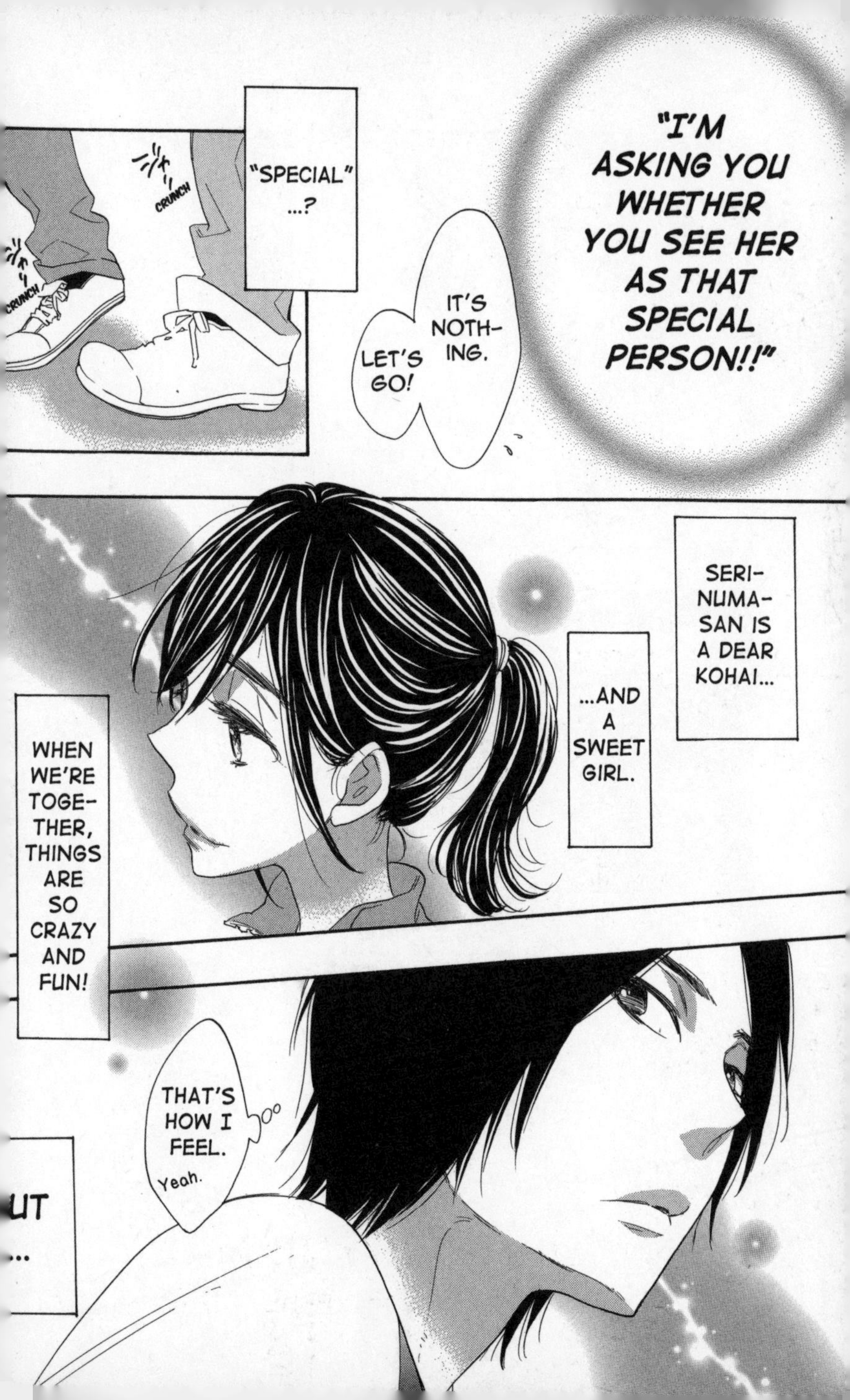
"I'M ASKING YOU WHETHER YOU SEE HER AS THAT SPECIAL PERSON!!"
IT'S NOTHING.
LET'S GO!
"SPECIAL" ...?
CRUNCH
CRUNCH
SERINUMA-SAN IS A DEAR KOHAI...
...AND A SWEET GIRL.
WHEN WE'RE TOGETHER, THINGS ARE SO CRAZY AND FUN!
THAT'S HOW I FEEL.
Yeah.
UT
...

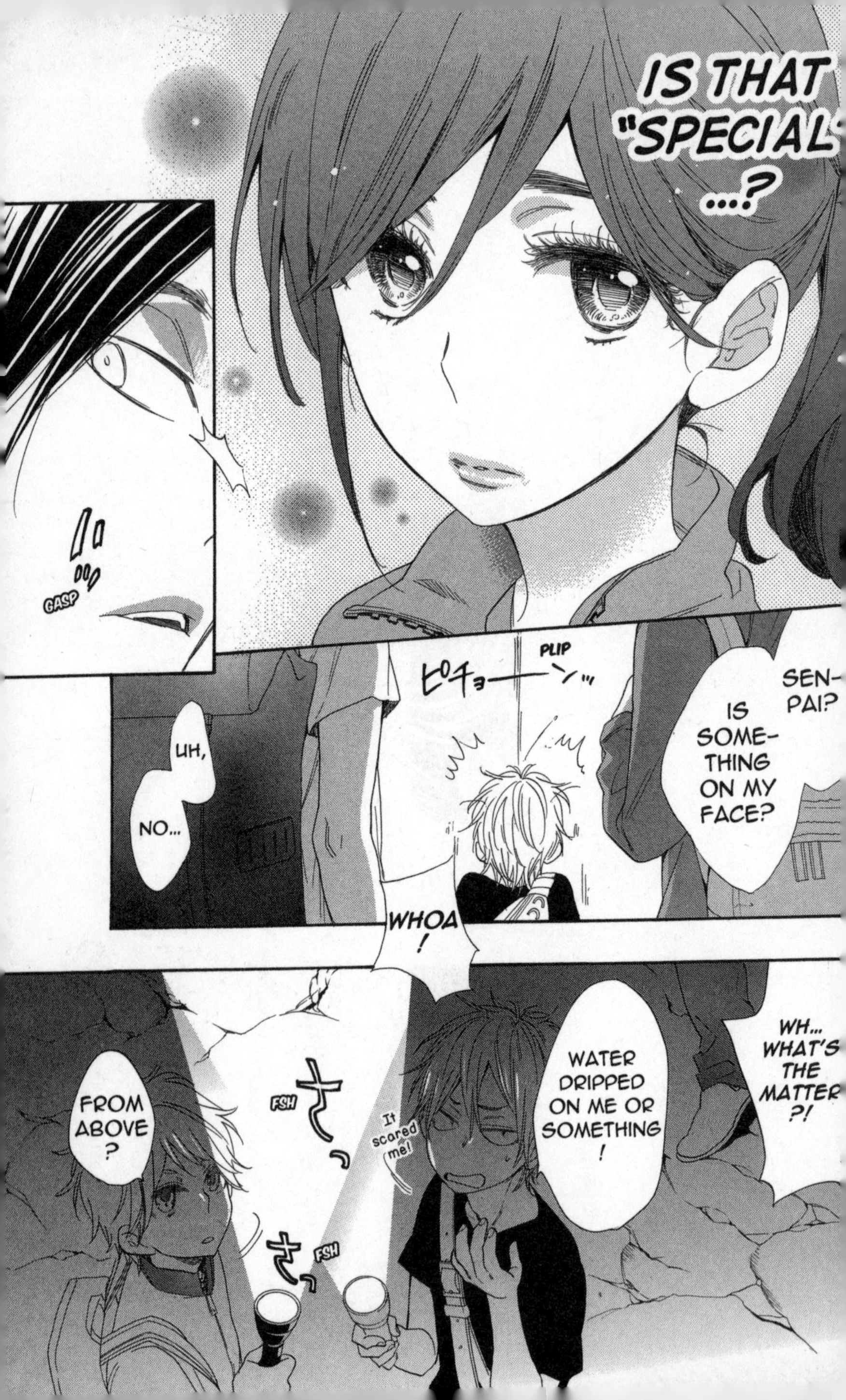
IS THAT "SPECIAL" ...?
GASP
SEN-PAI?
IS SOMETHING ON MY FACE?
PLIP
ピチョーン
UH,
NO...
WHOA!
WH... WHAT'S THE MATTER?!
WATER DRIPPED ON ME OR SOMETHING!
It scared me!
FSH
FSH
FROM ABOVE?

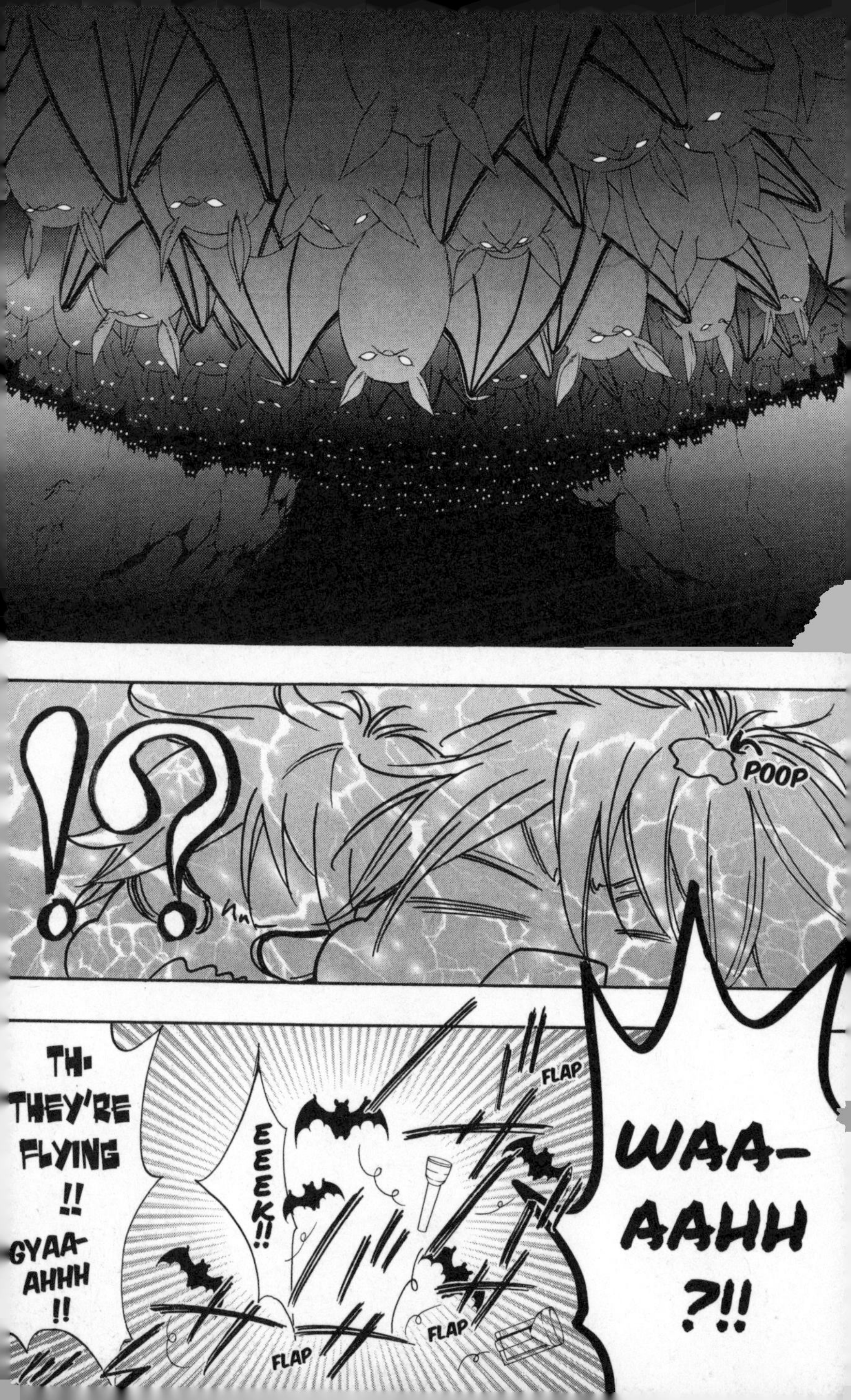
POOP
!?
WAA-AAHH ?!!
FLAP
EEEEK!!
FLAP
FLAP
TH-THEY'RE FLYING !!
GYAA-AHHH !!

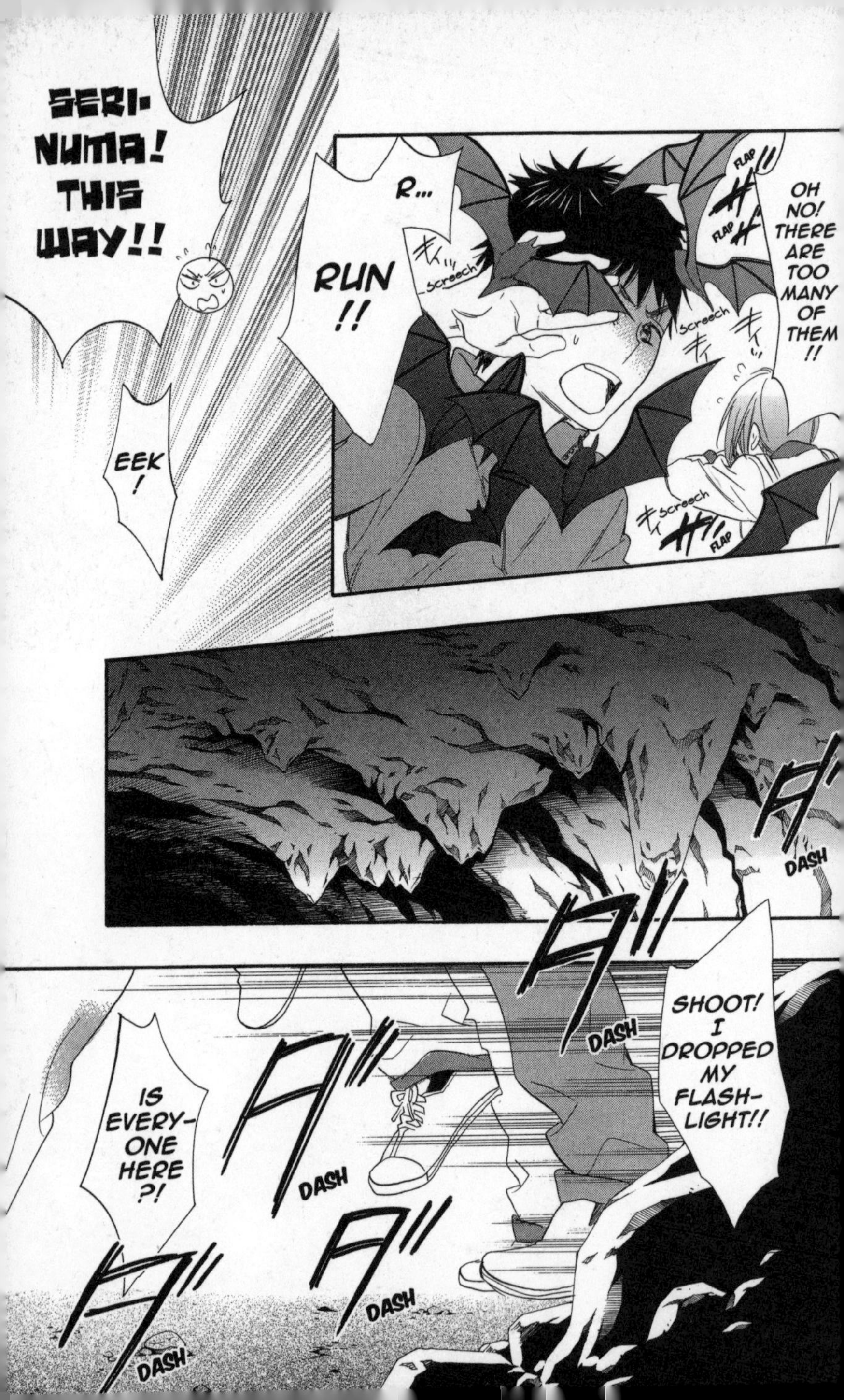
FLAP
FLAP
OH NO! THERE ARE TOO MANY OF THEM!!
Screech
Screech
FLAP
R...
RUN!!
Screech
SERI-NUMA! THIS WAY!!
EEK!
DASH
DASH
SHOOT! I DROPPED MY FLASHLIGHT!!
DASH
IS EVERYONE HERE?!
DASH
DASH

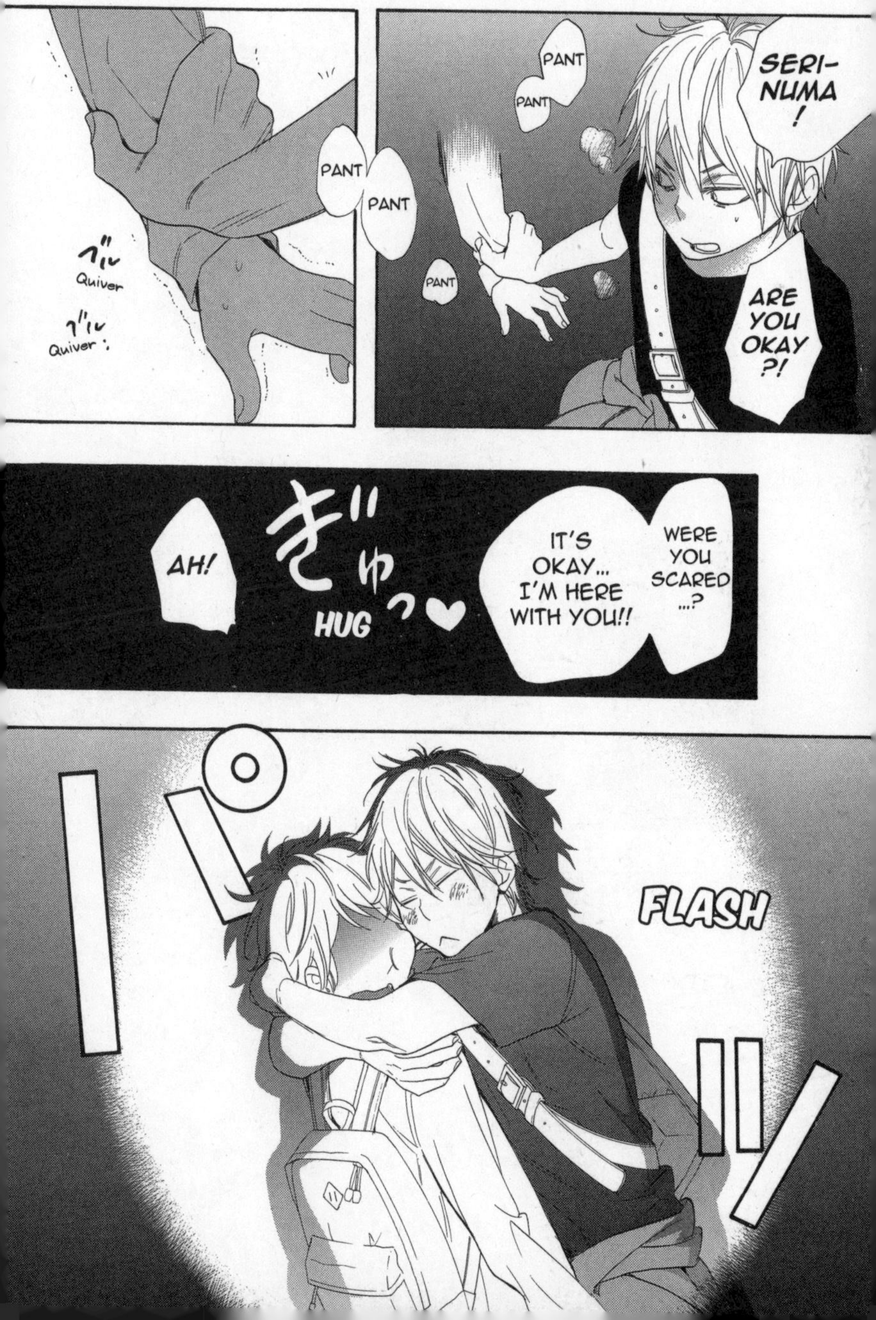
SERI-NUMA!
PANT
PANT
ARE YOU OKAY?!
PANT
PANT
PANT
ブル
Quiver
ブル
Quiver
WERE YOU SCARED...?
IT'S OKAY... I'M HERE WITH YOU!!
ぎゅっ
HUG
AH!
FLASH

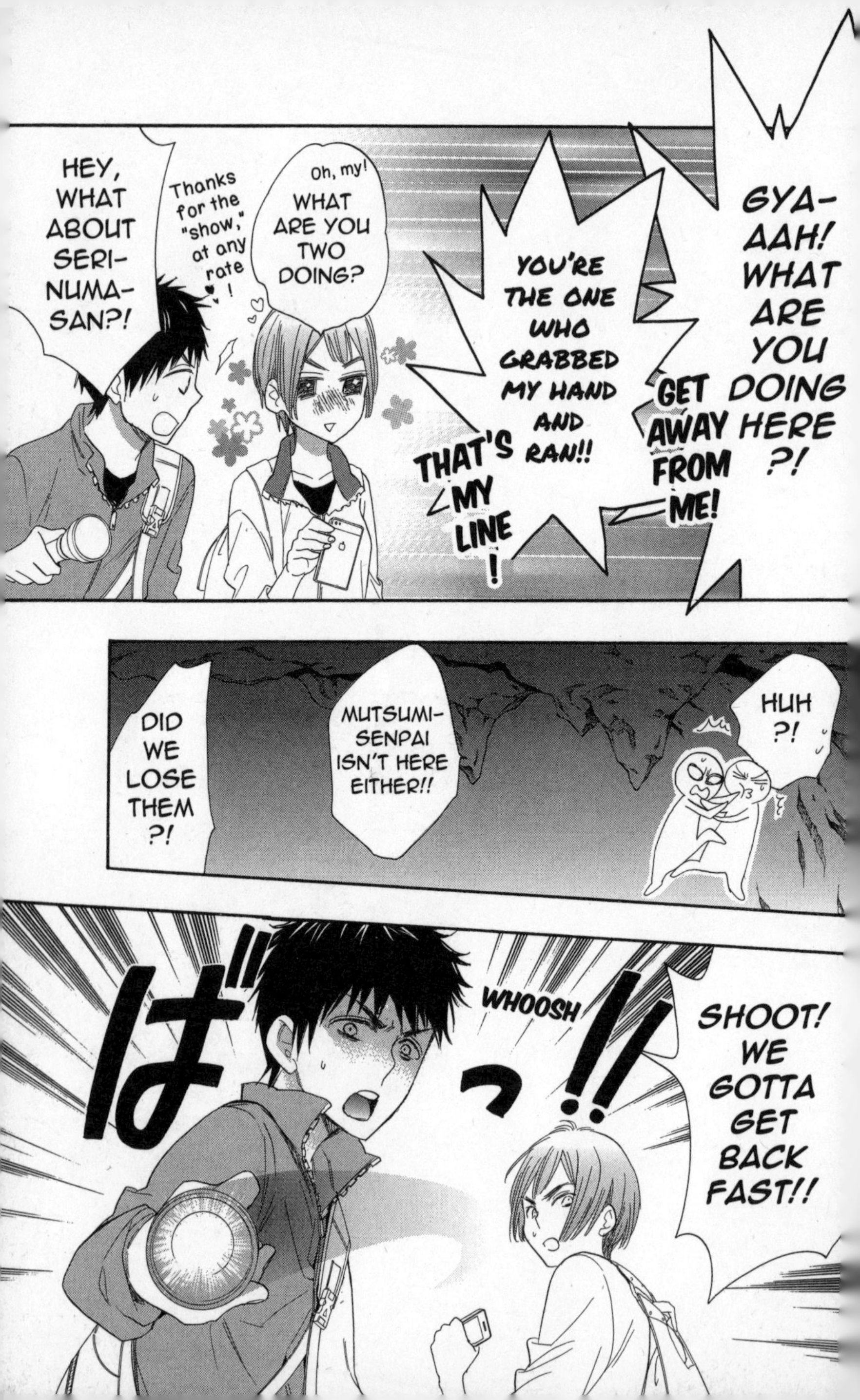
GYA-AAH! WHAT ARE YOU DOING HERE?!
GET AWAY FROM ME!
YOU'RE THE ONE WHO GRABBED MY HAND AND RAN!!
THAT'S MY LINE!
Oh, my! WHAT ARE YOU TWO DOING?
Thanks for the "show," at any rate ♥ !
HEY, WHAT ABOUT SERI-NUMA-SAN?!
HUH?!
MUTSUMI-SENPAI ISN'T HERE EITHER!!
DID WE LOSE THEM?!
SHOOT! WE GOTTA GET BACK FAST!!
WHOOSH
ばっ!!

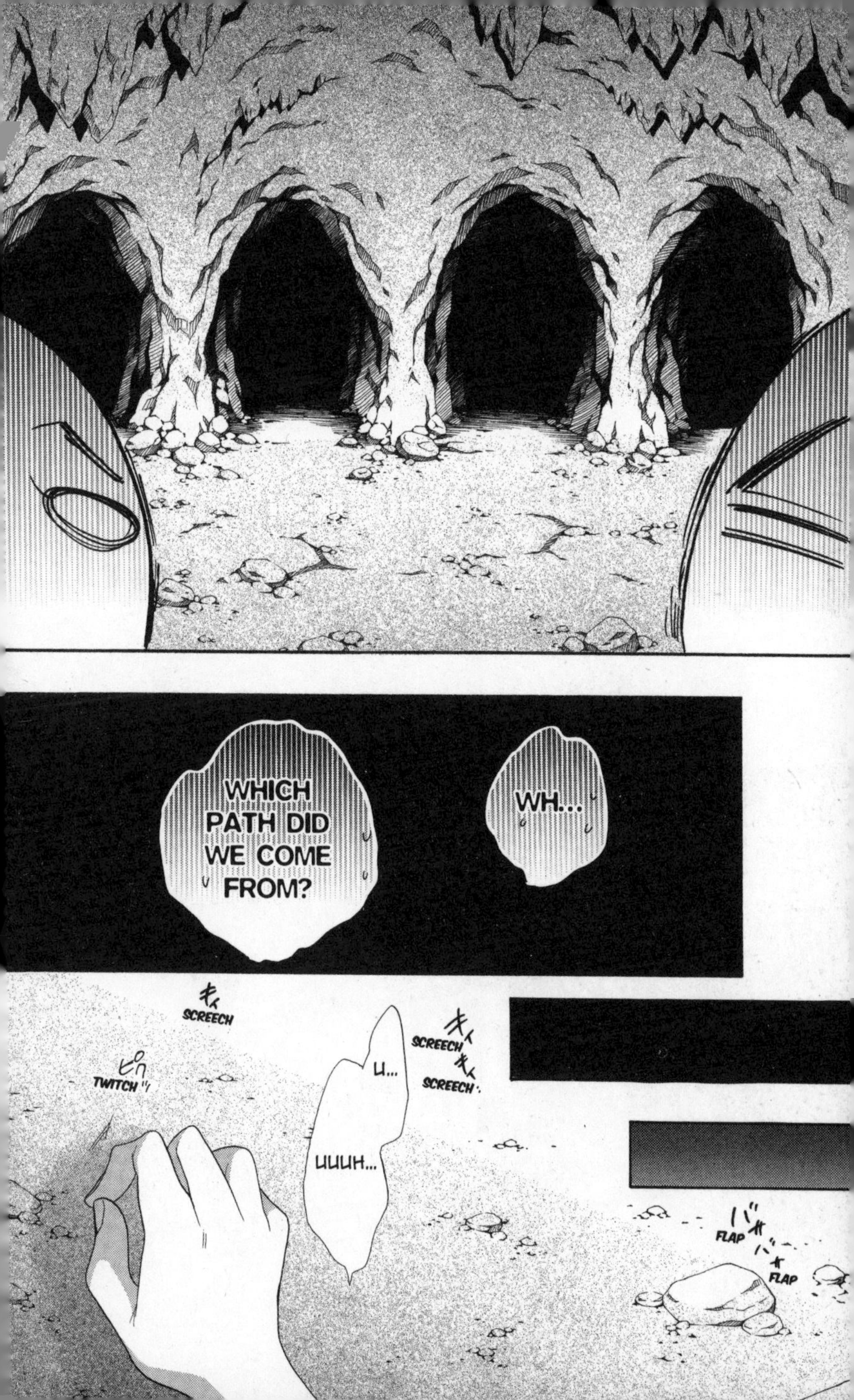

WH...
WHICH PATH DID WE COME FROM?
SCREECH
SCREECH
FLAP
FLAP
U...
UUUH...
SCREECH
TWITCH

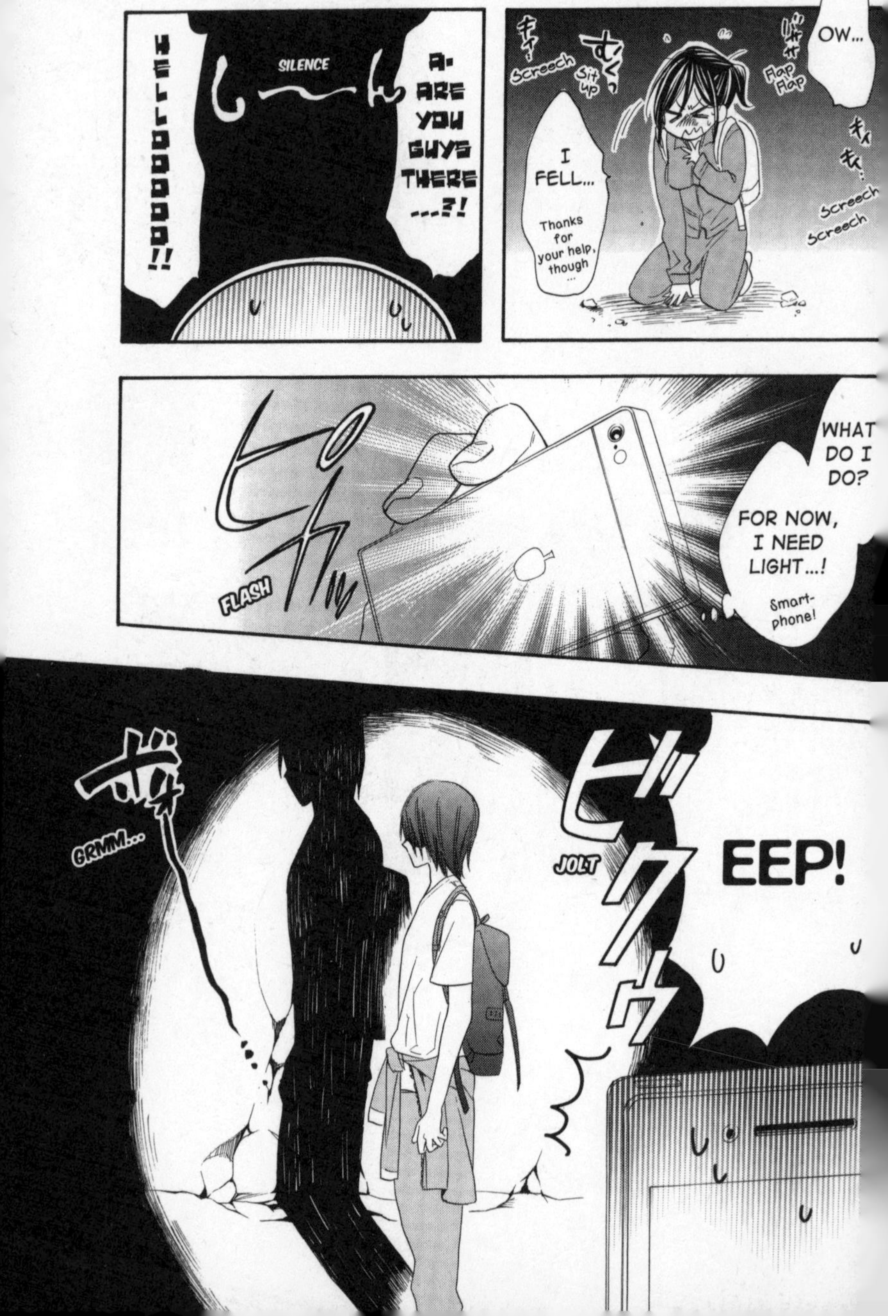
OW...
Flap Flap
Screech
Sit up
I FELL...
Thanks for your help, though ...
Screech Screech
A-ARE YOU GUYS THERE ...?!
SILENCE
HELLOOOOOO!!
WHAT DO I DO?
FOR NOW, I NEED LIGHT...!
Smart-phone!
FLASH
EEP!
JOLT
GRMM...

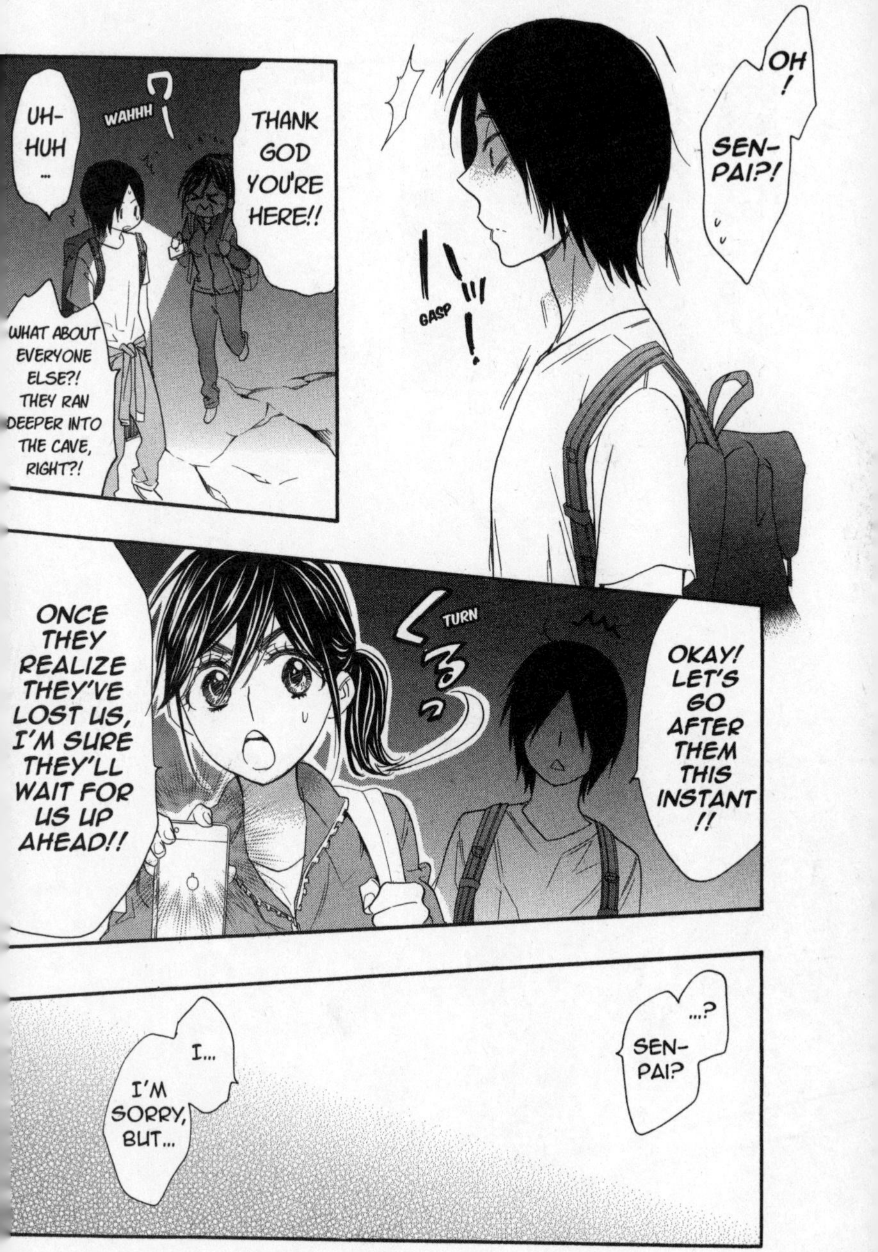
OH! SEN-PAI?!
GASP
THANK GOD YOU'RE HERE!!
WAHHH
UH-HUH...
WHAT ABOUT EVERYONE ELSE?! THEY RAN DEEPER INTO THE CAVE, RIGHT?!
OKAY! LET'S GO AFTER THEM THIS INSTANT!!
TURN
ONCE THEY REALIZE THEY'VE LOST US, I'M SURE THEY'LL WAIT FOR US UP AHEAD!!
...? SEN-PAI?
I... I'M SORRY, BUT...

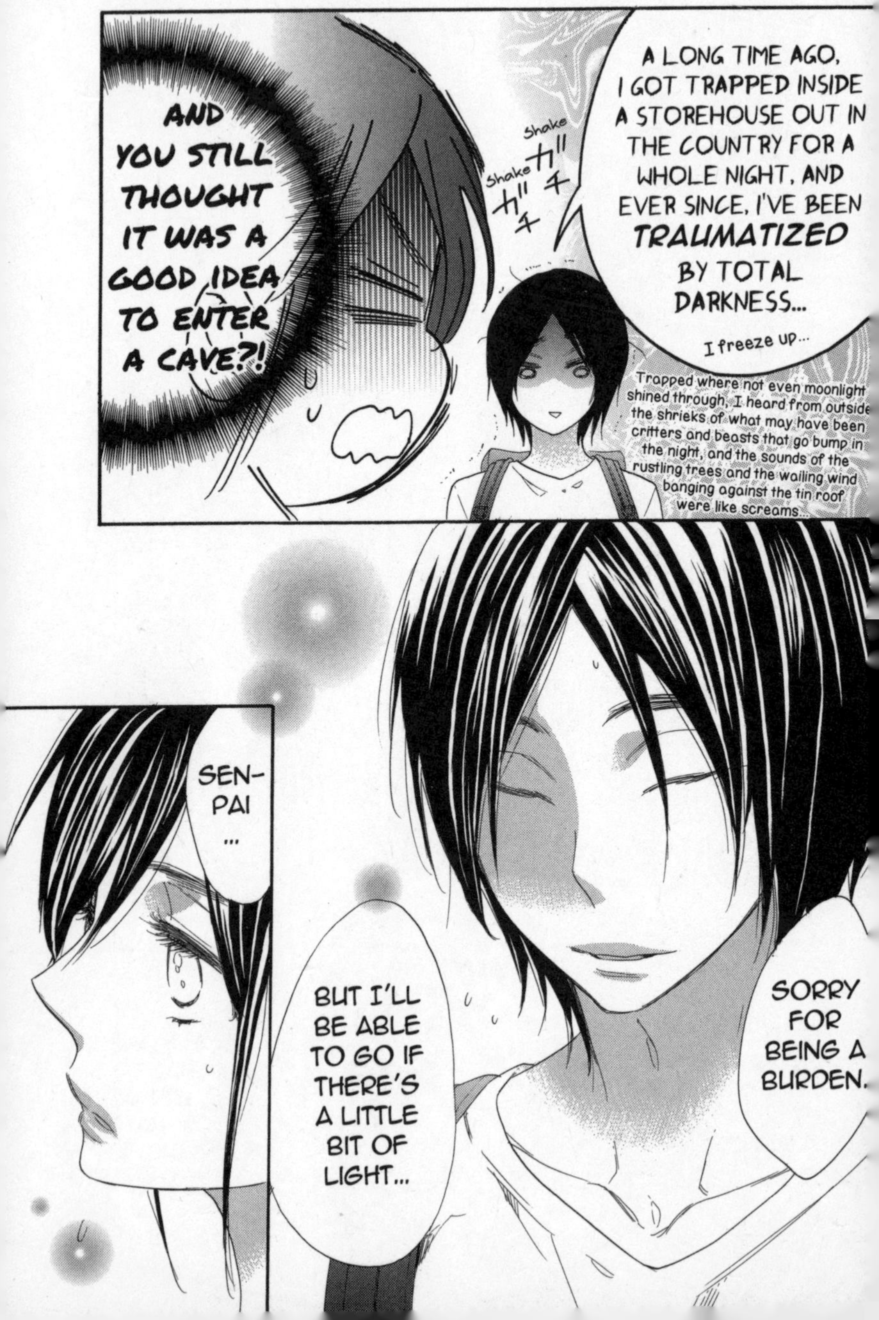
A LONG TIME AGO, I GOT TRAPPED INSIDE A STOREHOUSE OUT IN THE COUNTRY FOR A WHOLE NIGHT, AND EVER SINCE, I'VE BEEN TRAUMATIZED BY TOTAL DARKNESS...
I freeze up...
Shake
Shake
Trapped where not even moonlight shined through, I heard from outside the shrieks of what may have been critters and beasts that go bump in the night, and the sounds of the rustling trees and the wailing wind banging against the tin roof were like screams...
AND YOU STILL THOUGHT IT WAS A GOOD IDEA TO ENTER A CAVE?!
SORRY FOR BEING A BURDEN.
BUT I'LL BE ABLE TO GO IF THERE'S A LITTLE BIT OF LIGHT...
SEN-PAI...

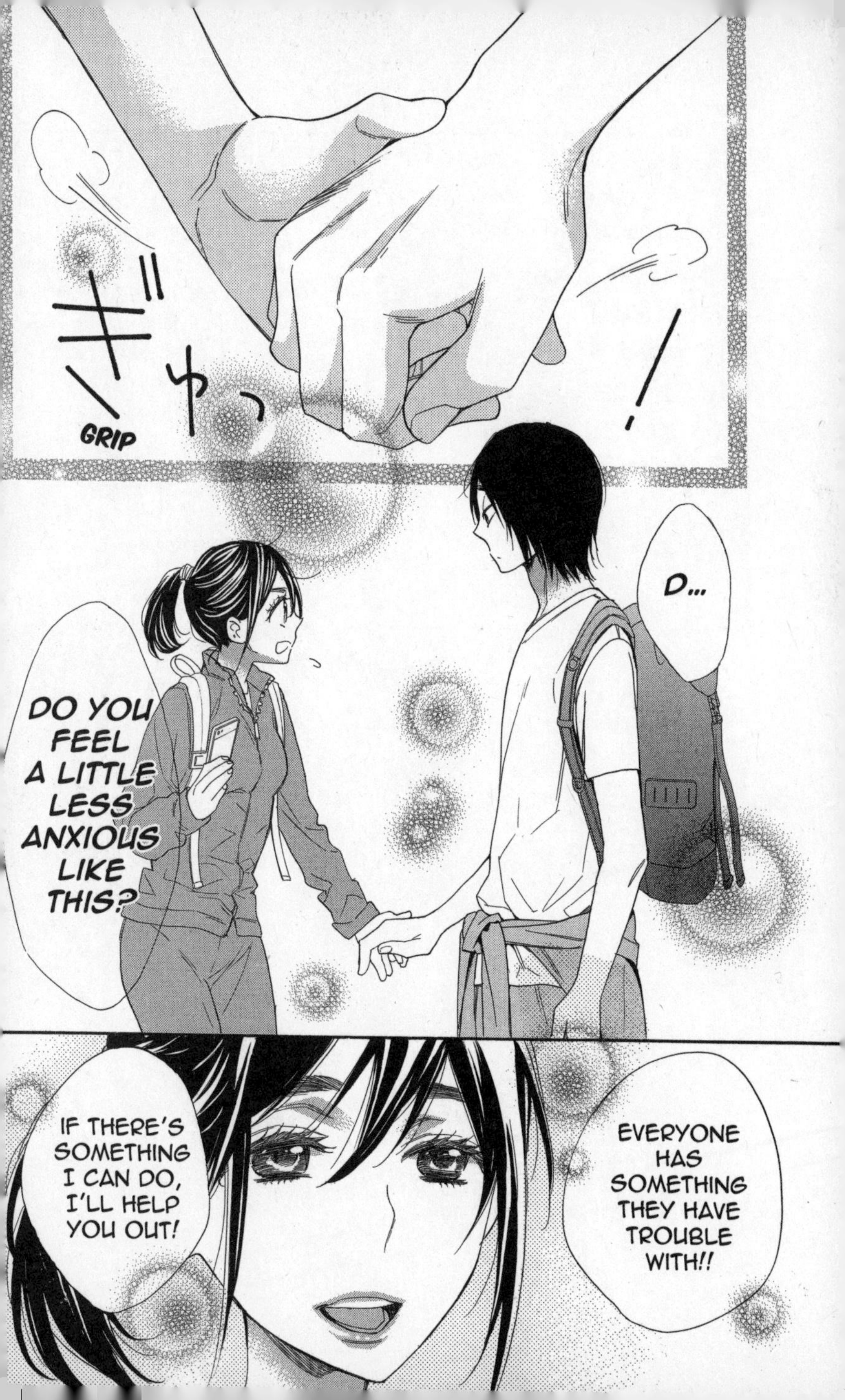
!
ギゅっ
GRIP
D...
DO YOU FEEL A LITTLE LESS ANXIOUS LIKE THIS?
EVERYONE HAS SOMETHING THEY HAVE TROUBLE WITH!!
IF THERE'S SOMETHING I CAN DO, I'LL HELP YOU OUT!

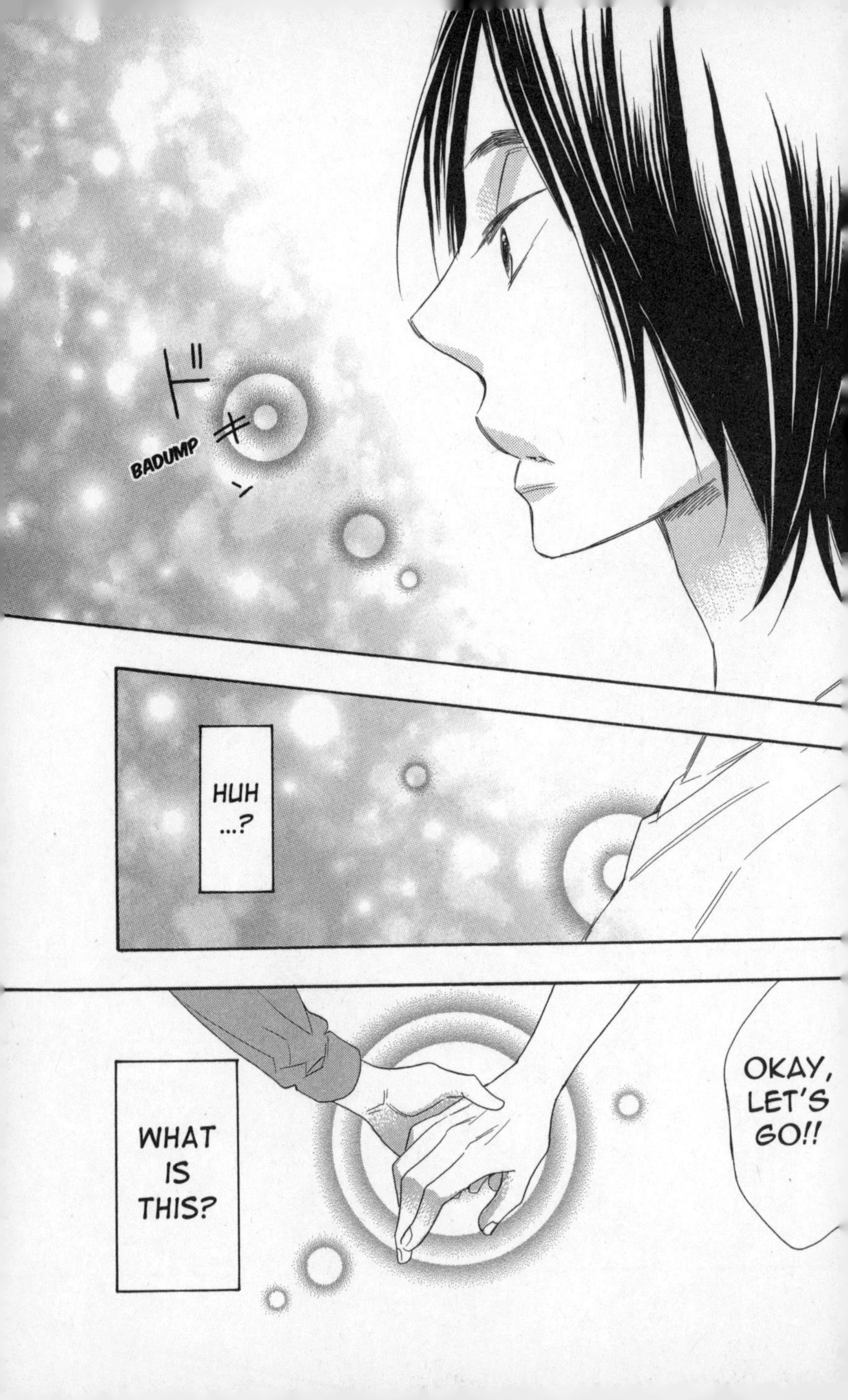
ドキン
BADUMP
HUH ...?
OKAY, LET'S GO!!
WHAT IS THIS?

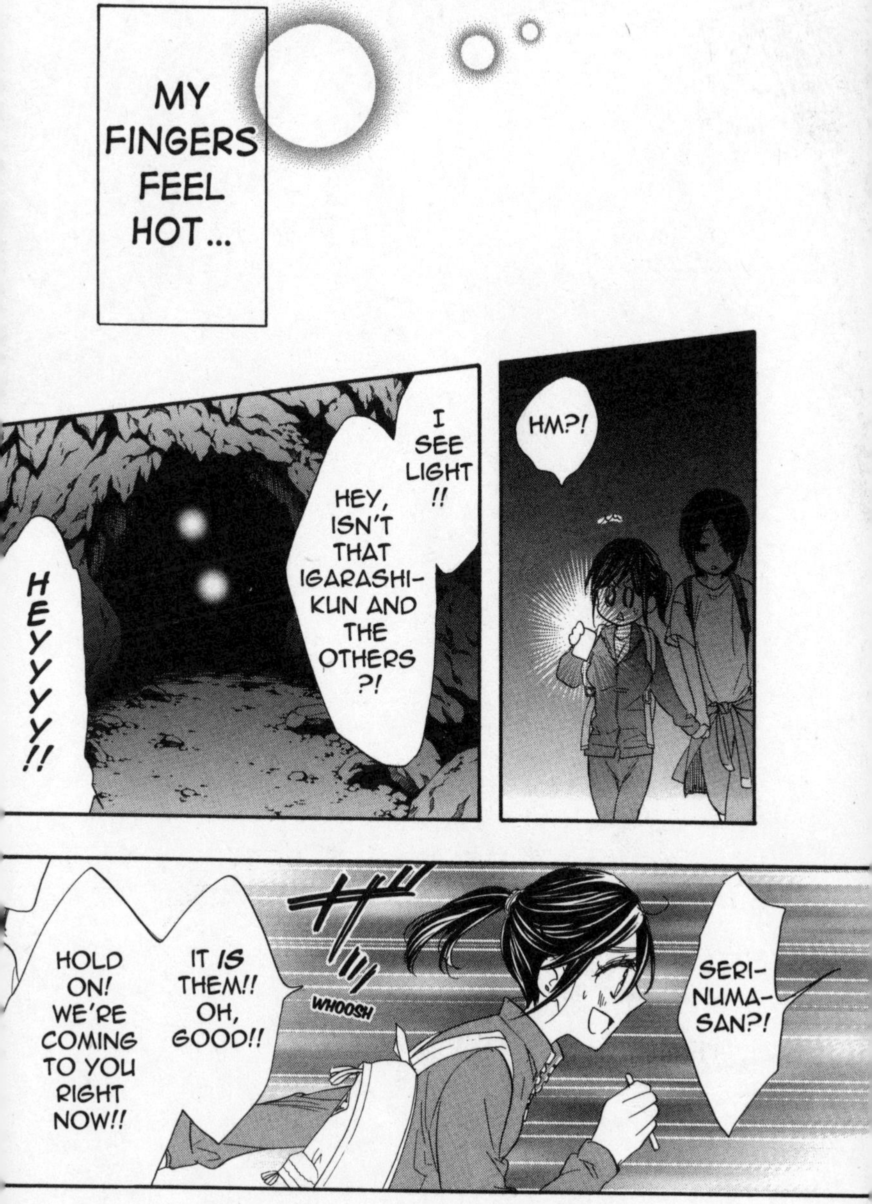
MY FINGERS FEEL HOT...
HM?!
I SEE LIGHT!!
HEY, ISN'T THAT IGARASHI-KUN AND THE OTHERS?!
HEYYYYY!!
SERI-NUMA-SAN?!
WHOOSH
IT IS THEM!! OH, GOOD!!
HOLD ON! WE'RE COMING TO YOU RIGHT NOW!!

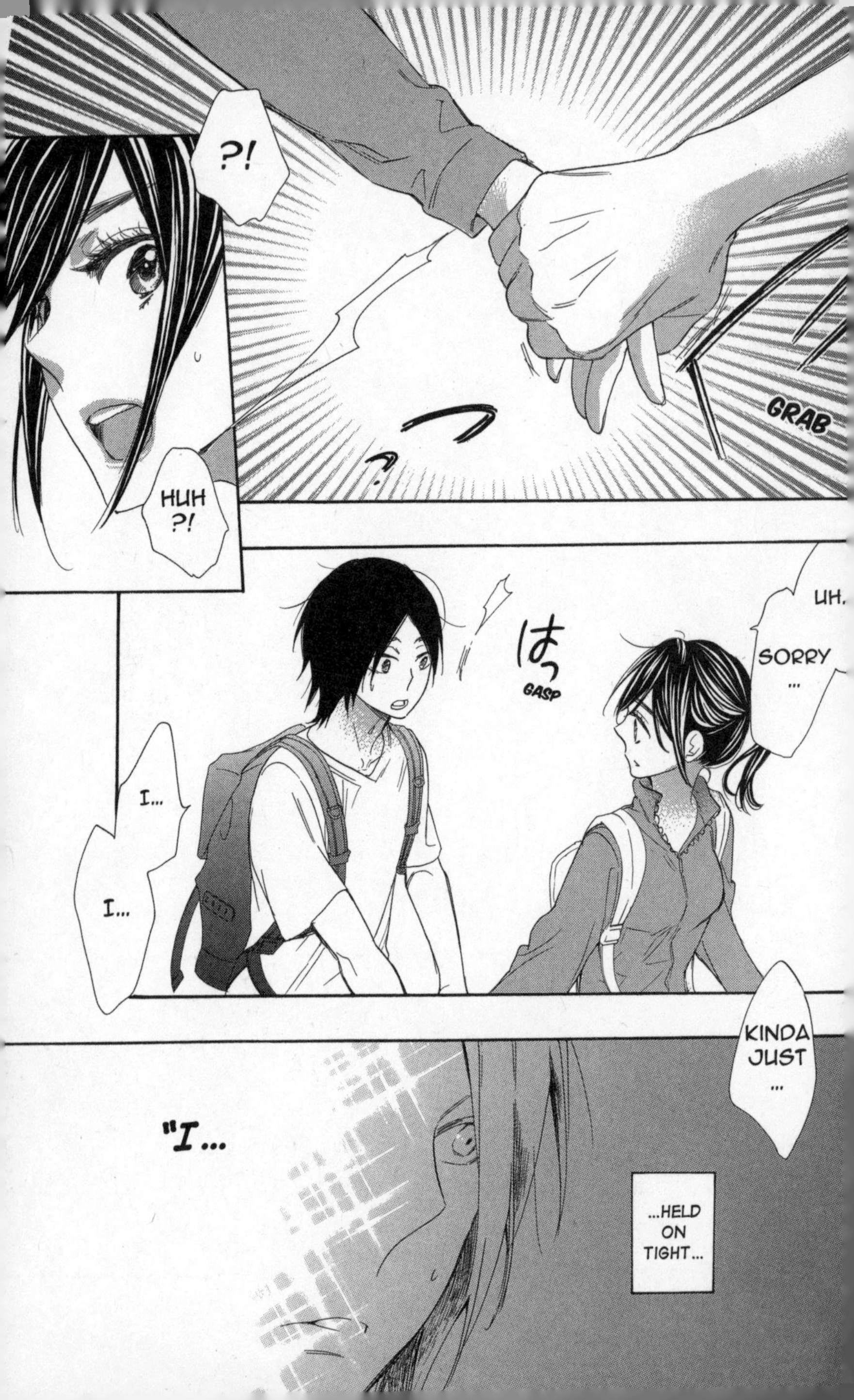
GRAB
?!
HUH ?!
UH, SORRY ...
はっ
GASP
I...
I...
KINDA JUST ...
...HELD ON TIGHT...
"I...

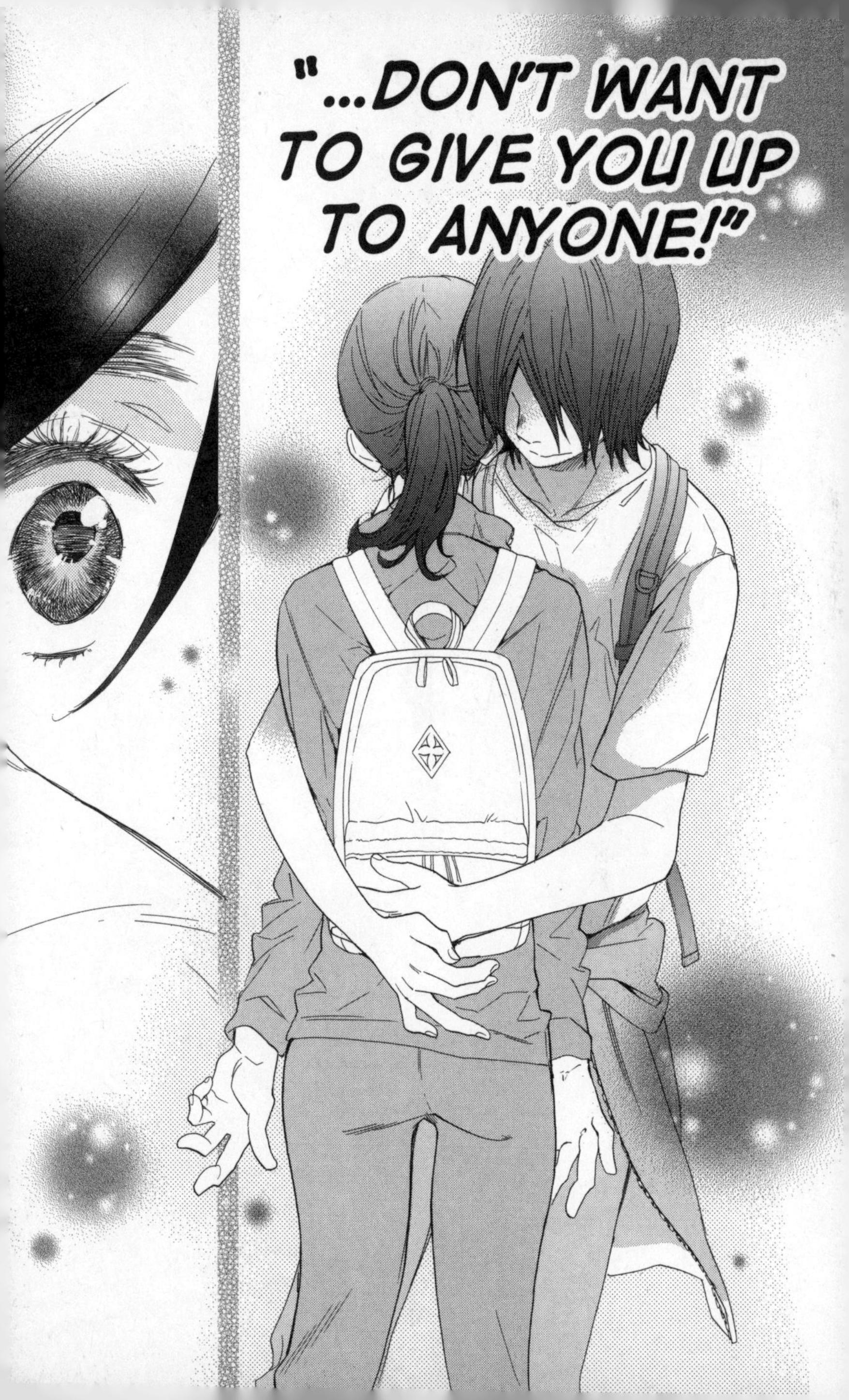
"...DON'T WANT TO GIVE YOU UP TO ANYONE!"

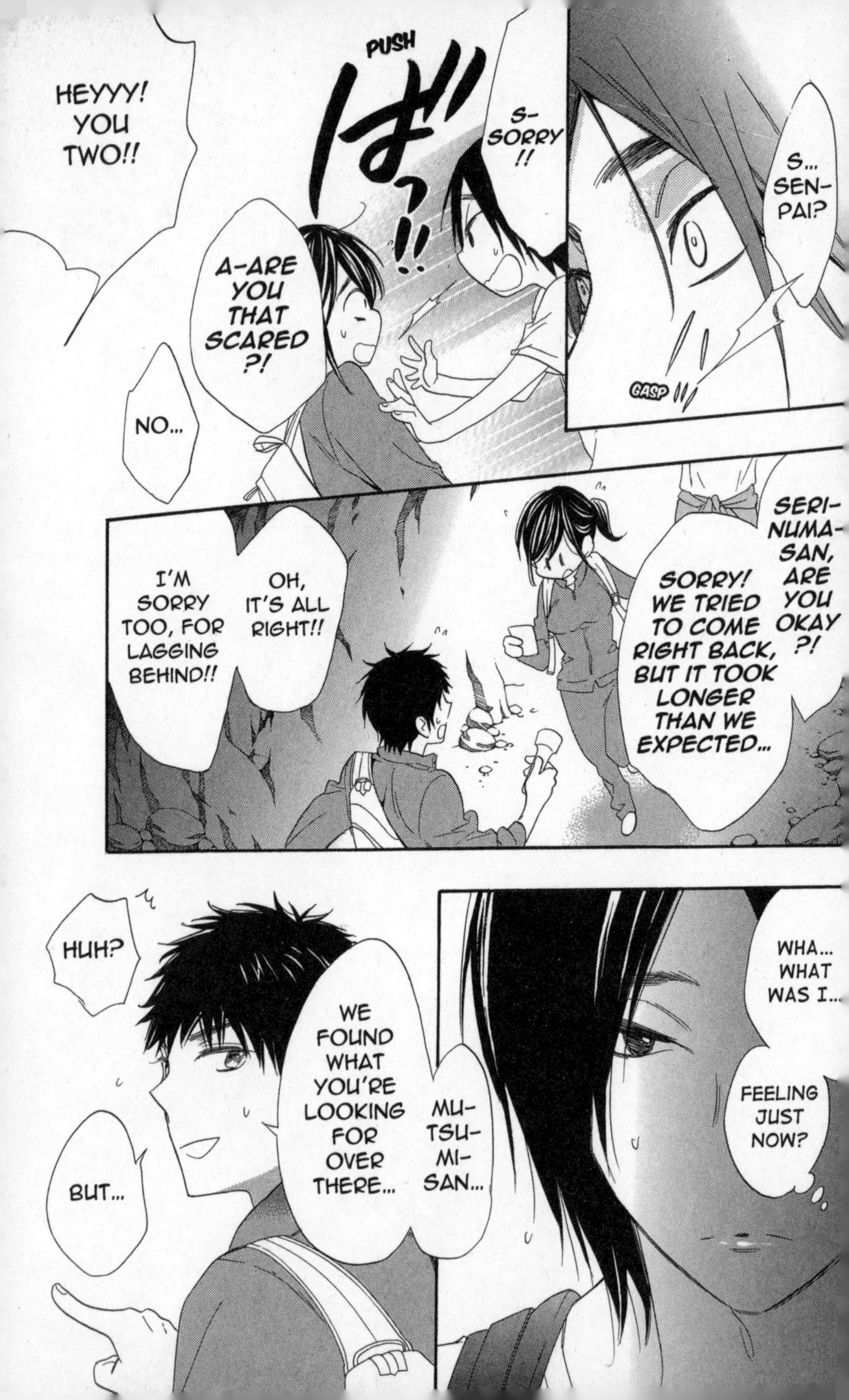
S... SEN-PAI?
GASP
PUSH
ぱっ!!
S-SORRY!!
A-ARE YOU THAT SCARED?!
NO...
HEYYY! YOU TWO!!
SERI-NUMA-SAN, ARE YOU OKAY?!
SORRY! WE TRIED TO COME RIGHT BACK, BUT IT TOOK LONGER THAN WE EXPECTED...
OH, IT'S ALL RIGHT!!
I'M SORRY TOO, FOR LAGGING BEHIND!!
WHA... WHAT WAS I... FEELING JUST NOW?
MU-TSU-MI-SAN...
WE FOUND WHAT YOU'RE LOOKING FOR OVER THERE...
HUH?
BUT...

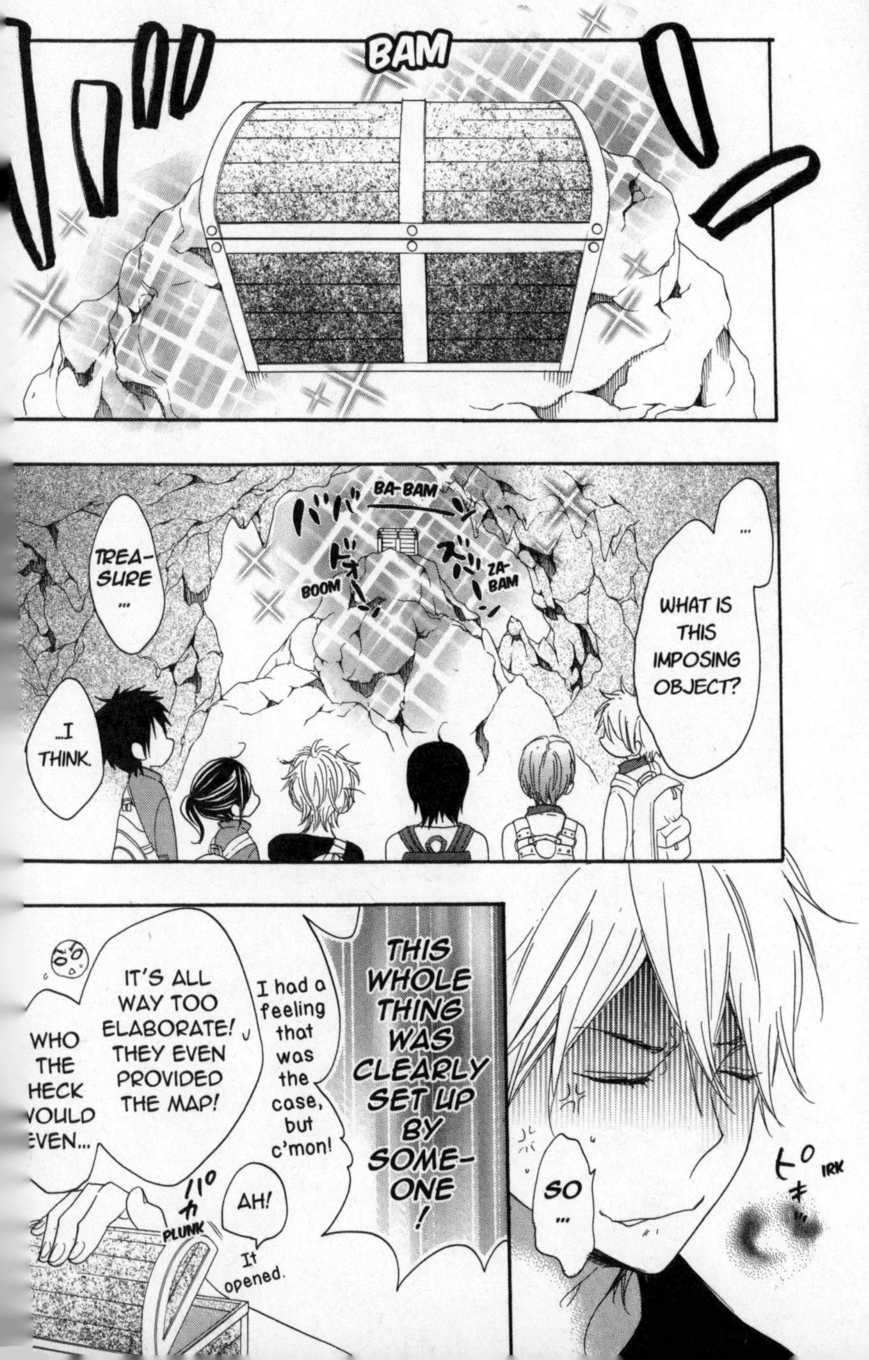
BAM
...
WHAT IS THIS IMPOSING OBJECT?
BA-BAM
ZA-BAM
BOOM
TREA-SURE ...
...I THINK.
IRK
SO ...
THIS WHOLE THING WAS CLEARLY SET UP BY SOME-ONE!
I had a feeling that was the case, but c'mon!
IT'S ALL WAY TOO ELABORATE! THEY EVEN PROVIDED THE MAP!
WHO THE HECK WOULD EVEN...
AH!
It opened.
PLUNK

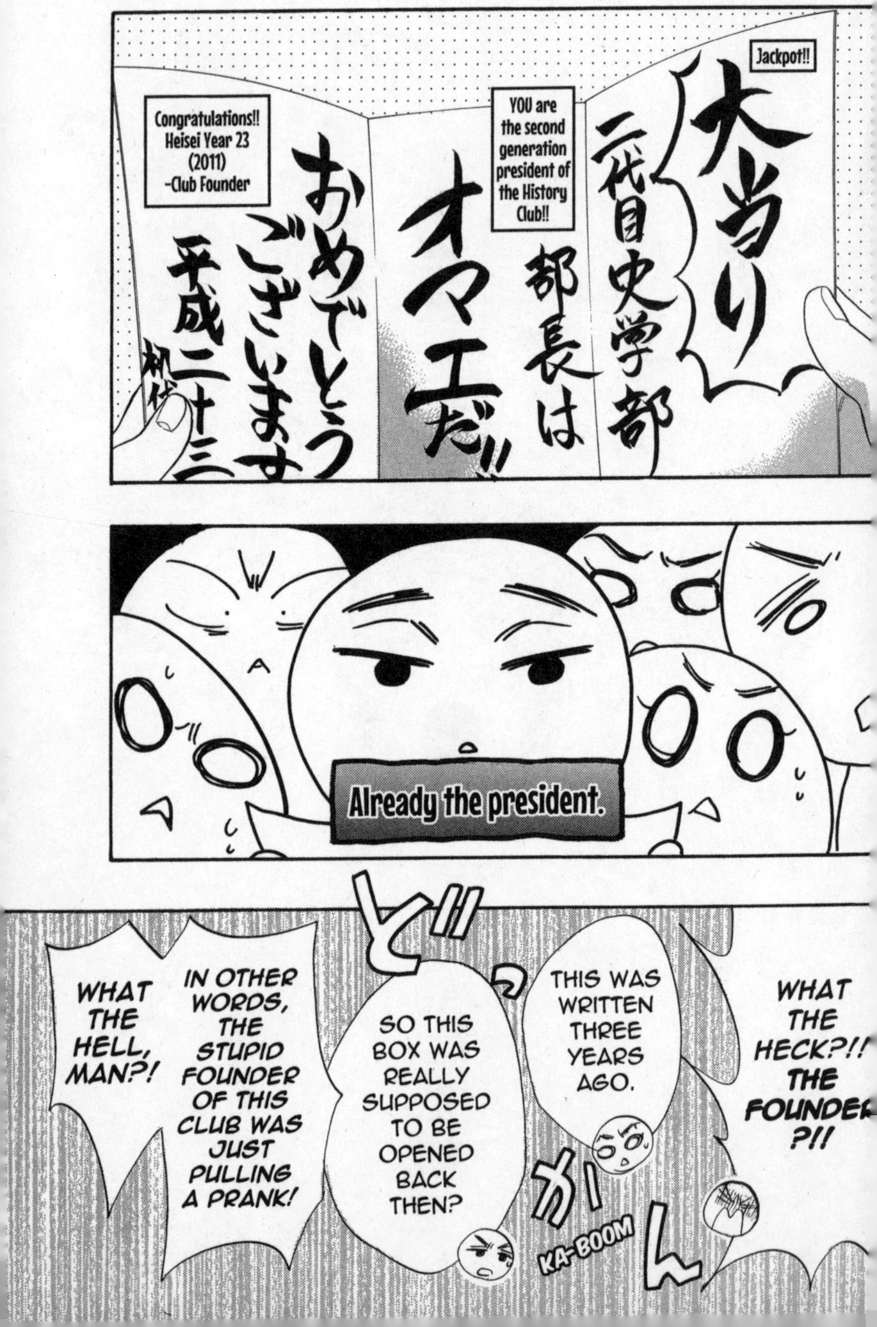
大当り
Jackpot!!
二代目史学部部長はオマエだ!!
YOU are the second generation president of the History Club!!
おめでとうございます
平成二十三
Congratulations!! Heisei Year 23 (2011) -Club Founder
Already the president.
どっ
WHAT THE HECK?!! THE FOUNDER?!!
THIS WAS WRITTEN THREE YEARS AGO.
SO THIS BOX WAS REALLY SUPPOSED TO BE OPENED BACK THEN?
IN OTHER WORDS, THE STUPID FOUNDER OF THIS CLUB WAS JUST PULLING A PRANK!
WHAT THE HELL, MAN?!
かーん
KA-BOOM

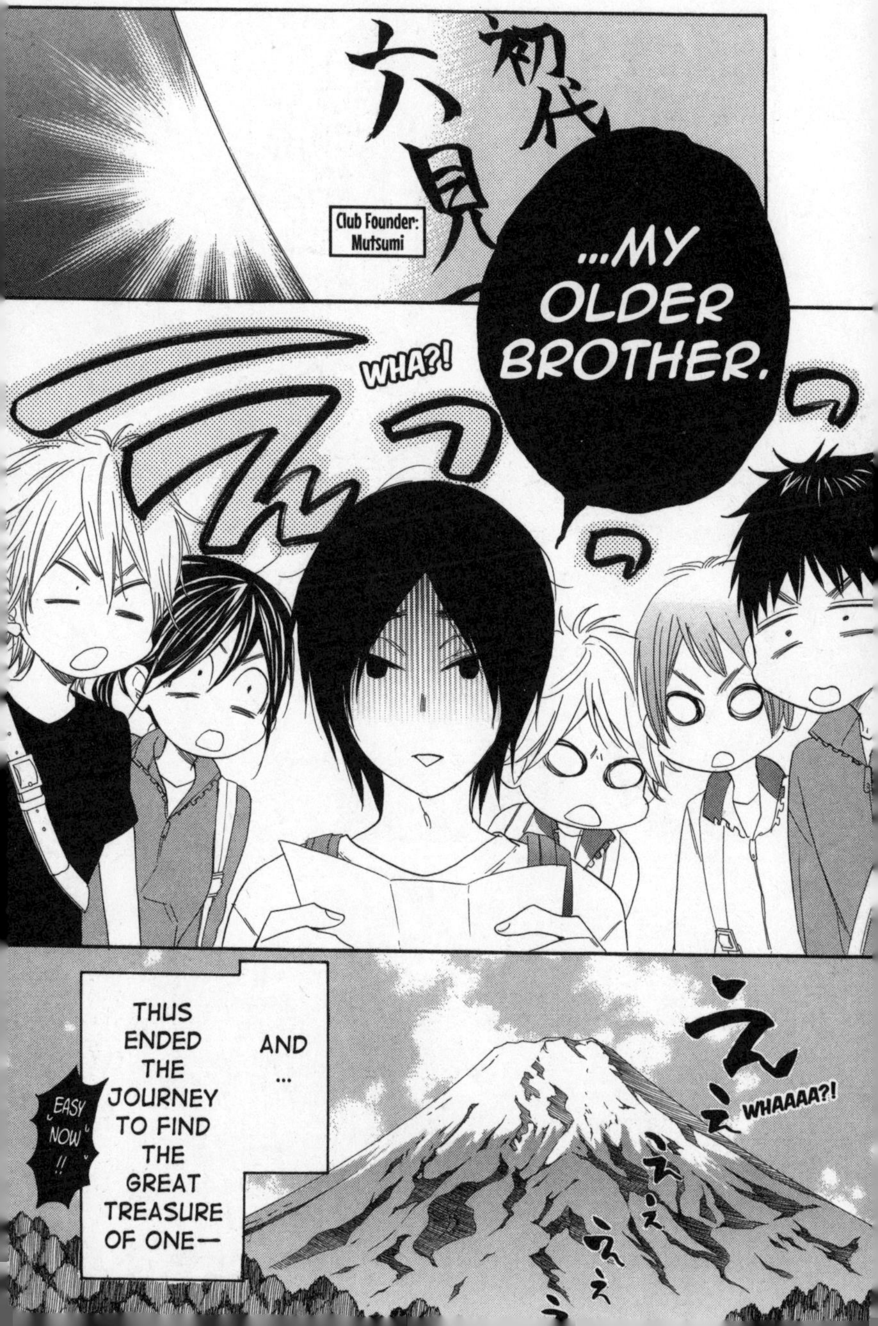

初代
六見
Club Founder: Mutsumi
...MY OLDER BROTHER.
WHA?!
WHAAAA?!
AND ...
THUS ENDED THE JOURNEY TO FIND THE GREAT TREASURE OF ONE—
EASY NOW!!

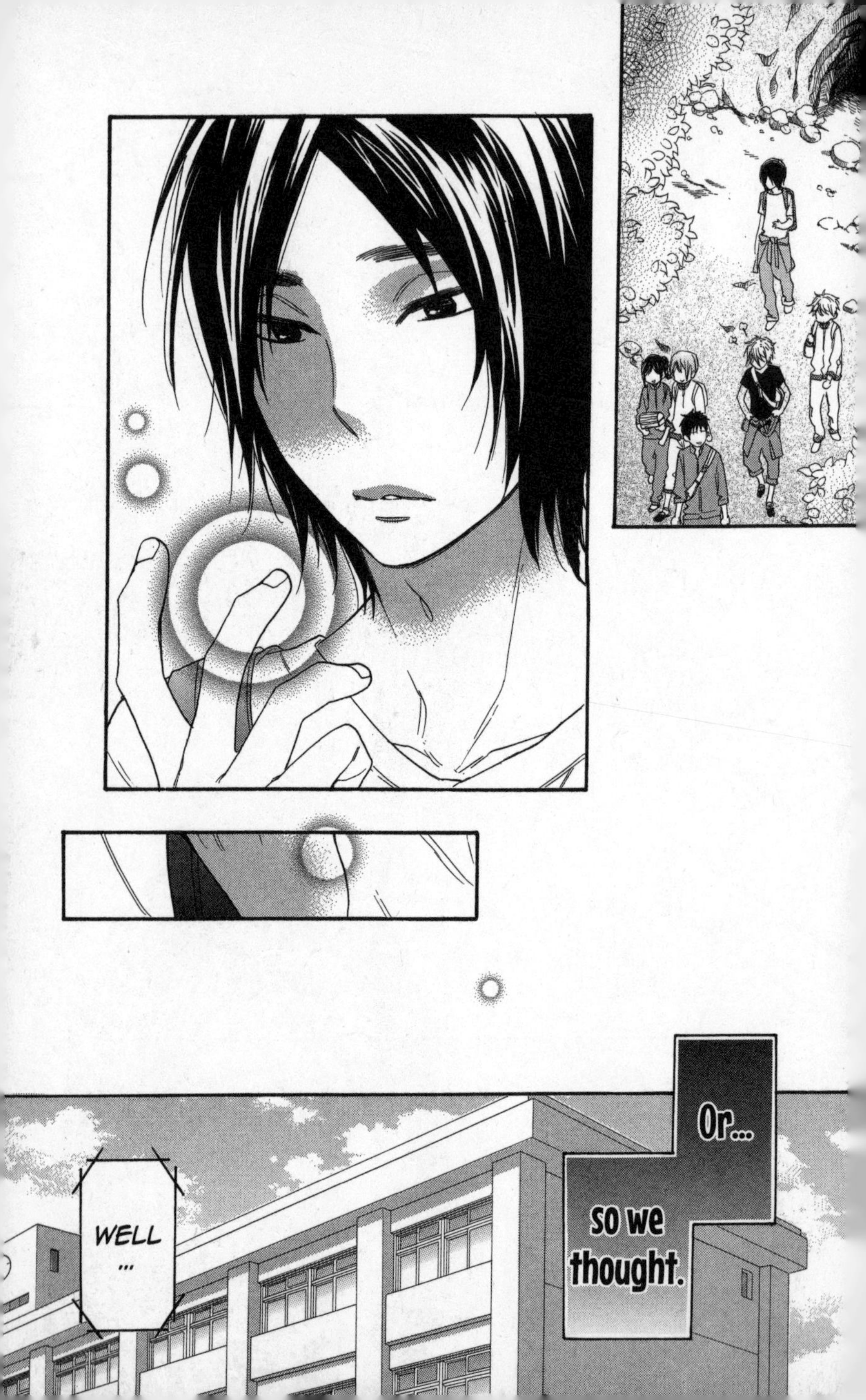
Or...
so we thought.
WELL ...

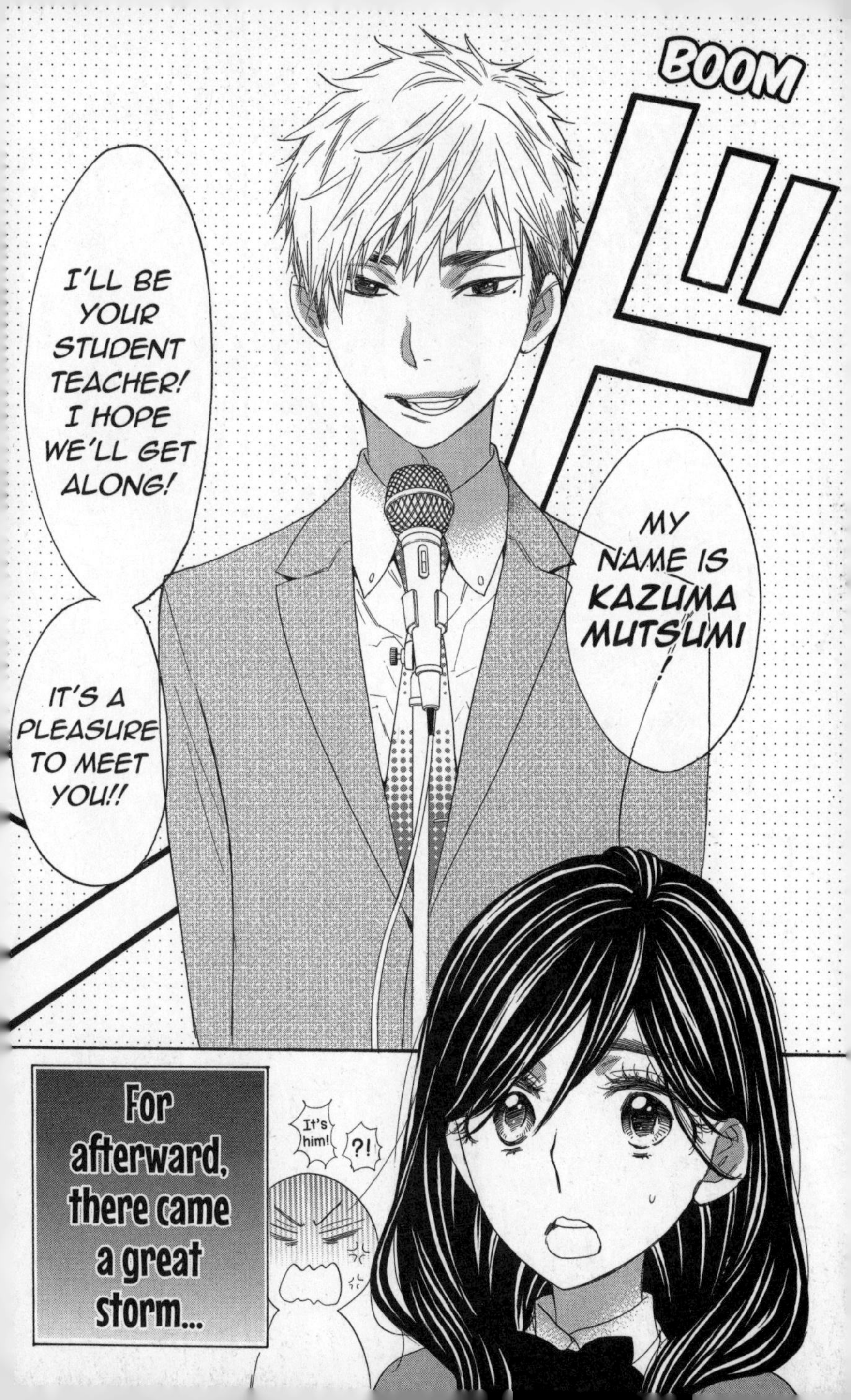
BOOM
MY NAME IS KAZUMA MUTSUMI!
I'LL BE YOUR STUDENT TEACHER! I HOPE WE'LL GET ALONG!
IT'S A PLEASURE TO MEET YOU!!
?!
It's him!
For afterward, there came a great storm...

#18 BROTHER, ATTACK

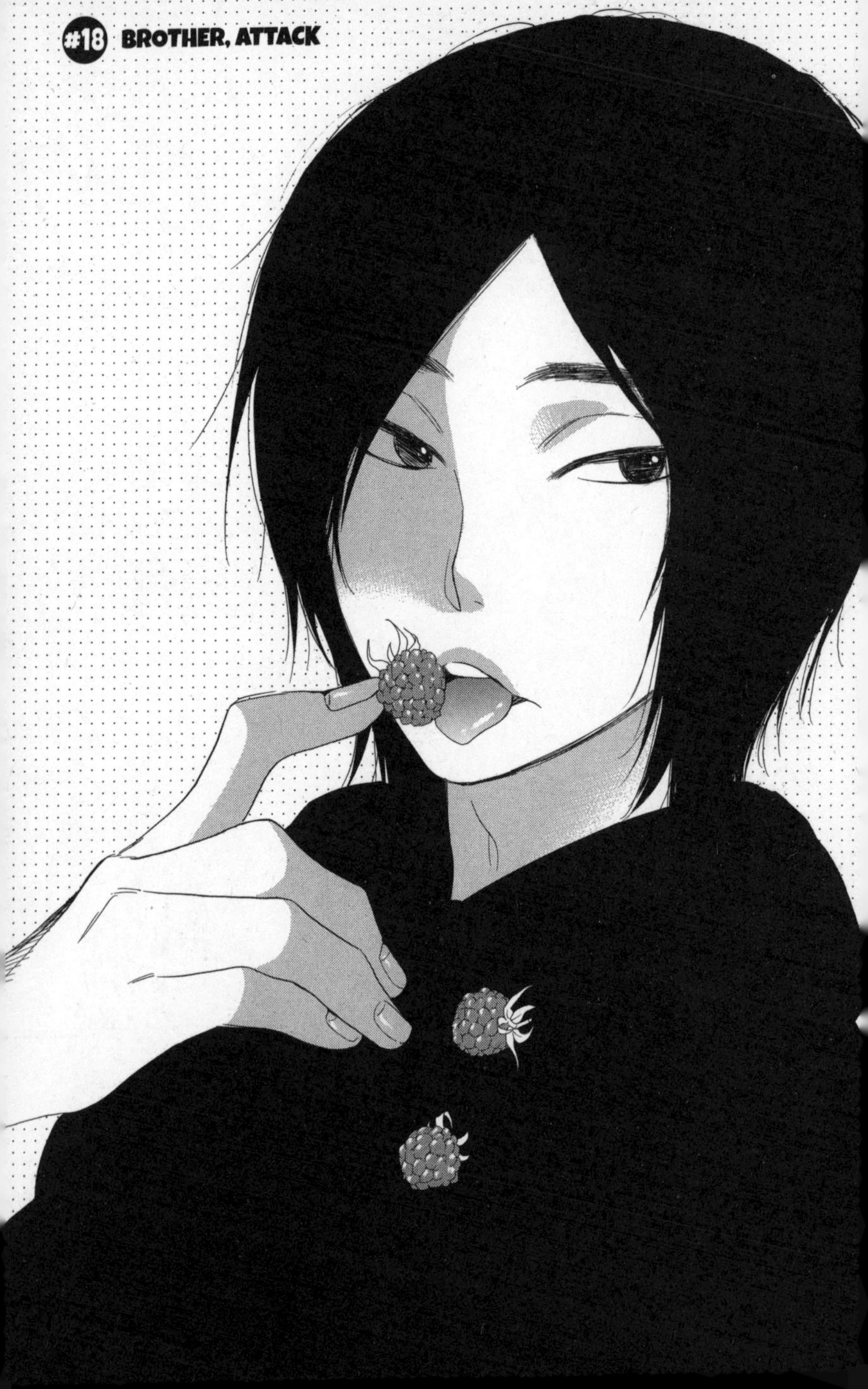

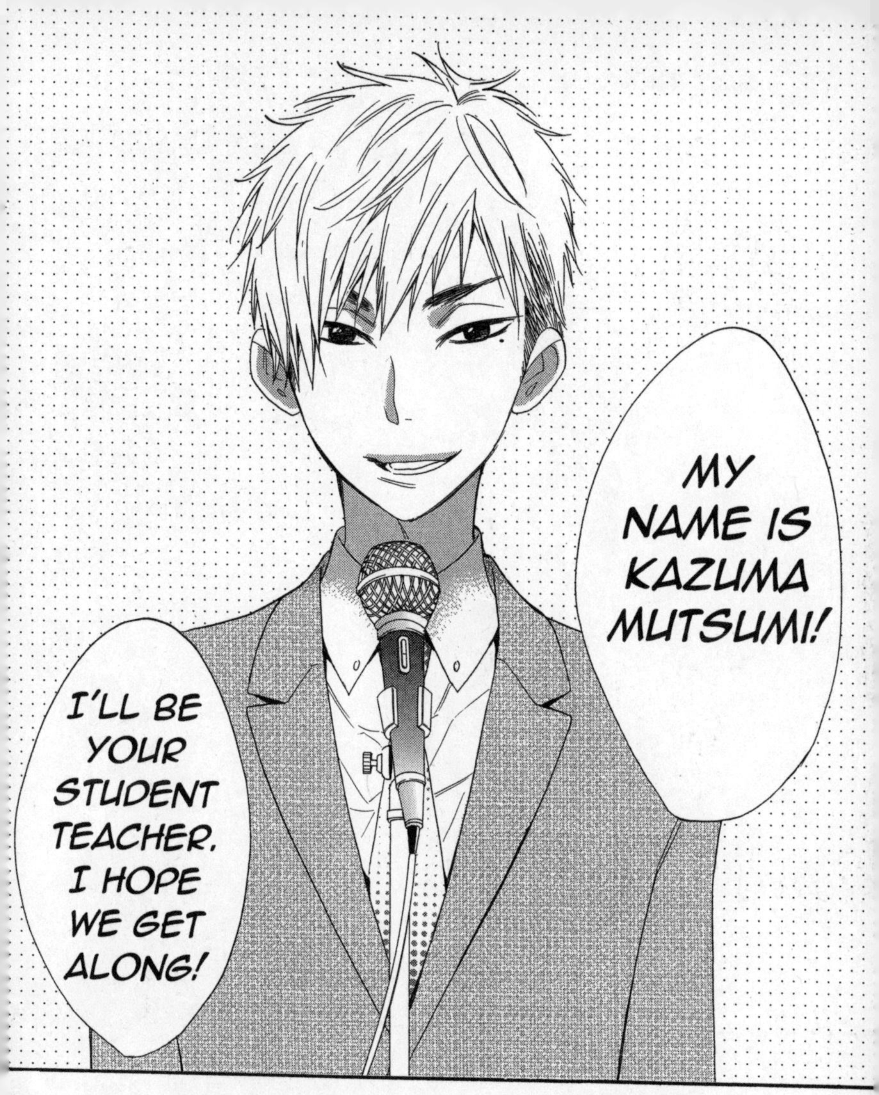
MY NAME IS KAZUMA MUTSUMI!
I'LL BE YOUR STUDENT TEACHER. I HOPE WE GET ALONG!

KiSS HiM, NOT ME!

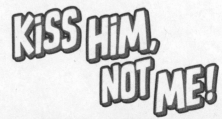

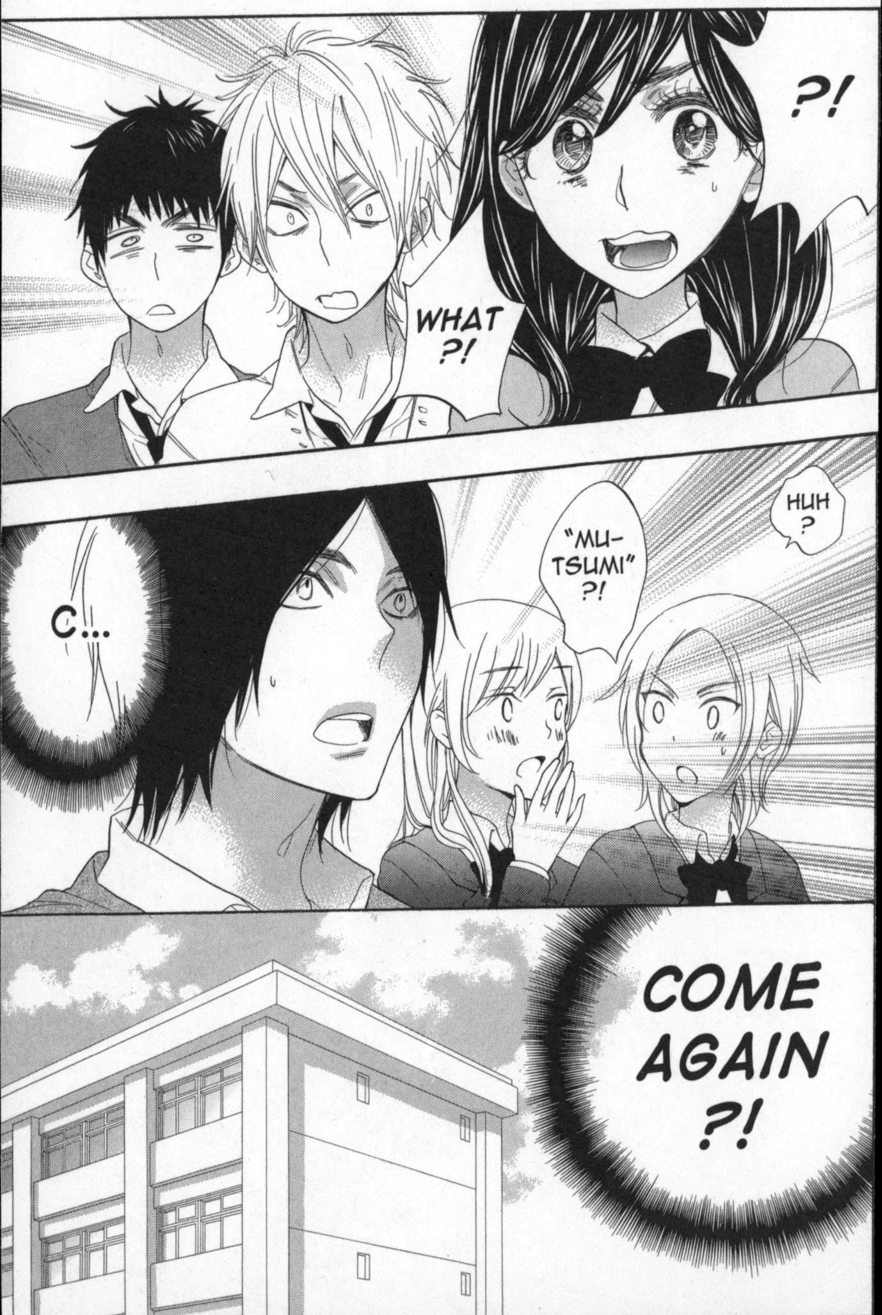
?!
WHAT ?!
HUH ?
"MU-TSUMI" ?!
C...
COME AGAIN ?!

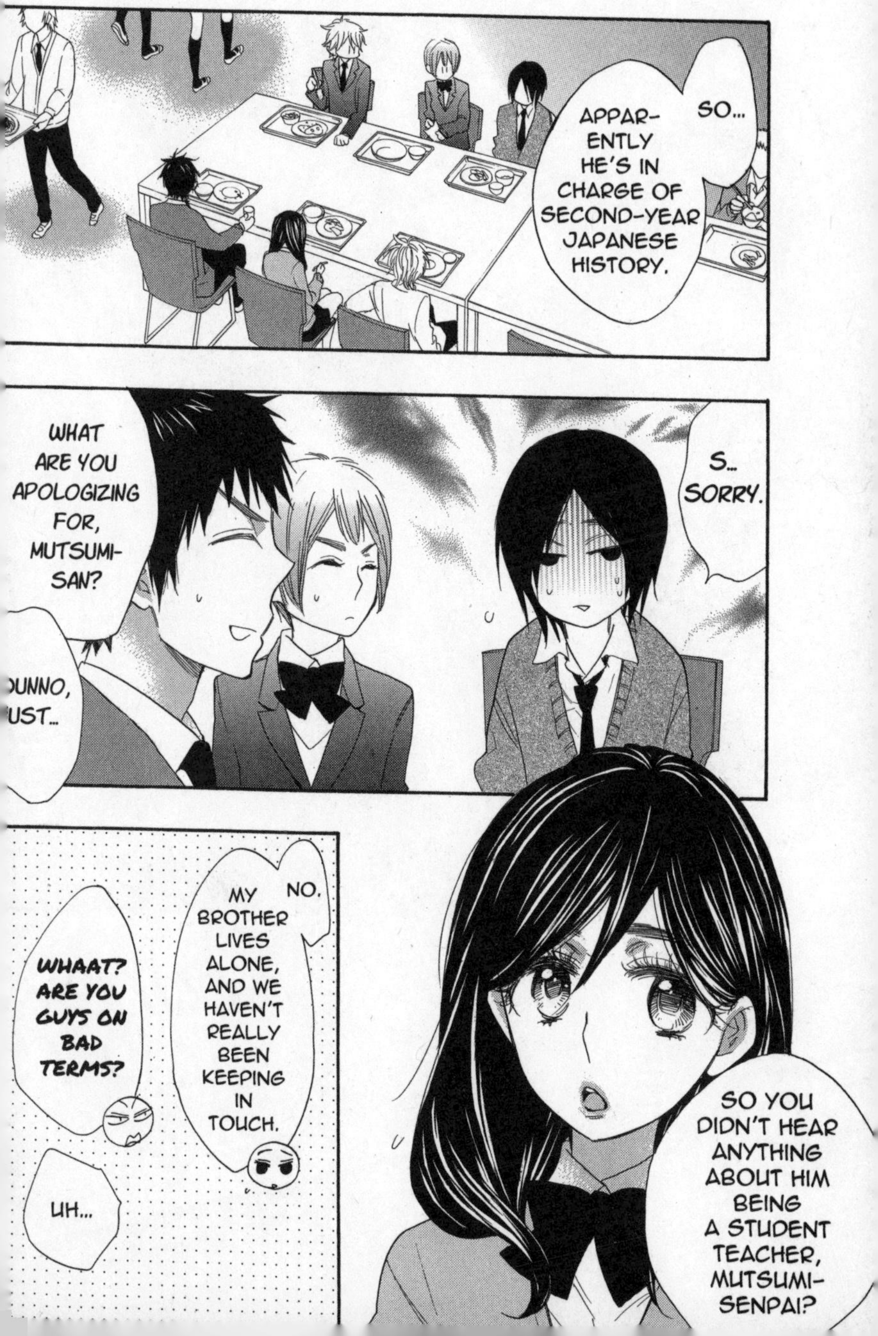
SO... APPARENTLY HE'S IN CHARGE OF SECOND-YEAR JAPANESE HISTORY.
S... SORRY.
WHAT ARE YOU APOLOGIZING FOR, MUTSUMI-SAN?
UNNO, UST...
SO YOU DIDN'T HEAR ANYTHING ABOUT HIM BEING A STUDENT TEACHER, MUTSUMI-SENPAI?
NO. MY BROTHER LIVES ALONE, AND WE HAVEN'T REALLY BEEN KEEPING IN TOUCH.
WHAAT? ARE YOU GUYS ON BAD TERMS?
UH...

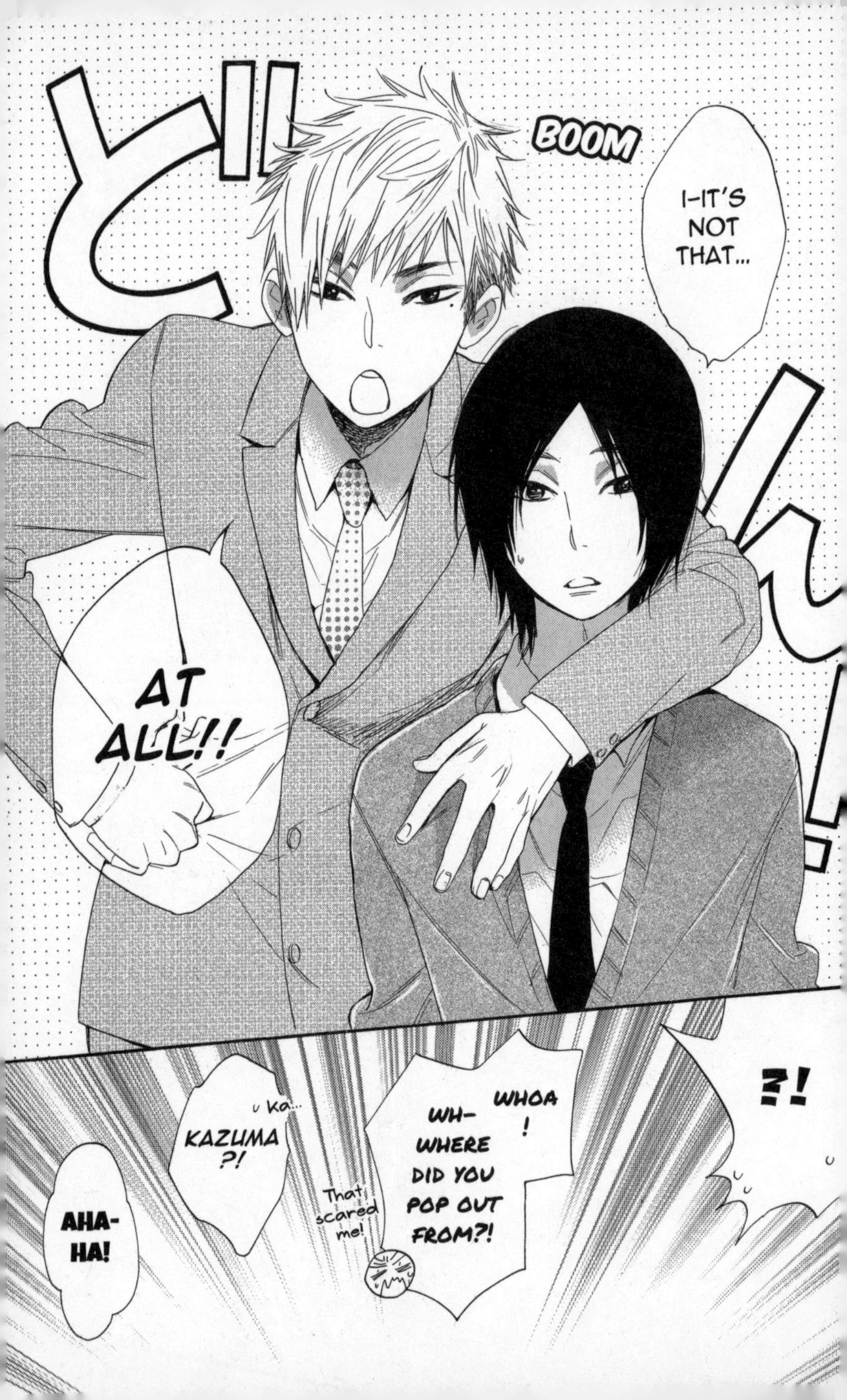

BOOM
I-IT'S NOT THAT...
AT ALL!!
?!
WHOA!
WH- WHERE DID YOU POP OUT FROM?!
That scared me!
Ka... KAZUMA?!
AHA-HA!

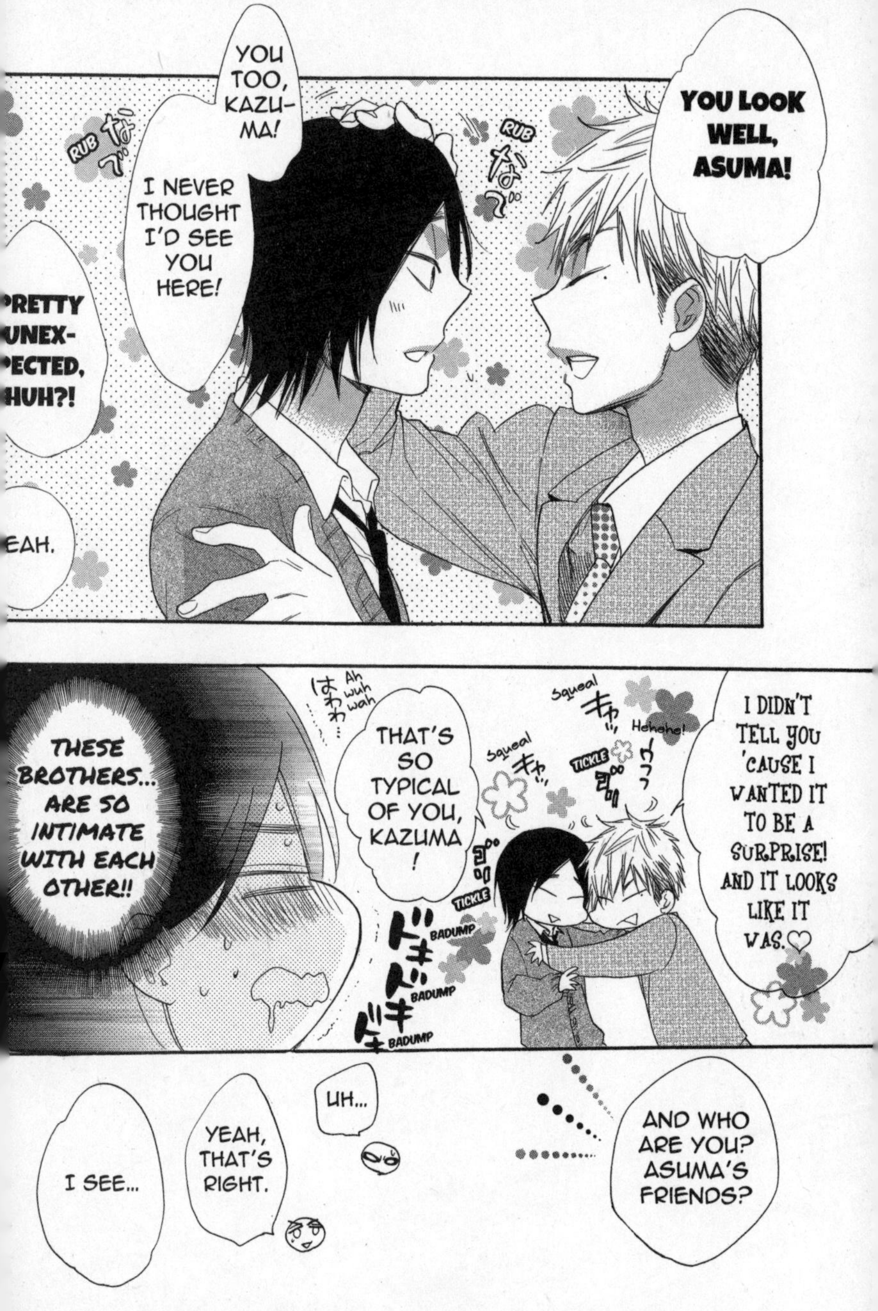
YOU LOOK WELL, ASUMA!
RUB なでっ
YOU TOO, KAZUMA!
RUB なでっ
I NEVER THOUGHT I'D SEE YOU HERE!
RETTY UNEX- ECTED, HUH?!
EAH.
I DIDN'T TELL YOU 'CAUSE I WANTED IT TO BE A SURPRISE! AND IT LOOKS LIKE IT WAS. ♡
Squeal キャッ
Hehehe ウフフ
TICKLE
Squeal キャッ
THAT'S SO TYPICAL OF YOU, KAZUMA!
Ah wuh wah はわわ……
TICKLE
BADUMP BADUMP BADUMP
THESE BROTHERS... ARE SO INTIMATE WITH EACH OTHER!!
AND WHO ARE YOU? ASUMA'S FRIENDS?
UH...
YEAH, THAT'S RIGHT.
I SEE...

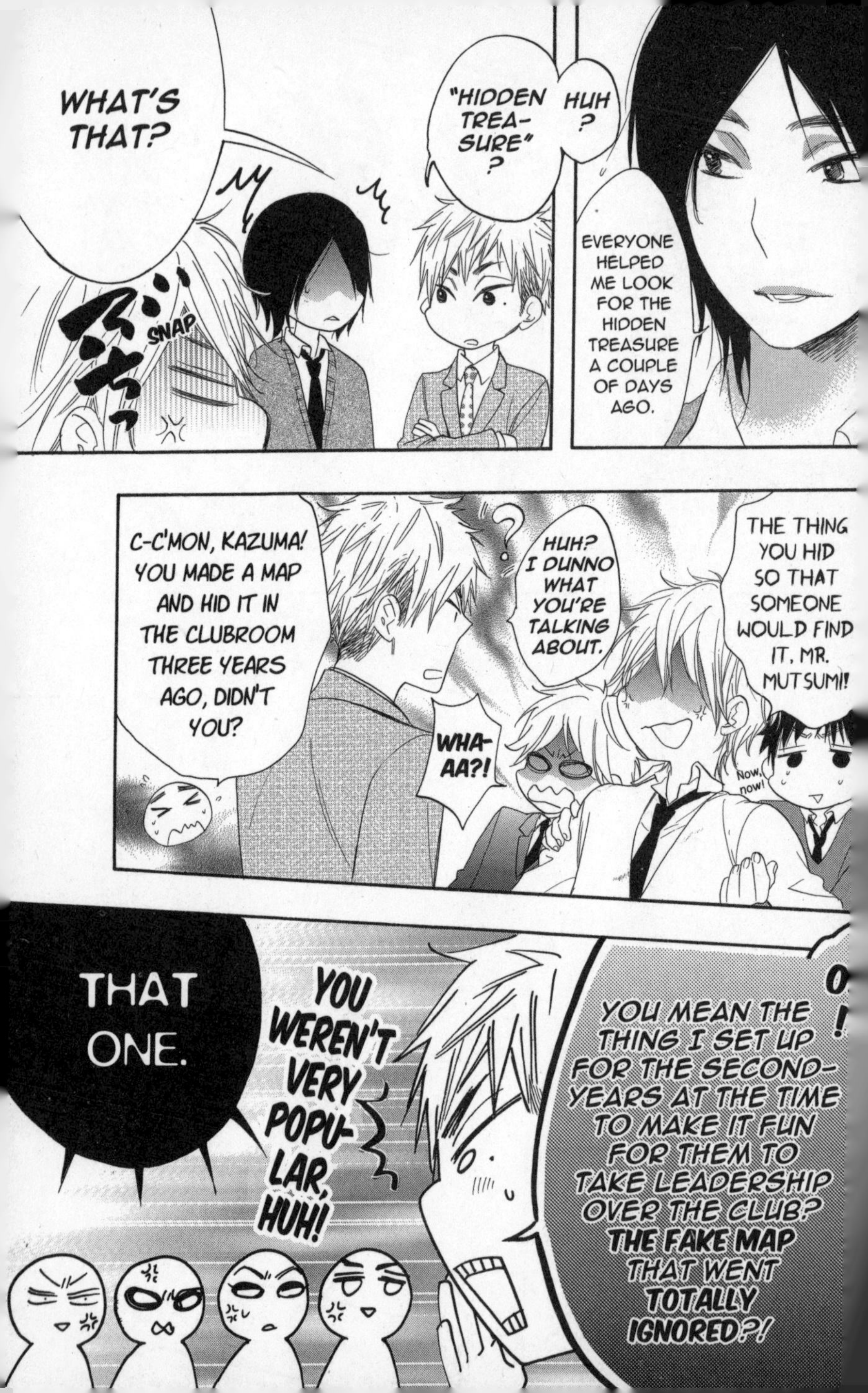
EVERYONE HELPED ME LOOK FOR THE HIDDEN TREASURE A COUPLE OF DAYS AGO.
HUH?
"HIDDEN TREASURE"?
WHAT'S THAT?
SNAP
THE THING YOU HID SO THAT SOMEONE WOULD FIND IT, MR. MUTSUMI!
Now, now!
HUH? I DUNNO WHAT YOU'RE TALKING ABOUT.
WHAAA?!
C-C'MON, KAZUMA! YOU MADE A MAP AND HID IT IN THE CLUBROOM THREE YEARS AGO, DIDN'T YOU?
O!
YOU MEAN THE THING I SET UP FOR THE SECOND-YEARS AT THE TIME TO MAKE IT FUN FOR THEM TO TAKE LEADERSHIP OVER THE CLUB? THE FAKE MAP THAT WENT TOTALLY IGNORED?!
YOU WEREN'T VERY POPULAR, HUH!
THAT ONE.

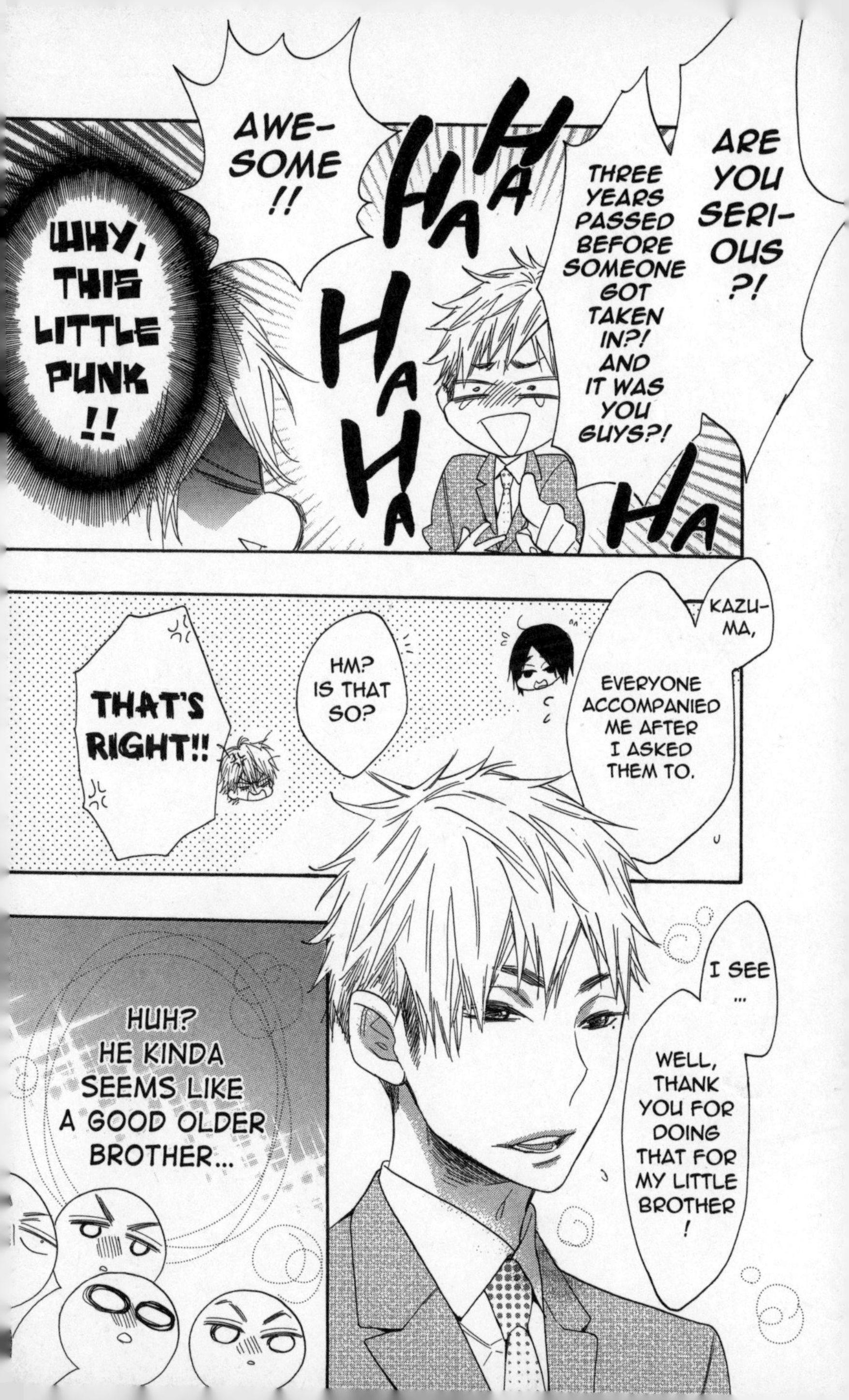

ARE YOU SERI-OUS?!
THREE YEARS PASSED BEFORE SOMEONE GOT TAKEN IN?! AND IT WAS YOU GUYS?!
HA HA HA HA HA HA HA
AWE-SOME!!
WHY, THIS LITTLE PUNK!!
KAZU-MA,
EVERYONE ACCOMPANIED ME AFTER I ASKED THEM TO.
HM? IS THAT SO?
THAT'S RIGHT!!
I SEE...
WELL, THANK YOU FOR DOING THAT FOR MY LITTLE BROTHER!
HUH? HE KINDA SEEMS LIKE A GOOD OLDER BROTHER...

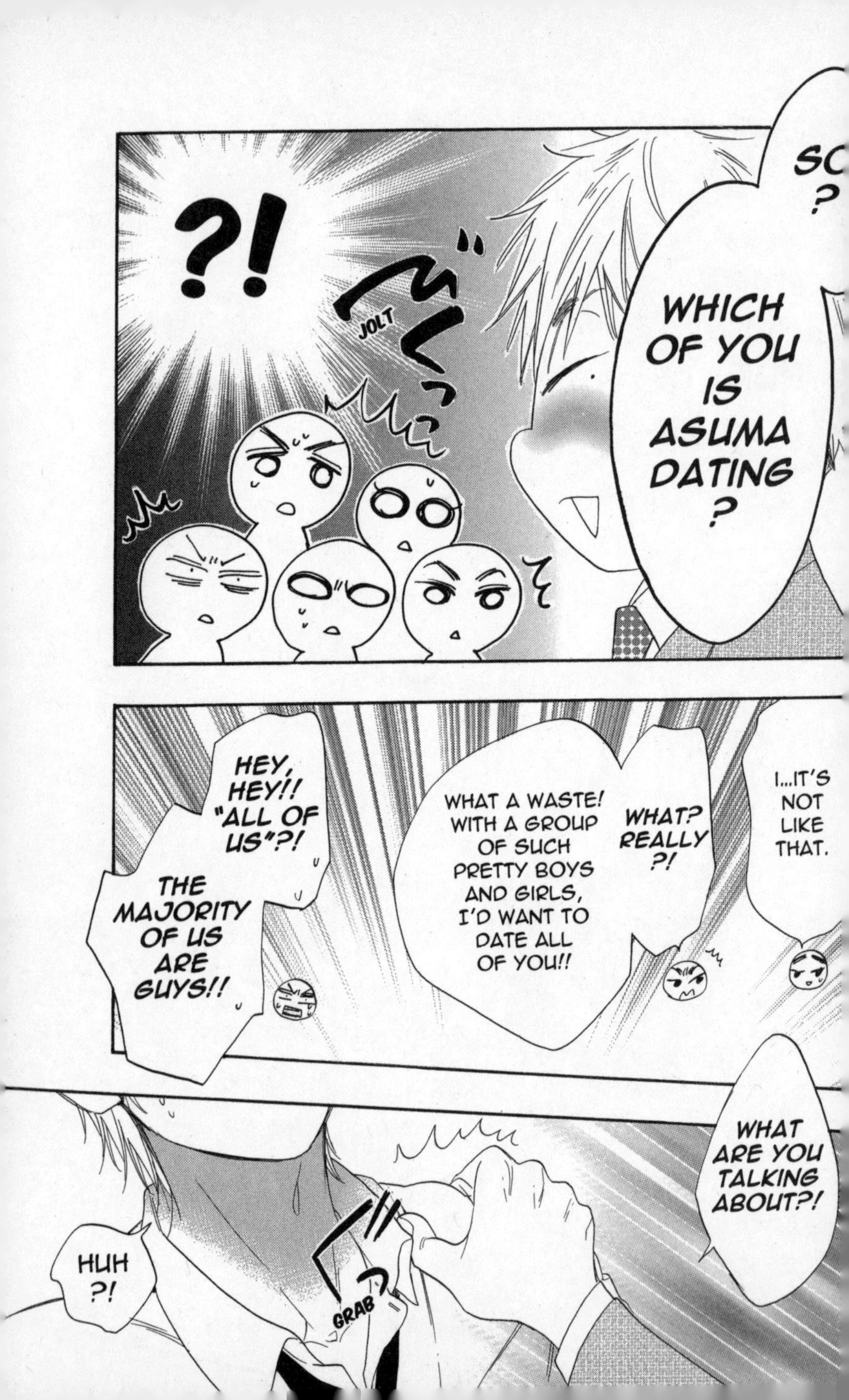
SO?
WHICH OF YOU IS ASUMA DATING?
?!
JOLT
I...IT'S NOT LIKE THAT.
WHAT? REALLY?!
WHAT A WASTE! WITH A GROUP OF SUCH PRETTY BOYS AND GIRLS, I'D WANT TO DATE ALL OF YOU!!
HEY, HEY!! "ALL OF US"?!
THE MAJORITY OF US ARE GUYS!!
WHAT ARE YOU TALKING ABOUT?!
GRAB
HUH?!

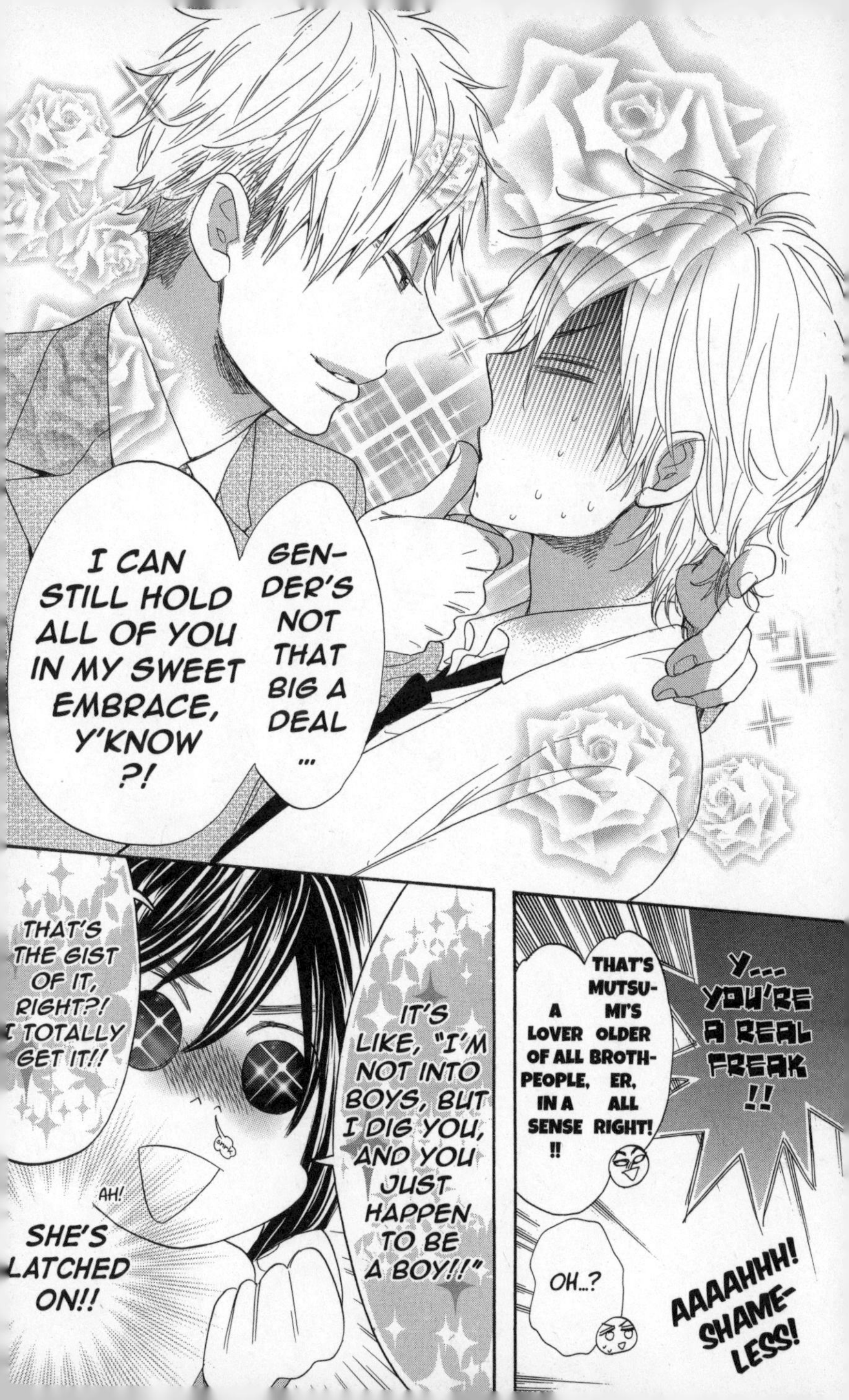
GEN-DER'S NOT THAT BIG A DEAL...
I CAN STILL HOLD ALL OF YOU IN MY SWEET EMBRACE, Y'KNOW?!
Y... YOU'RE A REAL FREAK!!
THAT'S MUTSU-MI'S OLDER BROTH-ER, ALL RIGHT!
A LOVER OF ALL PEOPLE, IN A SENSE!!
AAAAHHH! SHAME-LESS!
OH...?
IT'S LIKE, "I'M NOT INTO BOYS, BUT I DIG YOU, AND YOU JUST HAPPEN TO BE A BOY!!"
THAT'S THE GIST OF IT, RIGHT?! I TOTALLY GET IT!!
AH!
SHE'S LATCHED ON!!

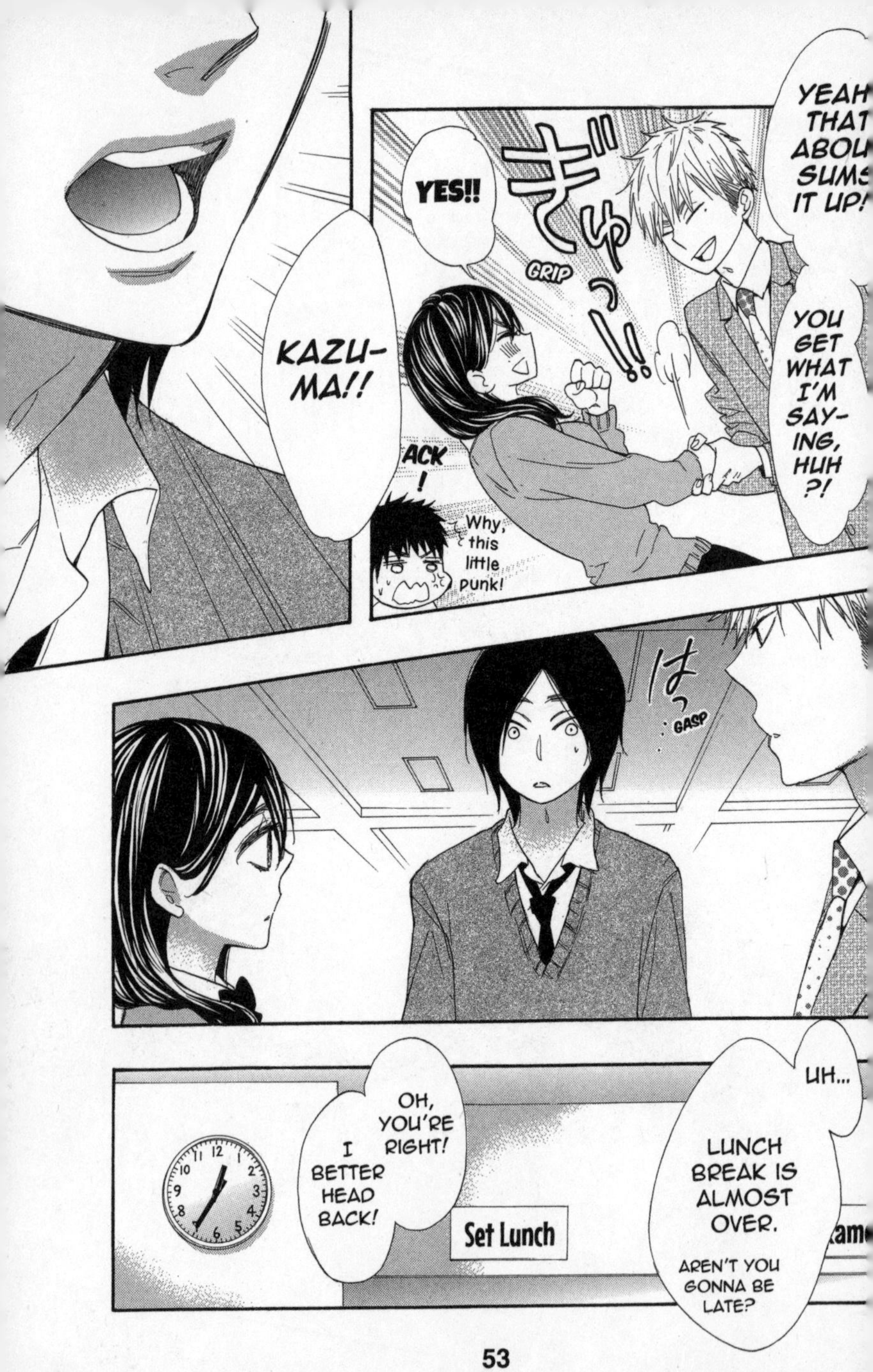
YEAH THAT ABOU SUMS IT UP!
YOU GET WHAT I'M SAY-ING, HUH?!
YES!!
ぎゅっ!!
GRIP
ACK!
Why, this little punk!
KAZU-MA!!
はっ
GASP
UH...
LUNCH BREAK IS ALMOST OVER.
AREN'T YOU GONNA BE LATE?
OH, YOU'RE RIGHT!
I BETTER HEAD BACK!
Set Lunch

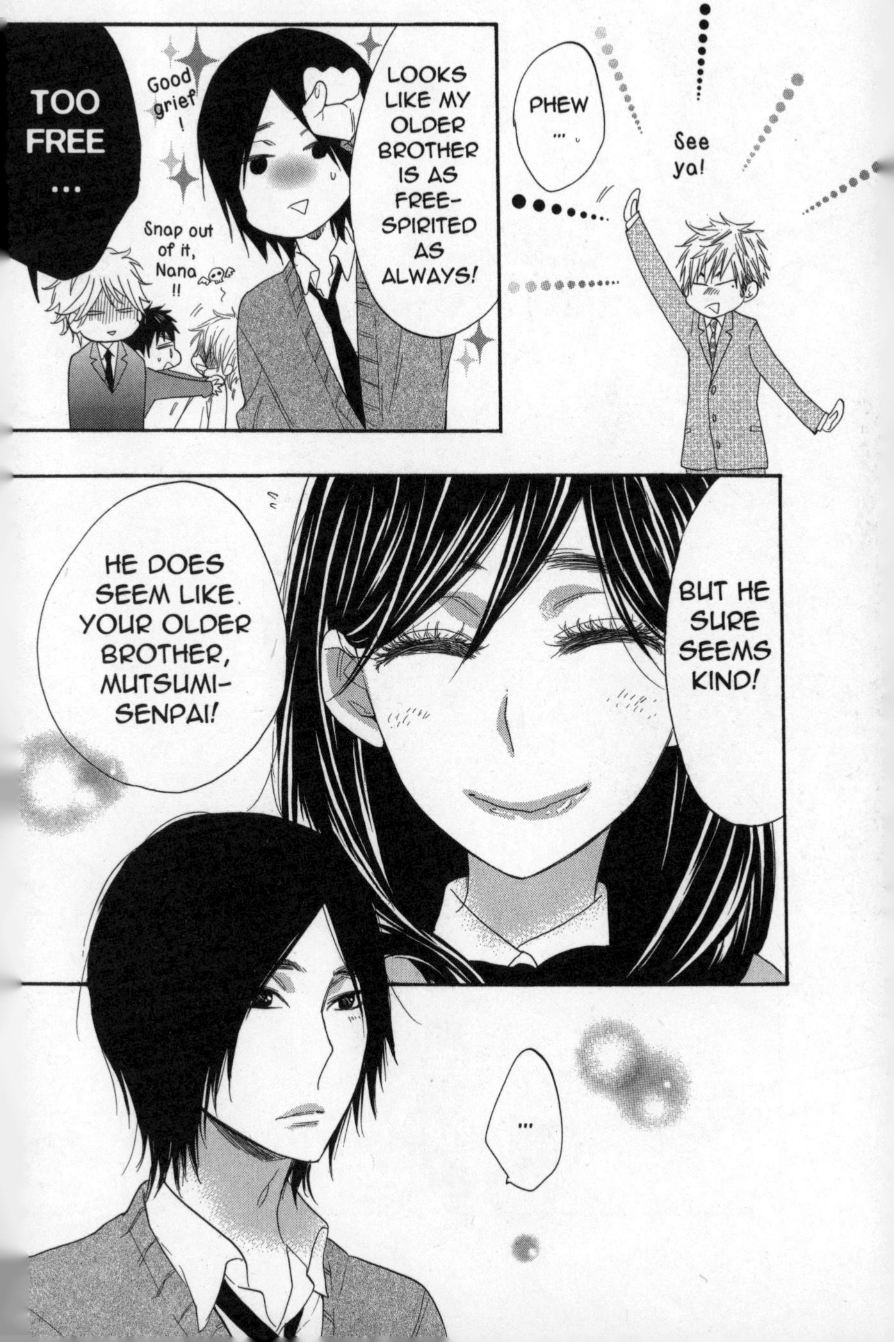
See ya!
PHEW...
LOOKS LIKE MY OLDER BROTHER IS AS FREE-SPIRITED AS ALWAYS!
Good grief!
Snap out of it, Nana!!
TOO FREE...
BUT HE SURE SEEMS KIND!
HE DOES SEEM LIKE YOUR OLDER BROTHER, MUTSUMI-SENPAI!
...

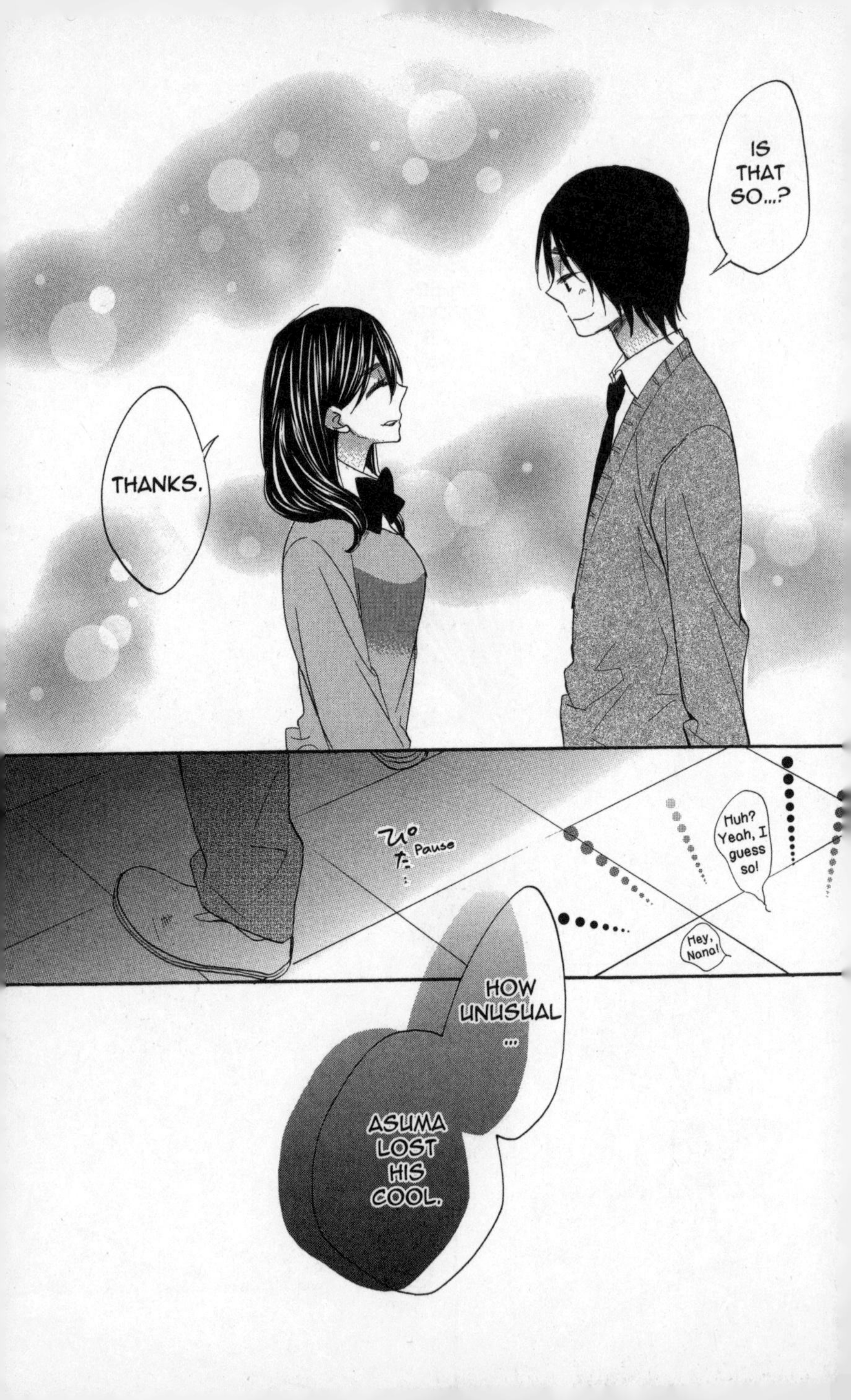
IS THAT SO...?
THANKS.
Huh? Yeah, I guess so!
Hey, Nana!
ぴた… Pause
HOW UNUSUAL...
ASUMA LOST HIS COOL.

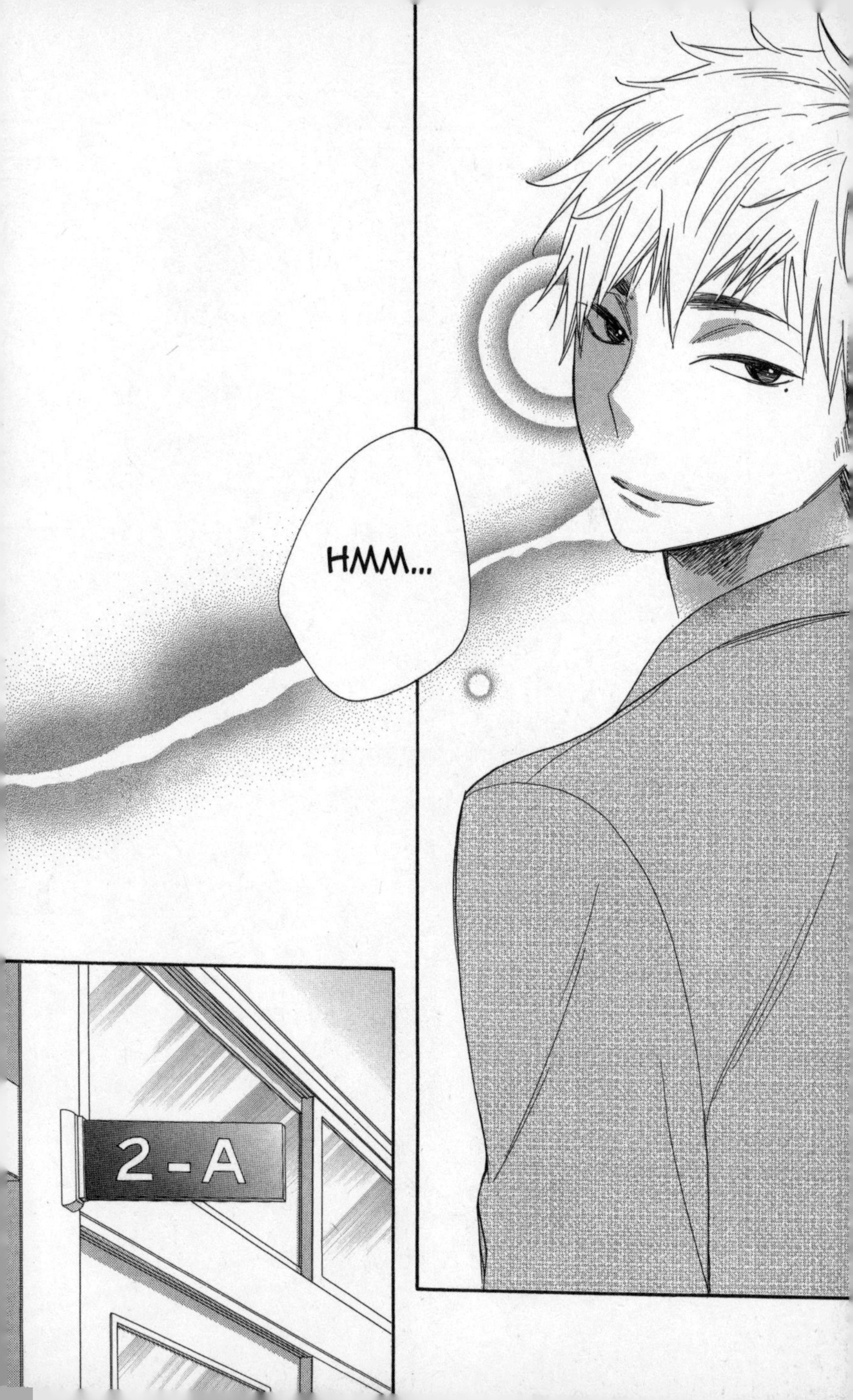
HMM...
2-A

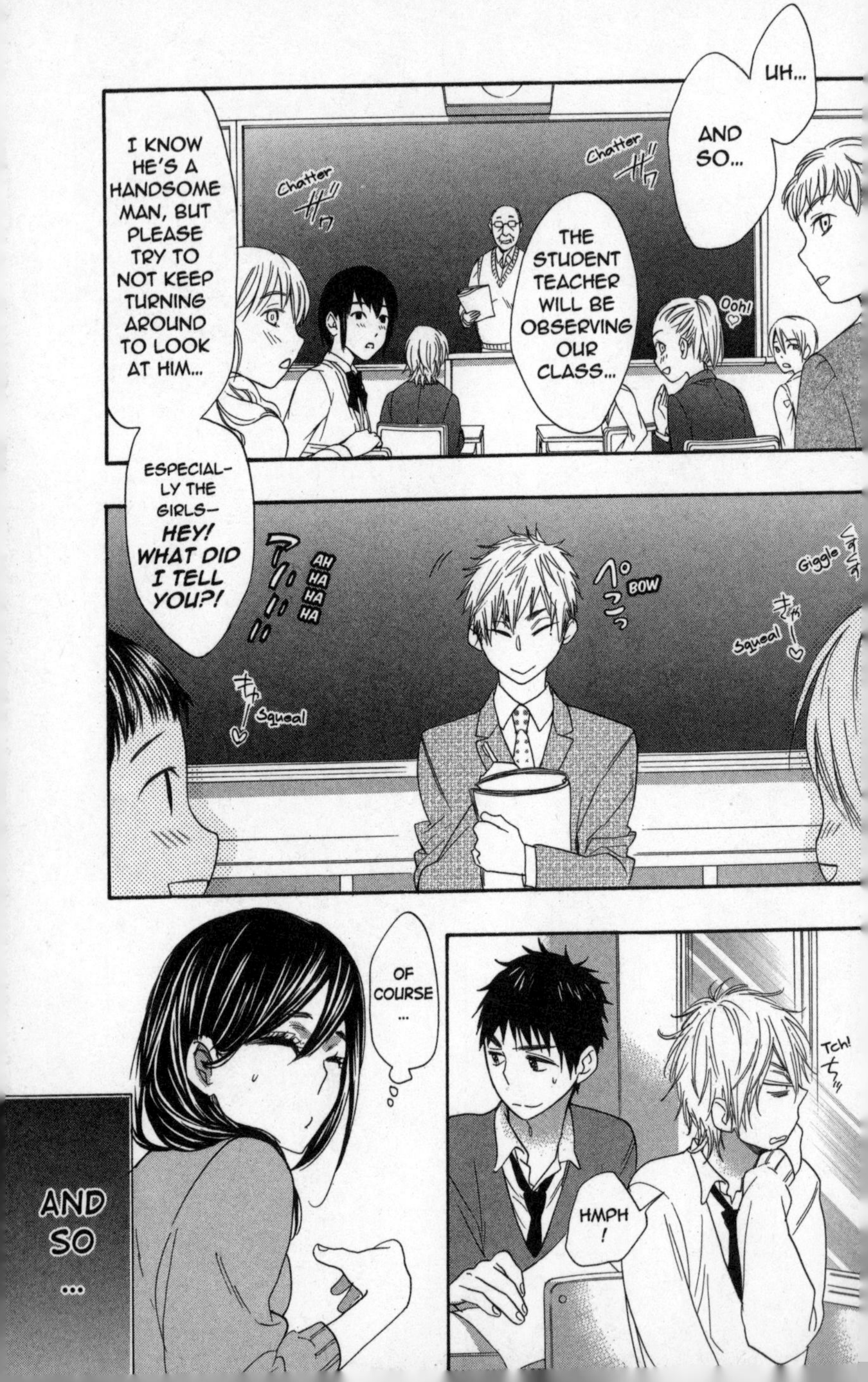
UH...
AND SO...
Chatter
Ooh!
THE STUDENT TEACHER WILL BE OBSERVING OUR CLASS...
Chatter
I KNOW HE'S A HANDSOME MAN, BUT PLEASE TRY TO NOT KEEP TURNING AROUND TO LOOK AT HIM...
ESPECIAL-LY THE GIRLS— HEY! WHAT DID I TELL YOU?!
Giggle
Squeal
BOW
AH HA HA HA
Squeal
Tch!
HMPH!
OF COURSE...
AND SO...

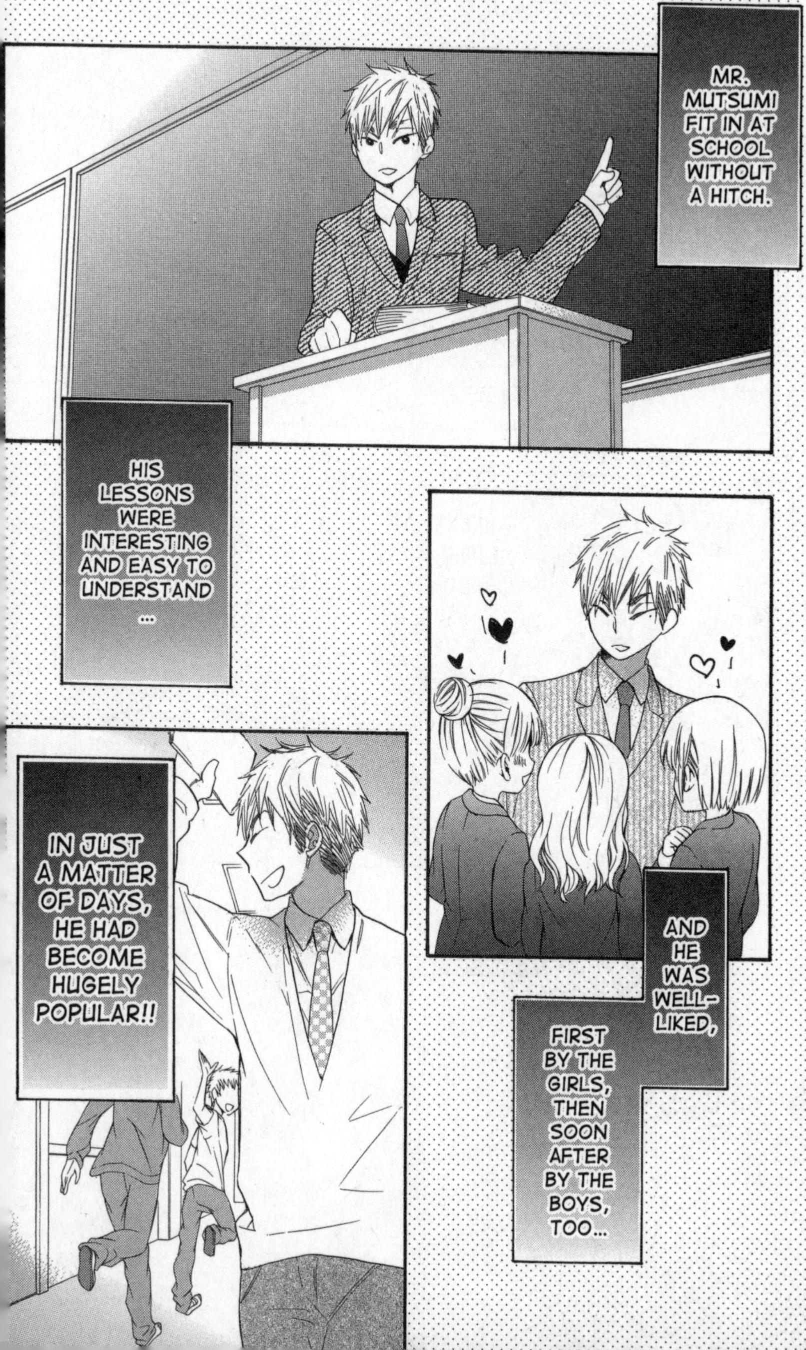
MR. MUTSUMI FIT IN AT SCHOOL WITHOUT A HITCH.
HIS LESSONS WERE INTERESTING AND EASY TO UNDERSTAND...
AND HE WAS WELL-LIKED,
FIRST BY THE GIRLS, THEN SOON AFTER BY THE BOYS, TOO...
IN JUST A MATTER OF DAYS, HE HAD BECOME HUGELY POPULAR!!

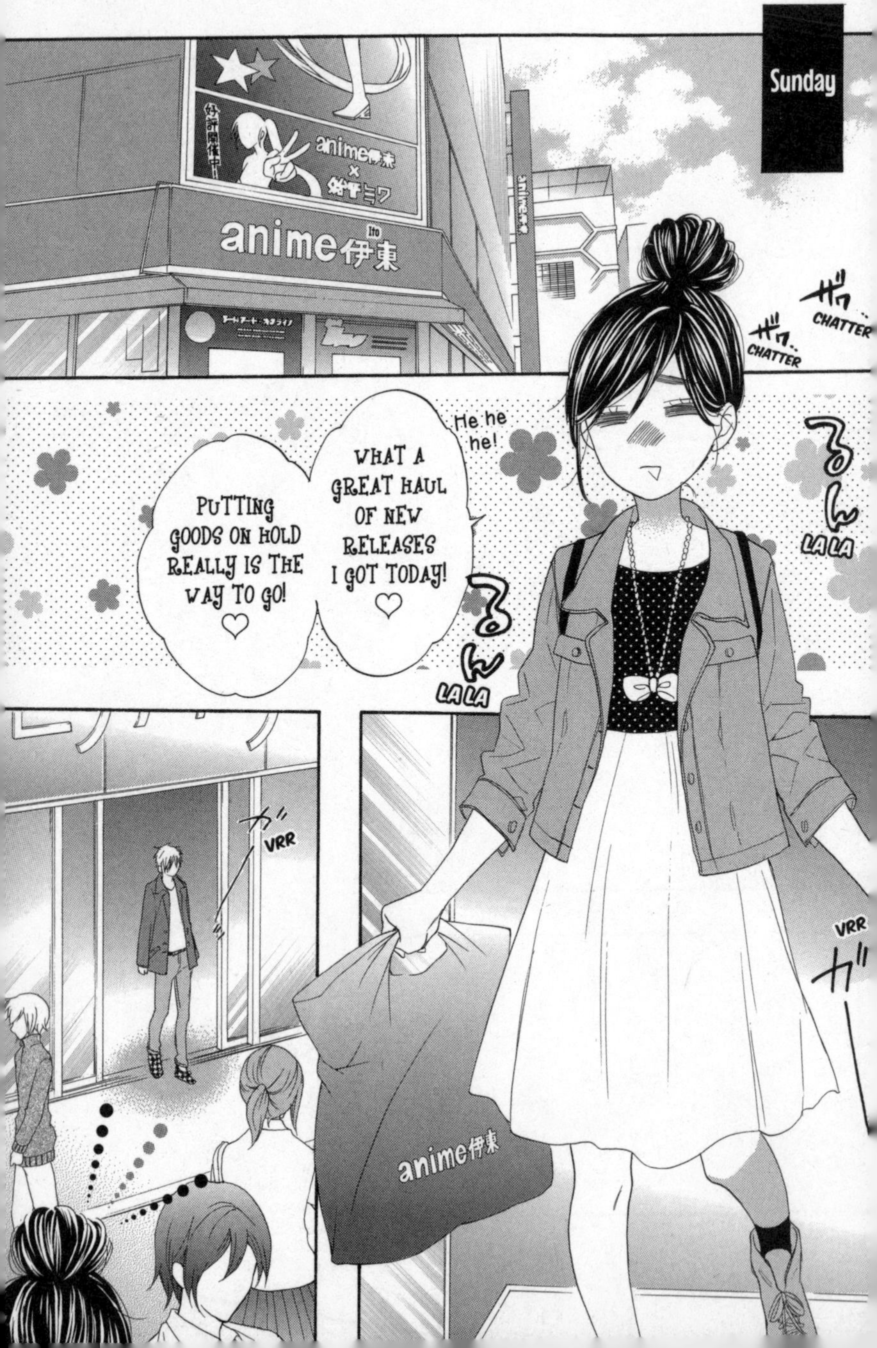
Sunday
ザワ CHATTER
ザワ CHATTER
anime伊東
Ito
好評開催中
anime伊東
×
He he he!
WHAT A GREAT HAUL OF NEW RELEASES I GOT TODAY! ♡
PUTTING GOODS ON HOLD REALLY IS THE WAY TO GO! ♡
るん LA LA
るん LA LA
ガ VRR
ガ VRR
anime伊東

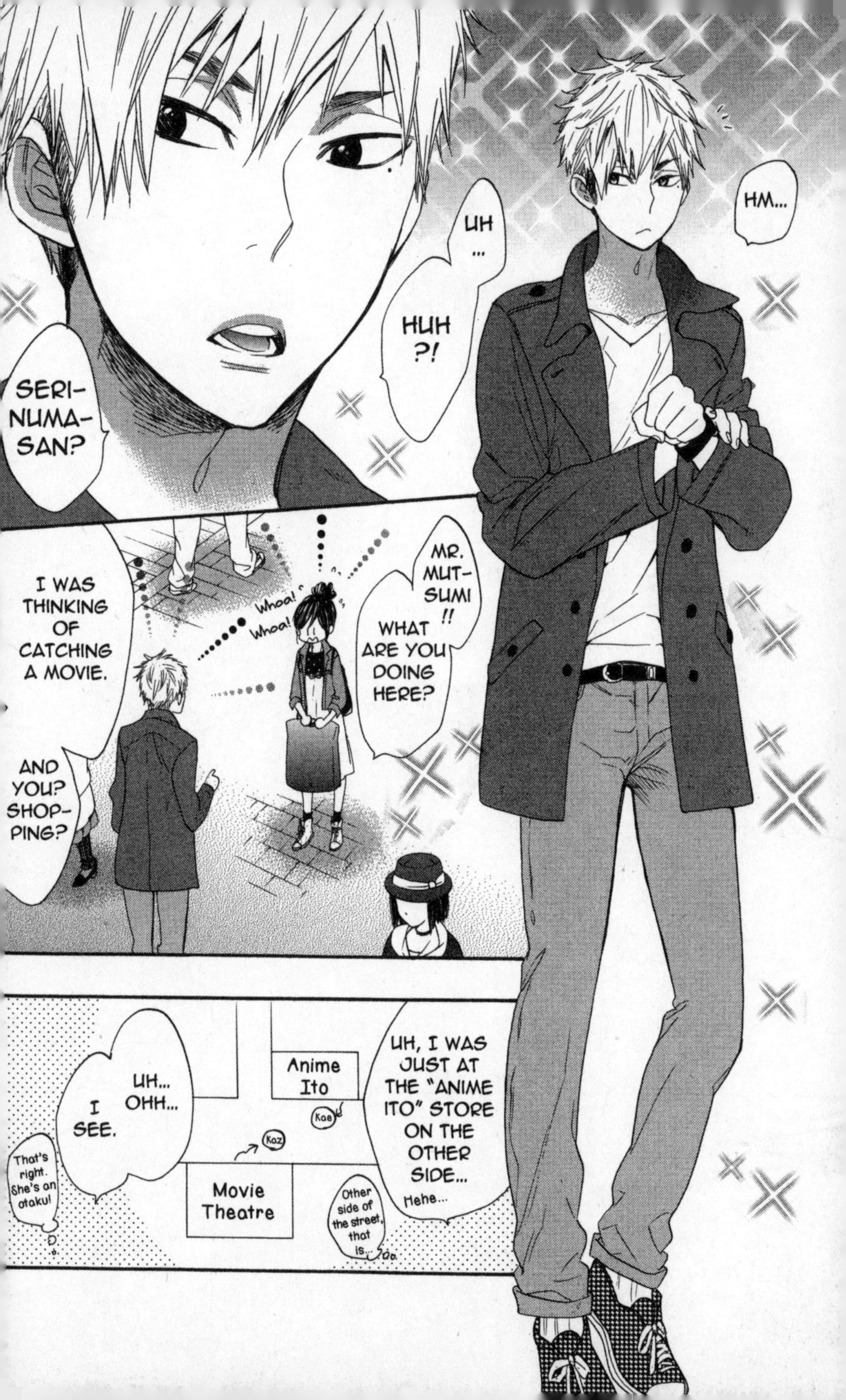
HM...
UH ...
HUH ?!
SERI-NUMA-SAN?
MR. MUT-SUMI !!
WHAT ARE YOU DOING HERE?
Whoa! Whoa!
I WAS THINKING OF CATCHING A MOVIE.
AND YOU? SHOP-PING?
UH, I WAS JUST AT THE "ANIME ITO" STORE ON THE OTHER SIDE...
Hehe...
Other side of the street, that is...
Anime Ito
Kae
Kaz
Movie Theatre
UH... OHH...
I SEE.
That's right. She's an otaku!

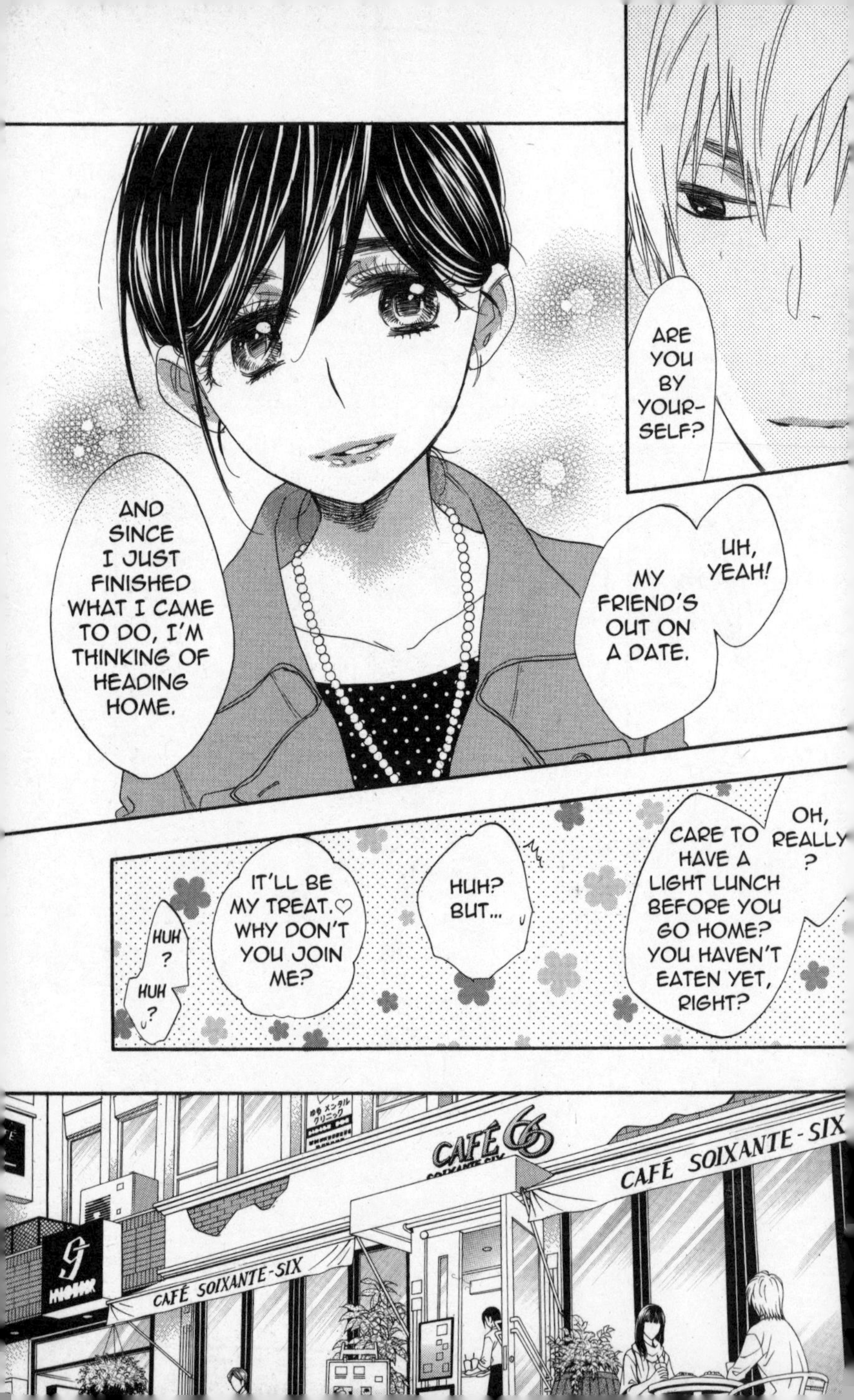
ARE YOU BY YOURSELF?
UH, YEAH!
MY FRIEND'S OUT ON A DATE.
AND SINCE I JUST FINISHED WHAT I CAME TO DO, I'M THINKING OF HEADING HOME.
OH, REALLY?
CARE TO HAVE A LIGHT LUNCH BEFORE YOU GO HOME? YOU HAVEN'T EATEN YET, RIGHT?
HUH? BUT...
IT'LL BE MY TREAT.♡ WHY DON'T YOU JOIN ME?
HUH? HUH?
CAFÉ SOIXANTE-SIX
CAFÉ 66
CAFÉ SOIXANTE-SIX

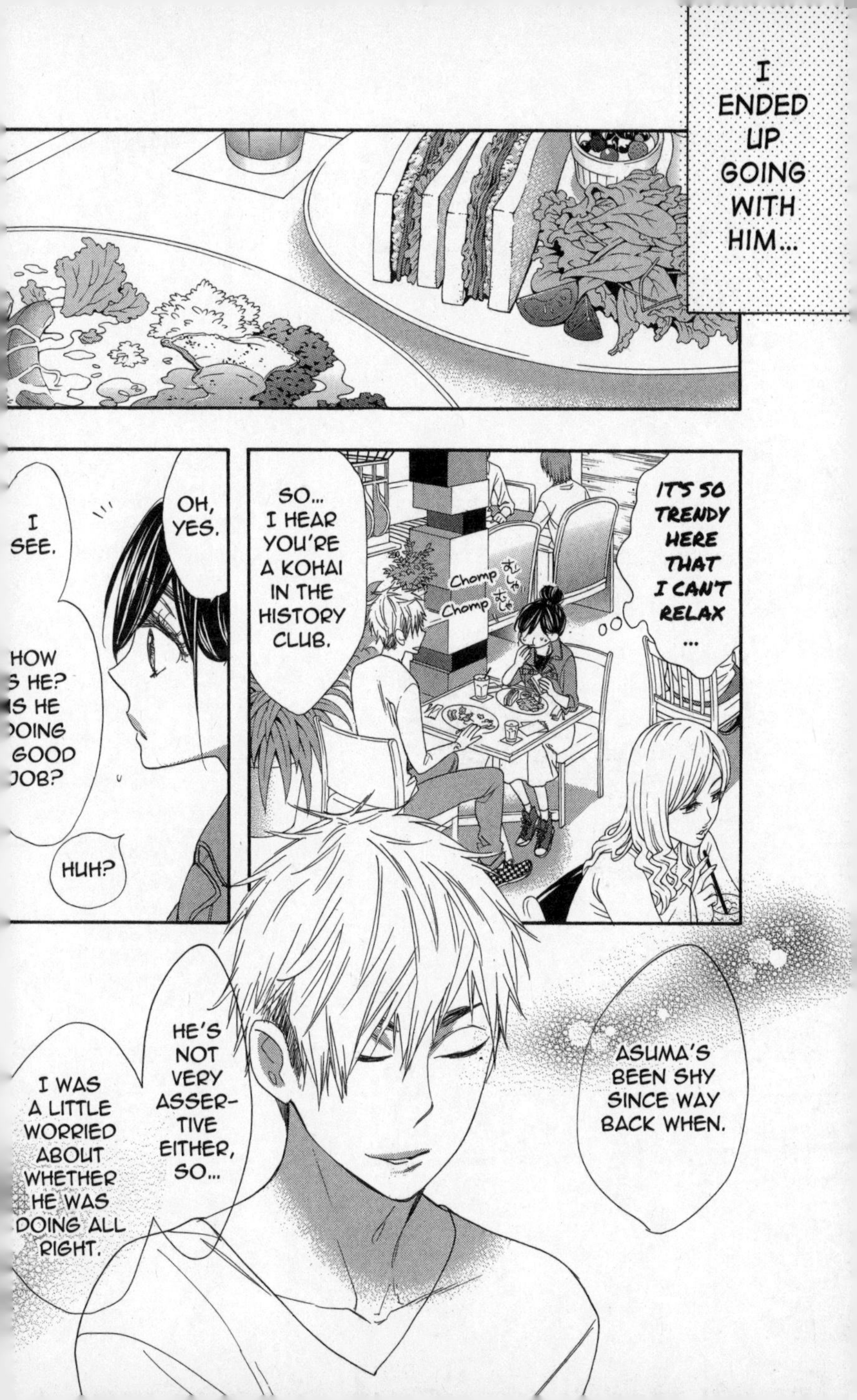
I ENDED UP GOING WITH HIM...
IT'S SO TRENDY HERE THAT I CAN'T RELAX ...
SO... I HEAR YOU'RE A KOHAI IN THE HISTORY CLUB.
Chomp むしゃ
Chomp むしゃ
OH, YES.
I SEE.
HOW IS HE? IS HE DOING A GOOD JOB?
HUH?
ASUMA'S BEEN SHY SINCE WAY BACK WHEN.
HE'S NOT VERY ASSER-TIVE EITHER, SO...
I WAS A LITTLE WORRIED ABOUT WHETHER HE WAS DOING ALL RIGHT.

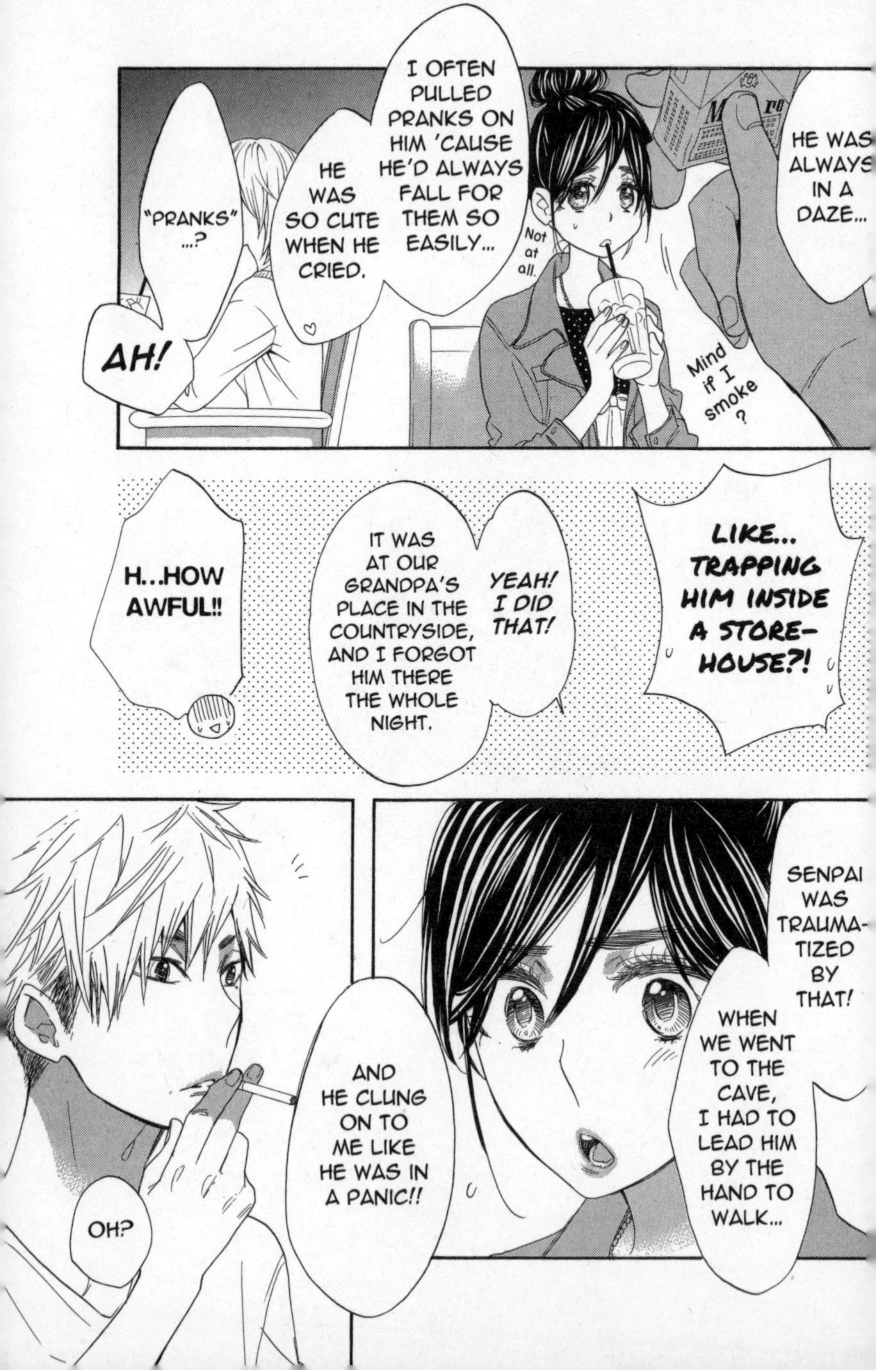
HE WAS ALWAYS IN A DAZE...
I OFTEN PULLED PRANKS ON HIM 'CAUSE HE'D ALWAYS FALL FOR THEM SO EASILY...
Mind if I smoke?
Not at all.
HE WAS SO CUTE WHEN HE CRIED.
"PRANKS" ...?
AH!
LIKE... TRAPPING HIM INSIDE A STORE-HOUSE?!
YEAH! I DID THAT!
IT WAS AT OUR GRANDPA'S PLACE IN THE COUNTRYSIDE, AND I FORGOT HIM THERE THE WHOLE NIGHT.
H...HOW AWFUL!!
SENPAI WAS TRAUMA-TIZED BY THAT!
WHEN WE WENT TO THE CAVE, I HAD TO LEAD HIM BY THE HAND TO WALK...
AND HE CLUNG ON TO ME LIKE HE WAS IN A PANIC!!
OH?

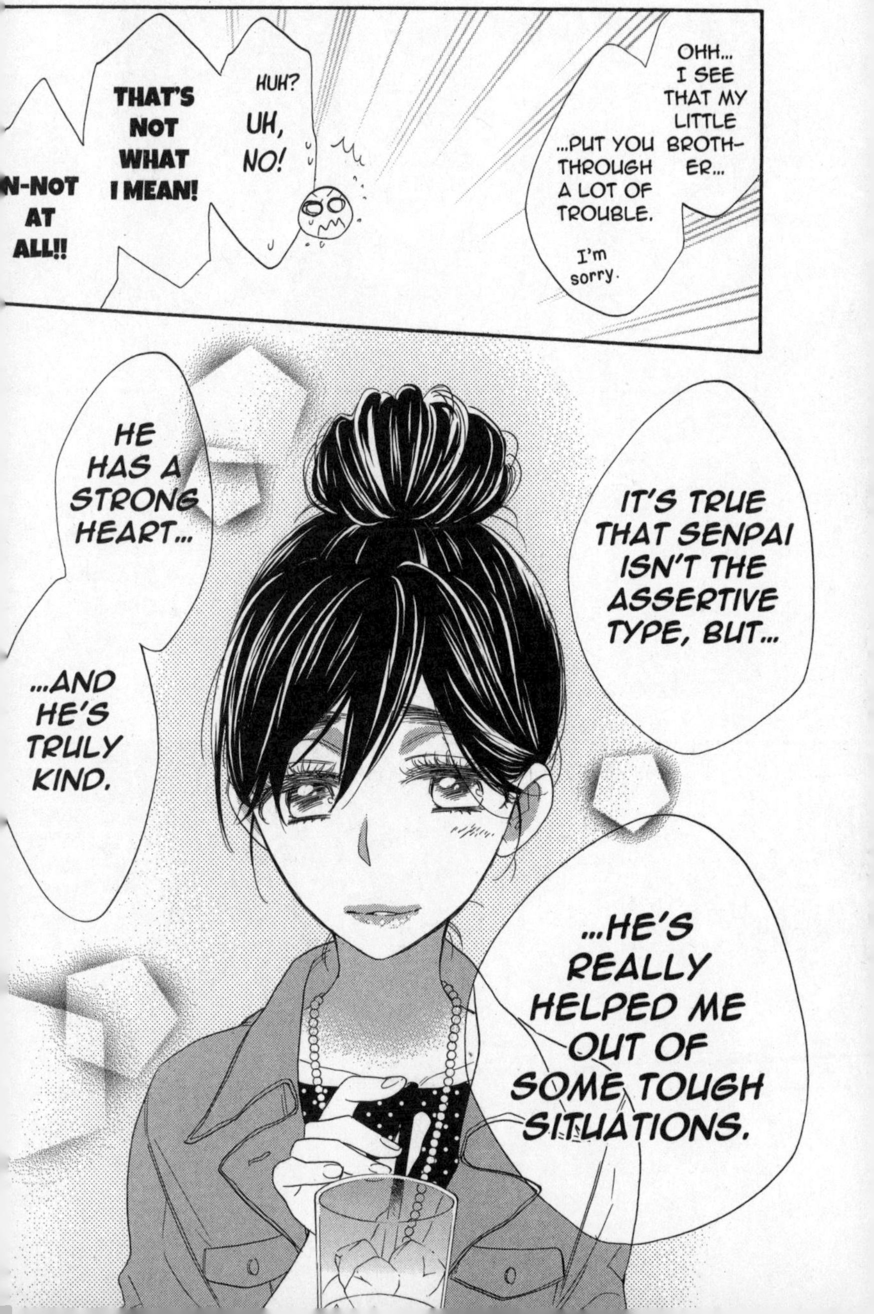
OHH... I SEE THAT MY LITTLE BROTH-ER...
...PUT YOU THROUGH A LOT OF TROUBLE.
I'm sorry.
HUH?
UH, NO!
THAT'S NOT WHAT I MEAN!
N-NOT AT ALL!!
IT'S TRUE THAT SENPAI ISN'T THE ASSERTIVE TYPE, BUT...
...HE'S REALLY HELPED ME OUT OF SOME TOUGH SITUATIONS.
HE HAS A STRONG HEART...
...AND HE'S TRULY KIND.

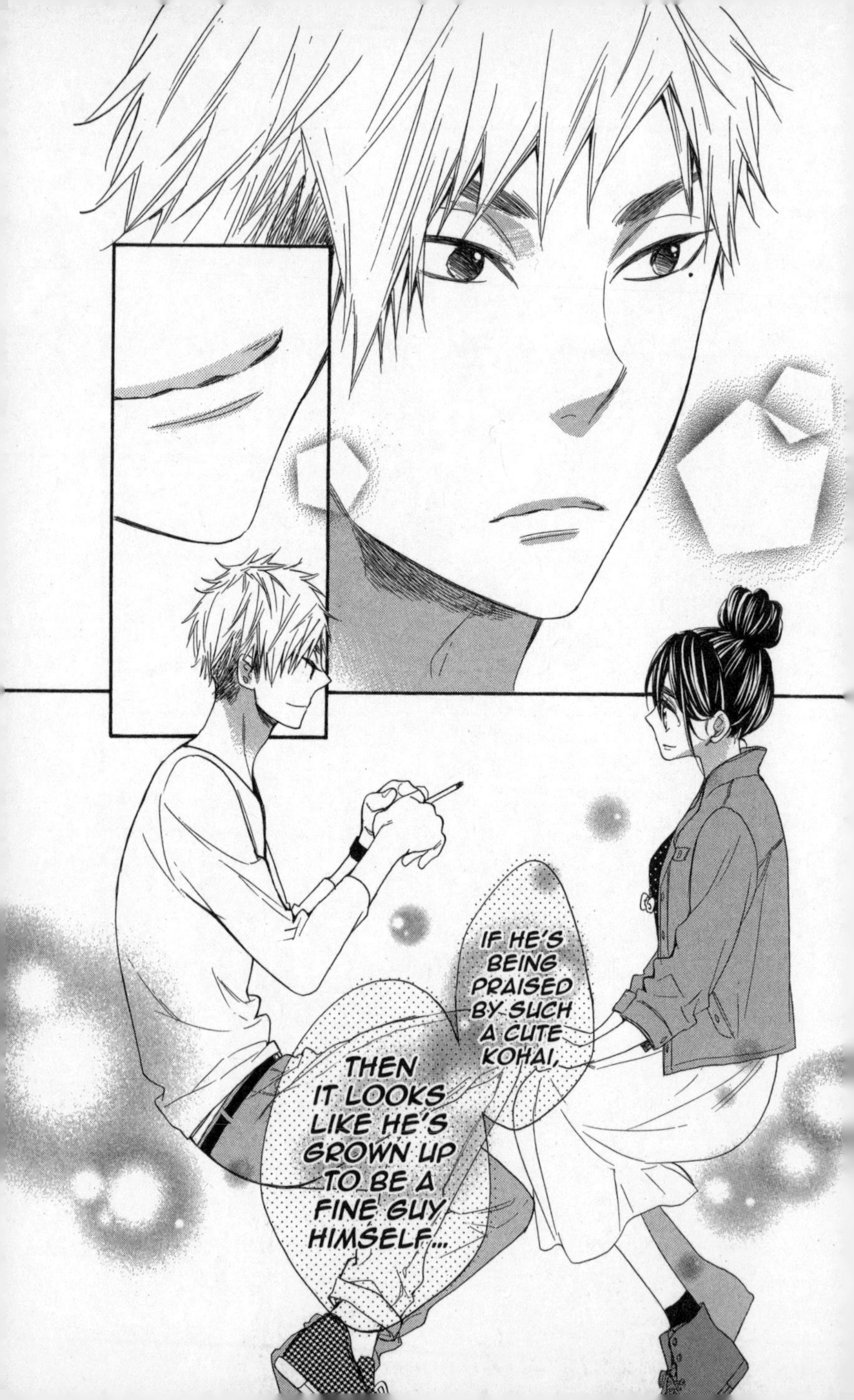
IF HE'S BEING PRAISED BY SUCH A CUTE KOHAI,
THEN IT LOOKS LIKE HE'S GROWN UP TO BE A FINE GUY HIMSELF...

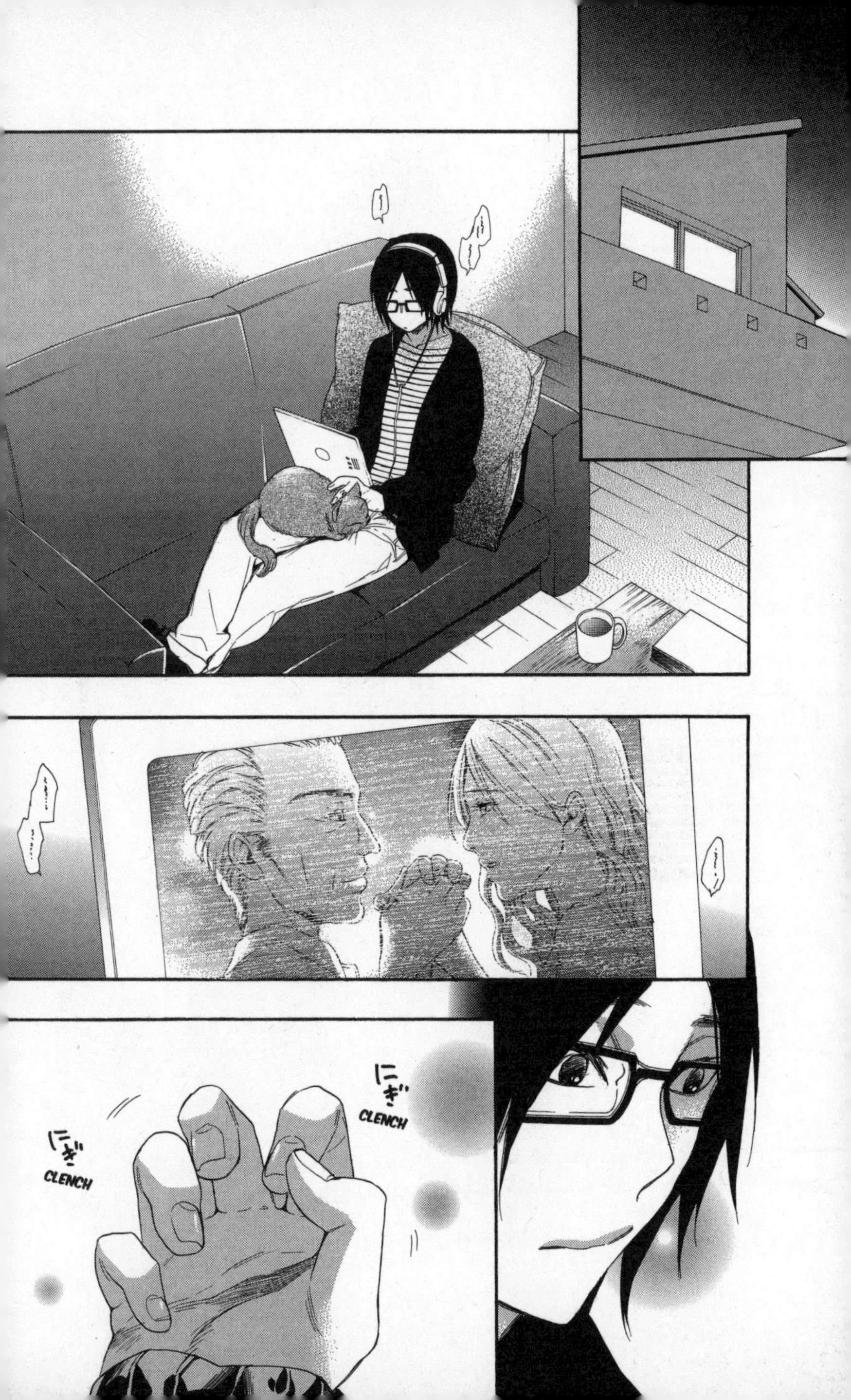
にぎ
CLENCH
にぎ
CLENCH

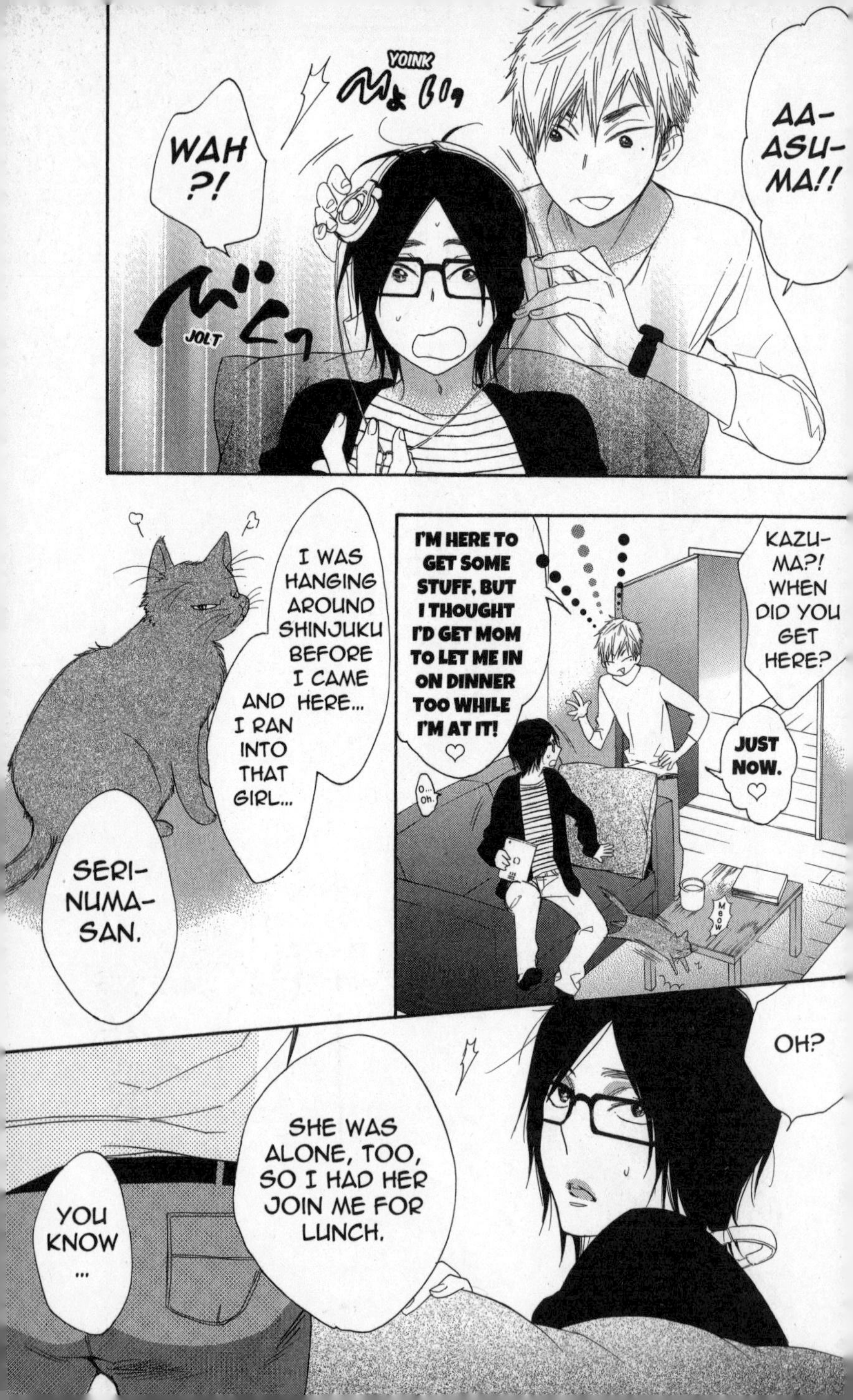
AA-ASUMA!!
YOINK
WAH?!
JOLT
KAZUMA?! WHEN DID YOU GET HERE?
I'M HERE TO GET SOME STUFF, BUT I THOUGHT I'D GET MOM TO LET ME IN ON DINNER TOO WHILE I'M AT IT! ♡
JUST NOW. ♡
O... Oh.
Meow
I WAS HANGING AROUND SHINJUKU BEFORE I CAME HERE...
AND I RAN INTO THAT GIRL...
SERI-NUMA-SAN.
OH?
SHE WAS ALONE, TOO, SO I HAD HER JOIN ME FOR LUNCH.
YOU KNOW...

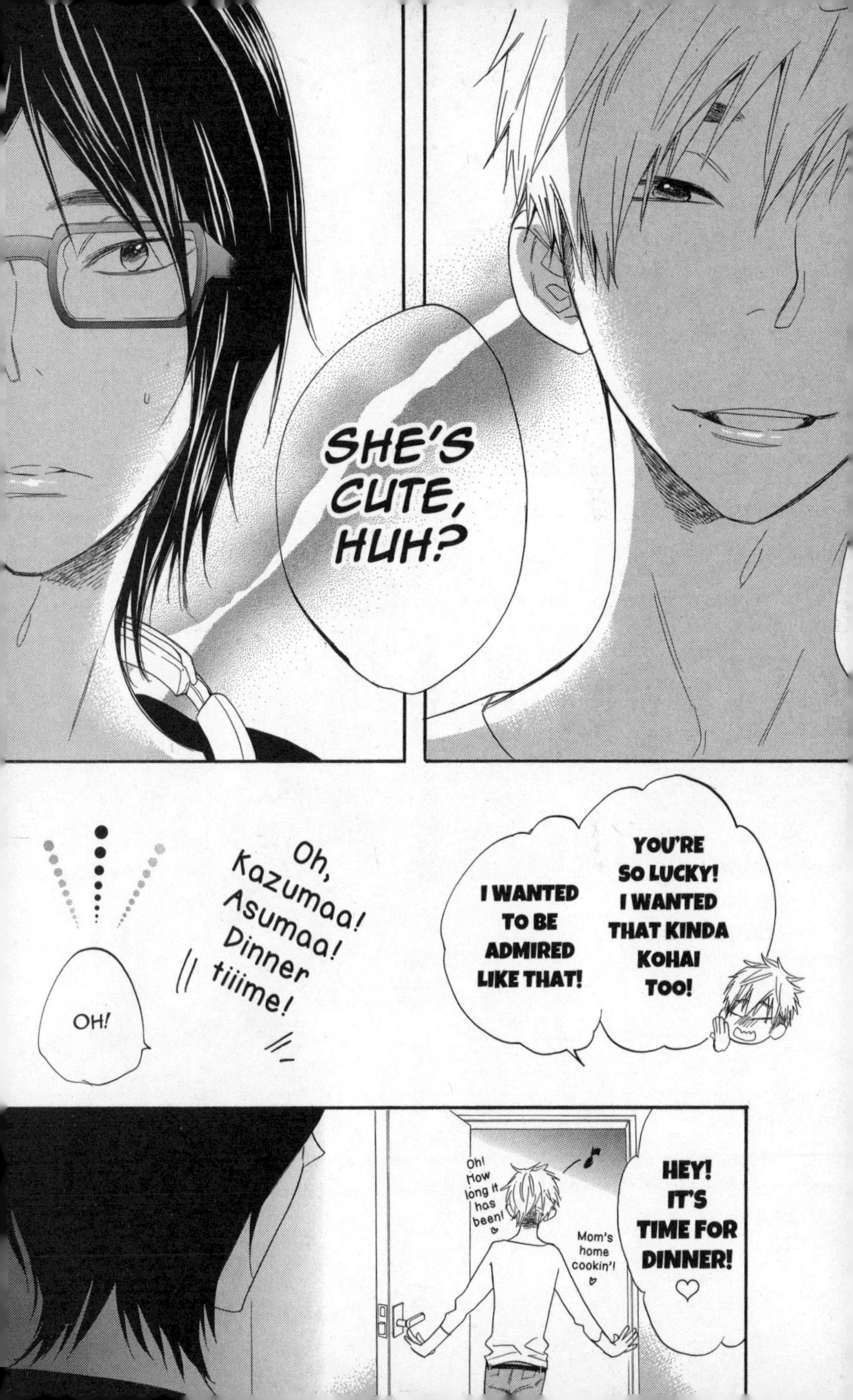
SHE'S CUTE, HUH?
YOU'RE SO LUCKY! I WANTED THAT KINDA KOHAI TOO!
I WANTED TO BE ADMIRED LIKE THAT!
Oh, Kazumaa! Asumaa! Dinner tiiime!
OH!
HEY! IT'S TIME FOR DINNER! ♡
Mom's home cookin'! ♡
Oh! How long it has been! ♡

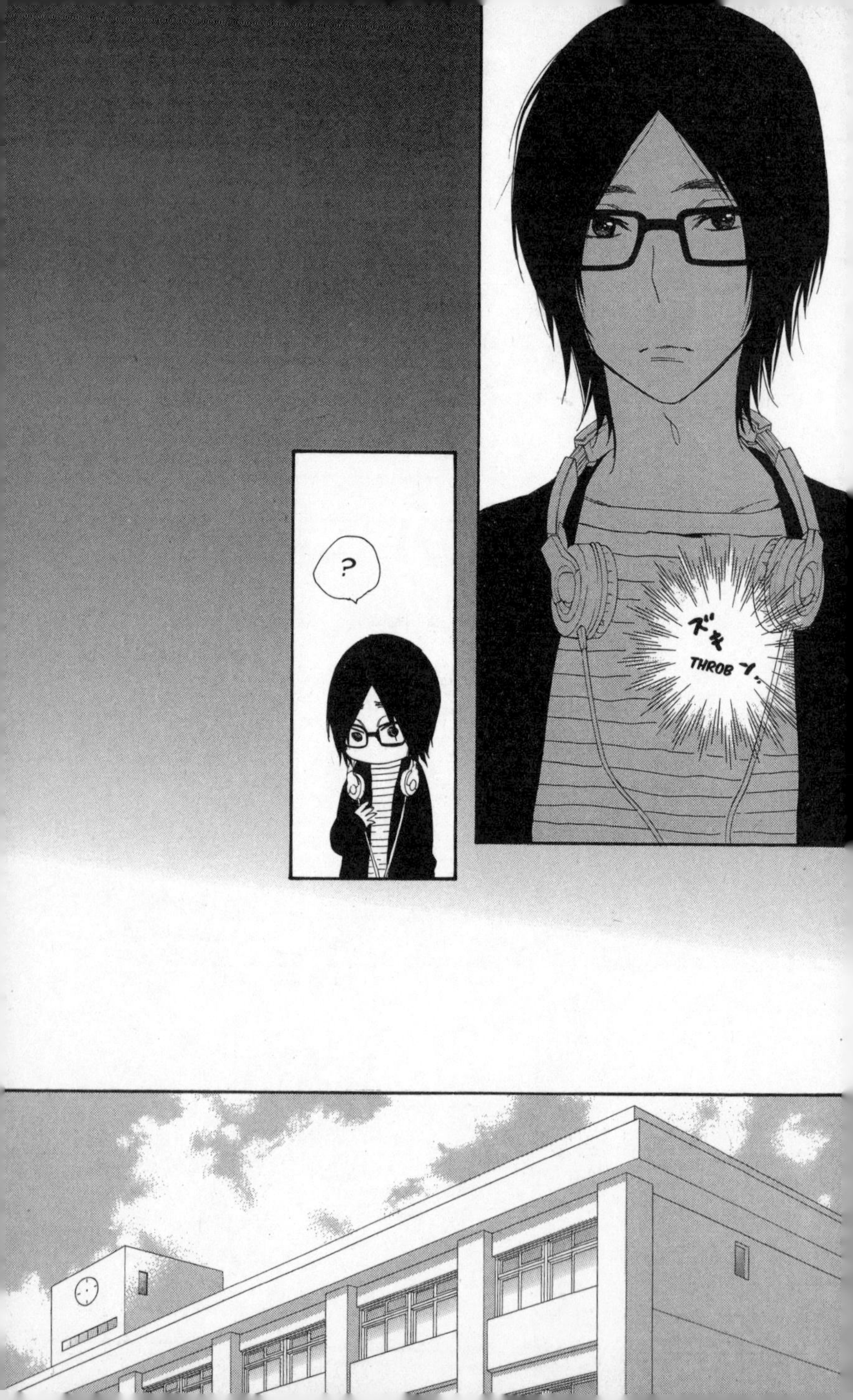
ドキ
THROB
?

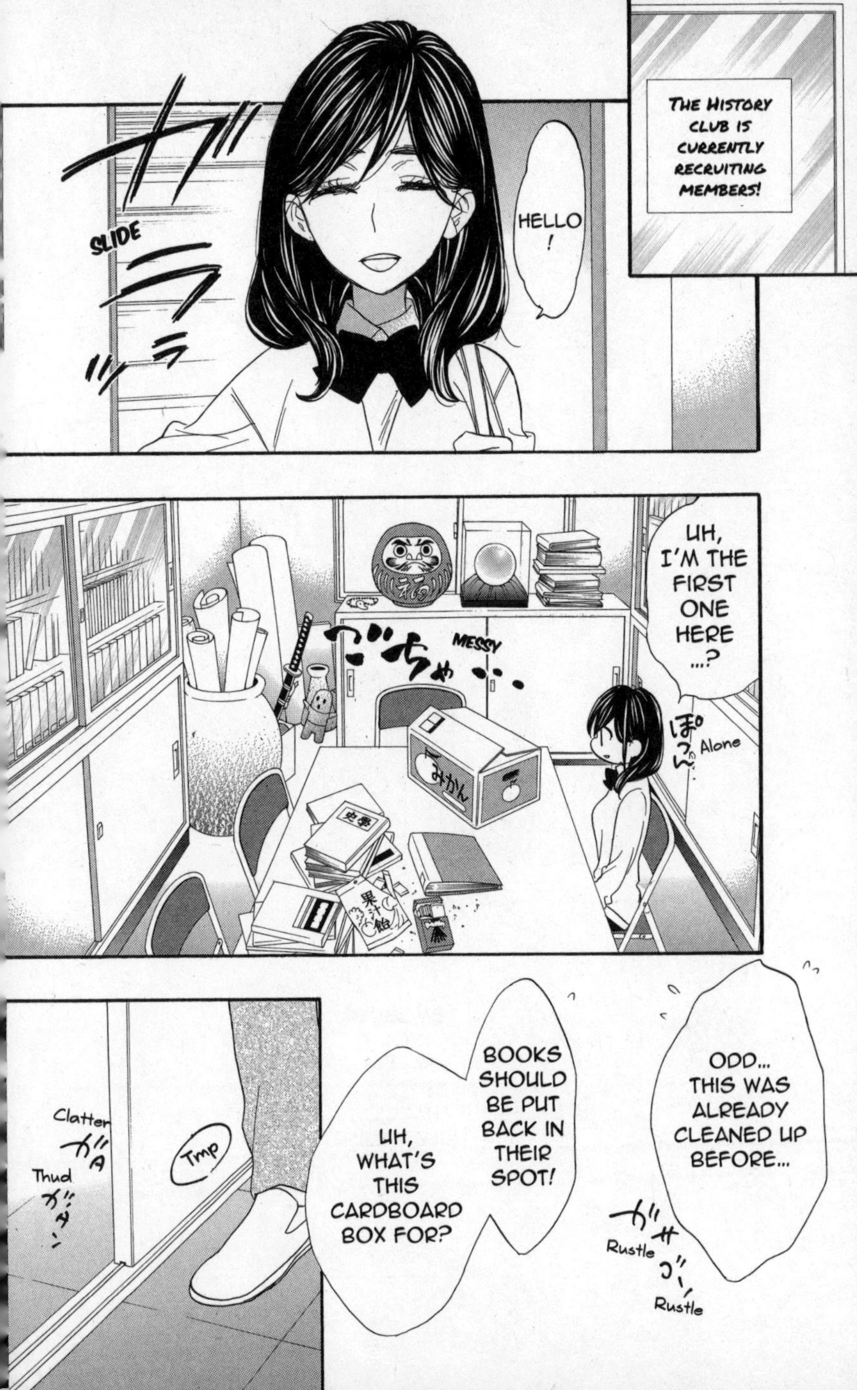
THE HISTORY CLUB IS CURRENTLY RECRUITING MEMBERS!
HELLO!
SLIDE
UH, I'M THE FIRST ONE HERE ...?
Alone
MESSY
ODD... THIS WAS ALREADY CLEANED UP BEFORE...
Rustle
Rustle
BOOKS SHOULD BE PUT BACK IN THEIR SPOT!
UH, WHAT'S THIS CARDBOARD BOX FOR?
Tmp
Clatter
Thud

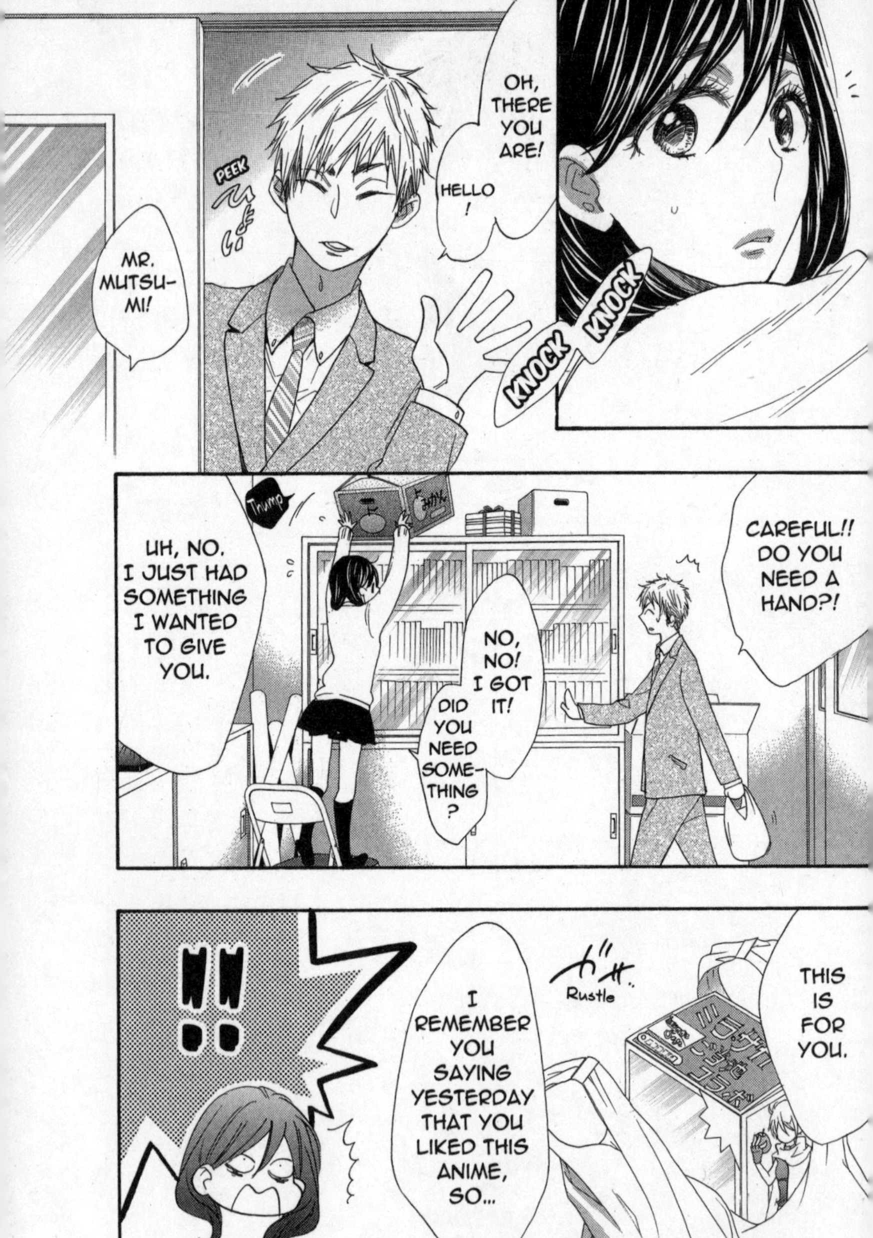
KNOCK KNOCK
OH, THERE YOU ARE!
HELLO!
PEEK
MR. MUTSUMI!
CAREFUL!! DO YOU NEED A HAND?!
NO, NO! I GOT IT!
DID YOU NEED SOMETHING?
Thump
UH, NO. I JUST HAD SOMETHING I WANTED TO GIVE YOU.
THIS IS FOR YOU.
Rustle
I REMEMBER YOU SAYING YESTERDAY THAT YOU LIKED THIS ANIME, SO...
!!

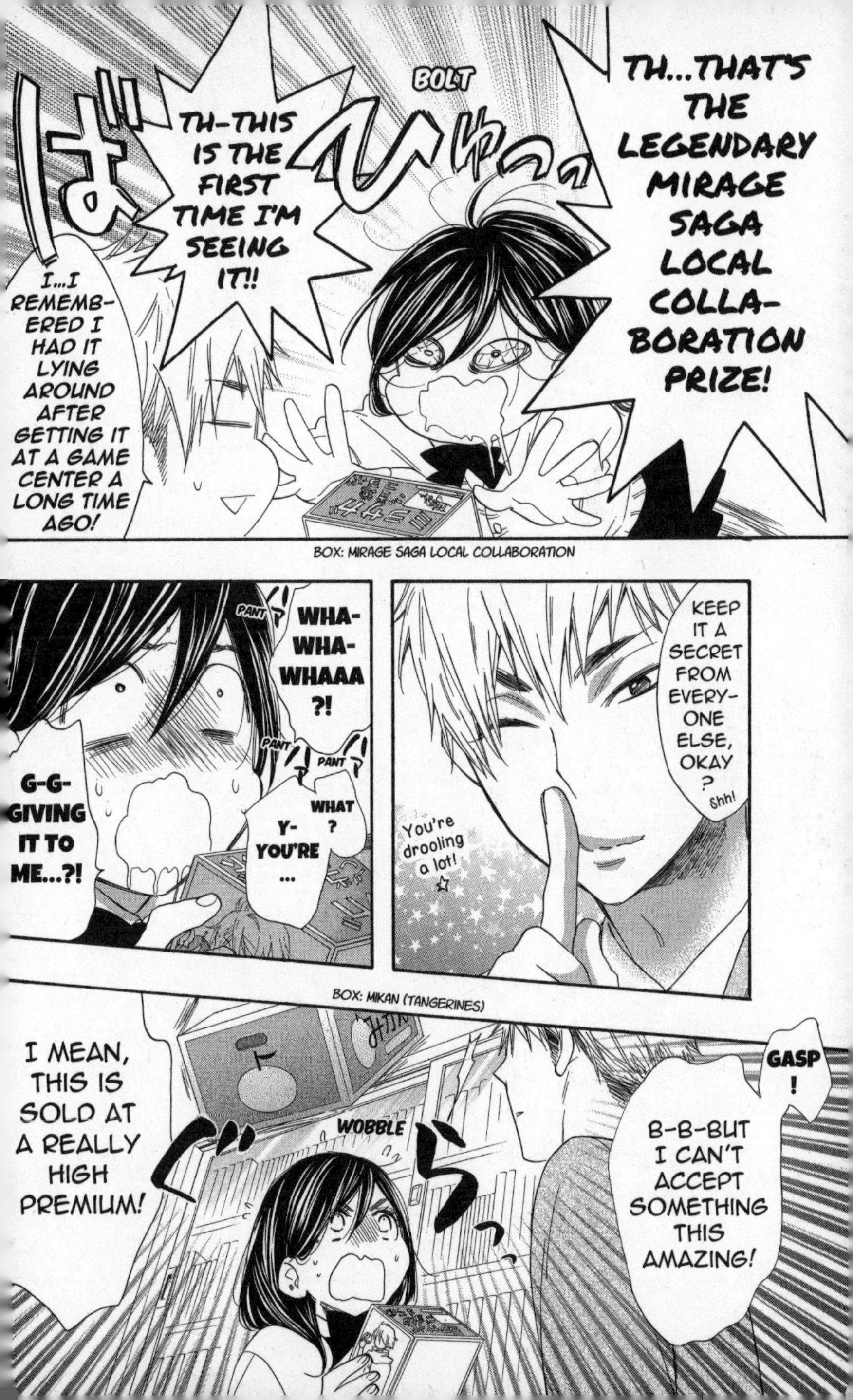
TH...THAT'S THE LEGENDARY MIRAGE SAGA LOCAL COLLABORATION PRIZE!
BOLT
TH-THIS IS THE FIRST TIME I'M SEEING IT!!
I...I REMEMBERED I HAD IT LYING AROUND AFTER GETTING IT AT A GAME CENTER A LONG TIME AGO!
BOX: MIRAGE SAGA LOCAL COLLABORATION
KEEP IT A SECRET FROM EVERYONE ELSE, OKAY?
Shh!
You're drooling a lot!
PANT
WHA-WHA-WHAAA?!
PANT
PANT
WHAT?
Y-YOU'RE...
G-G-GIVING IT TO ME...?!
BOX: MIKAN (TANGERINES)
GASP!
B-B-BUT I CAN'T ACCEPT SOMETHING THIS AMAZING!
WOBBLE
I MEAN, THIS IS SOLD AT A REALLY HIGH PREMIUM!

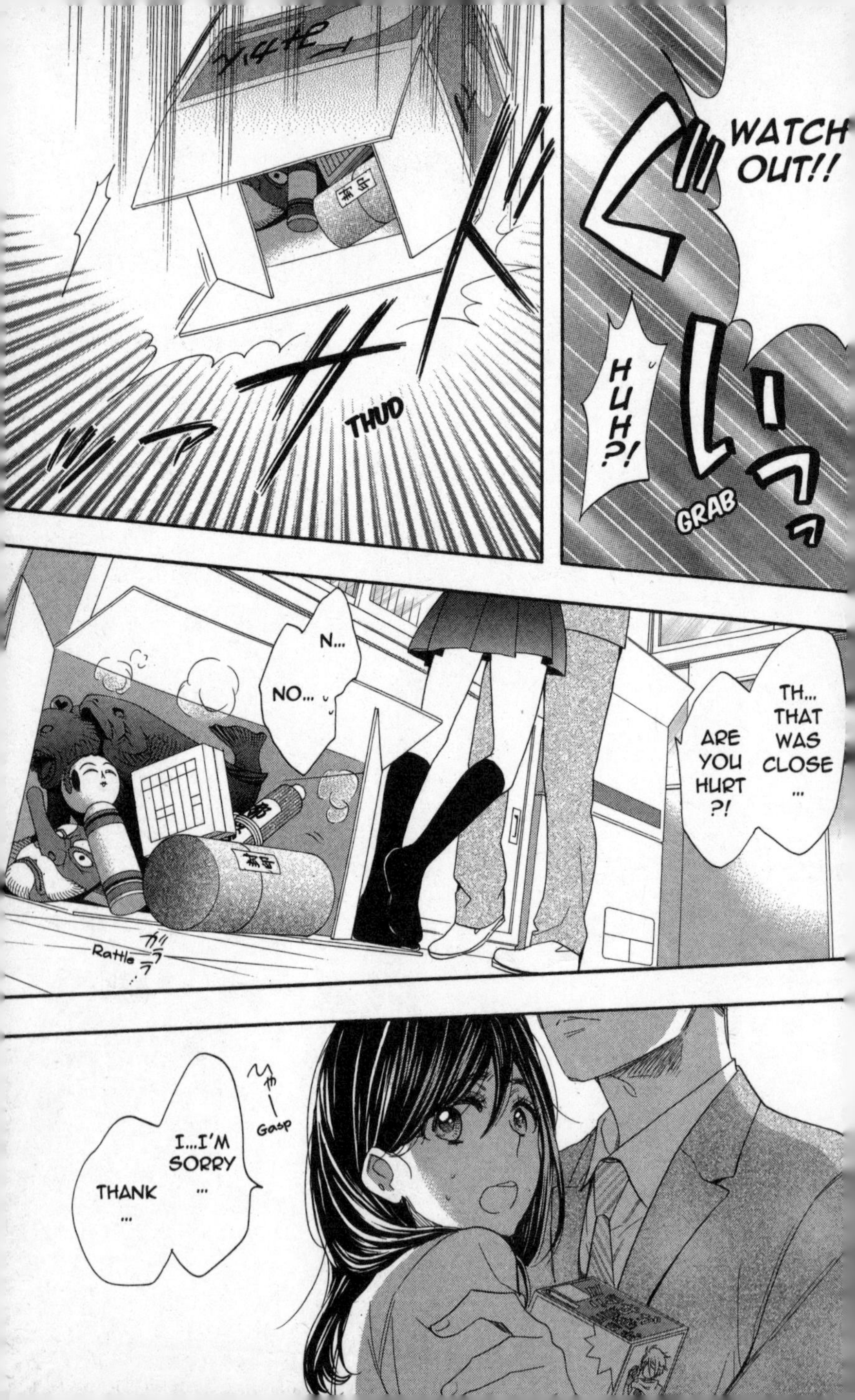
WATCH OUT!!
HUH?!
GRAB
THUD
TH... THAT WAS CLOSE ...
ARE YOU HURT ?!
N... NO...
Rattle
Gasp
I...I'M SORRY ... THANK ...

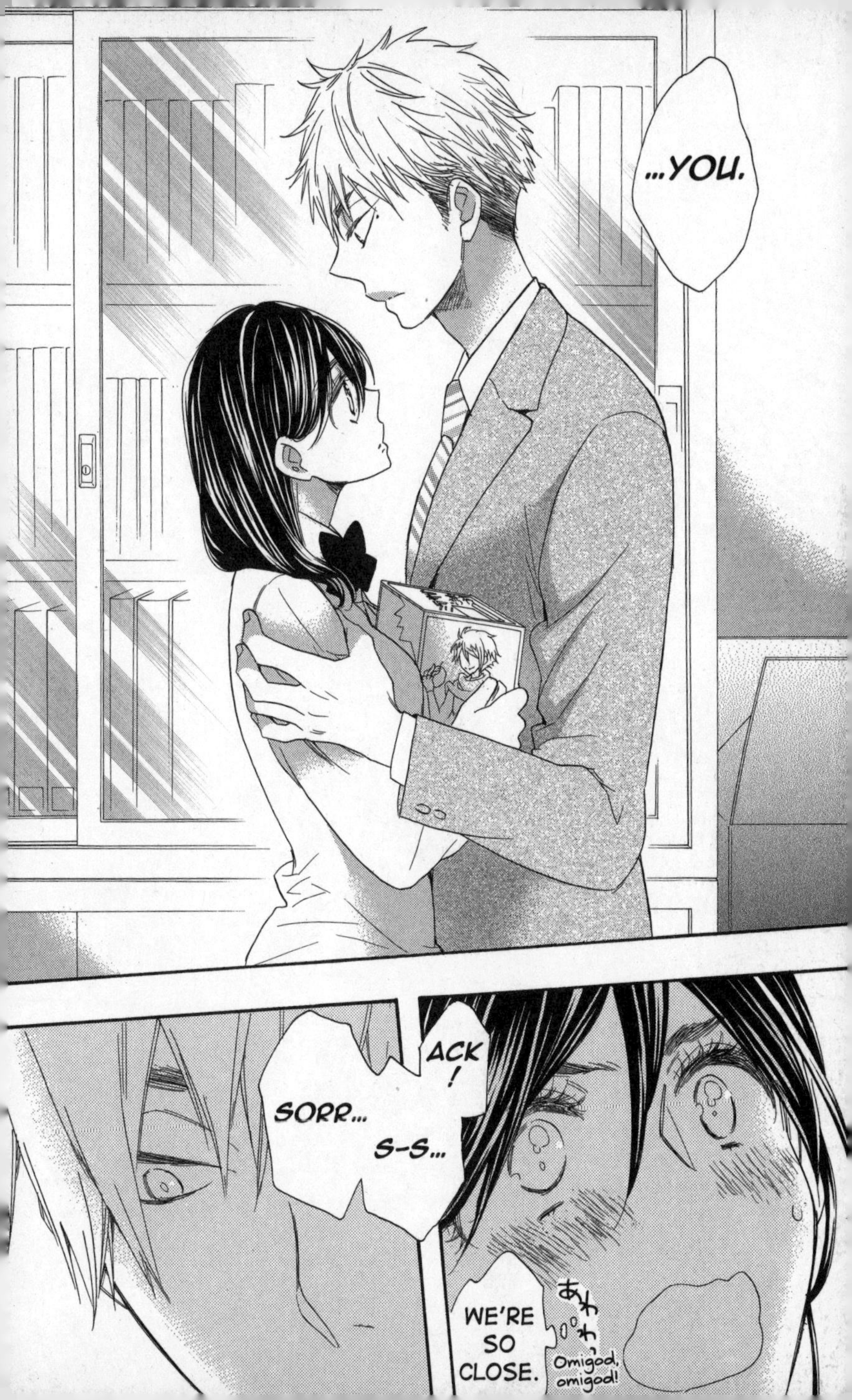
...YOU.
ACK!
SORR...
S-S...
あわわ
Omigod, omigod!
WE'RE SO CLOSE.

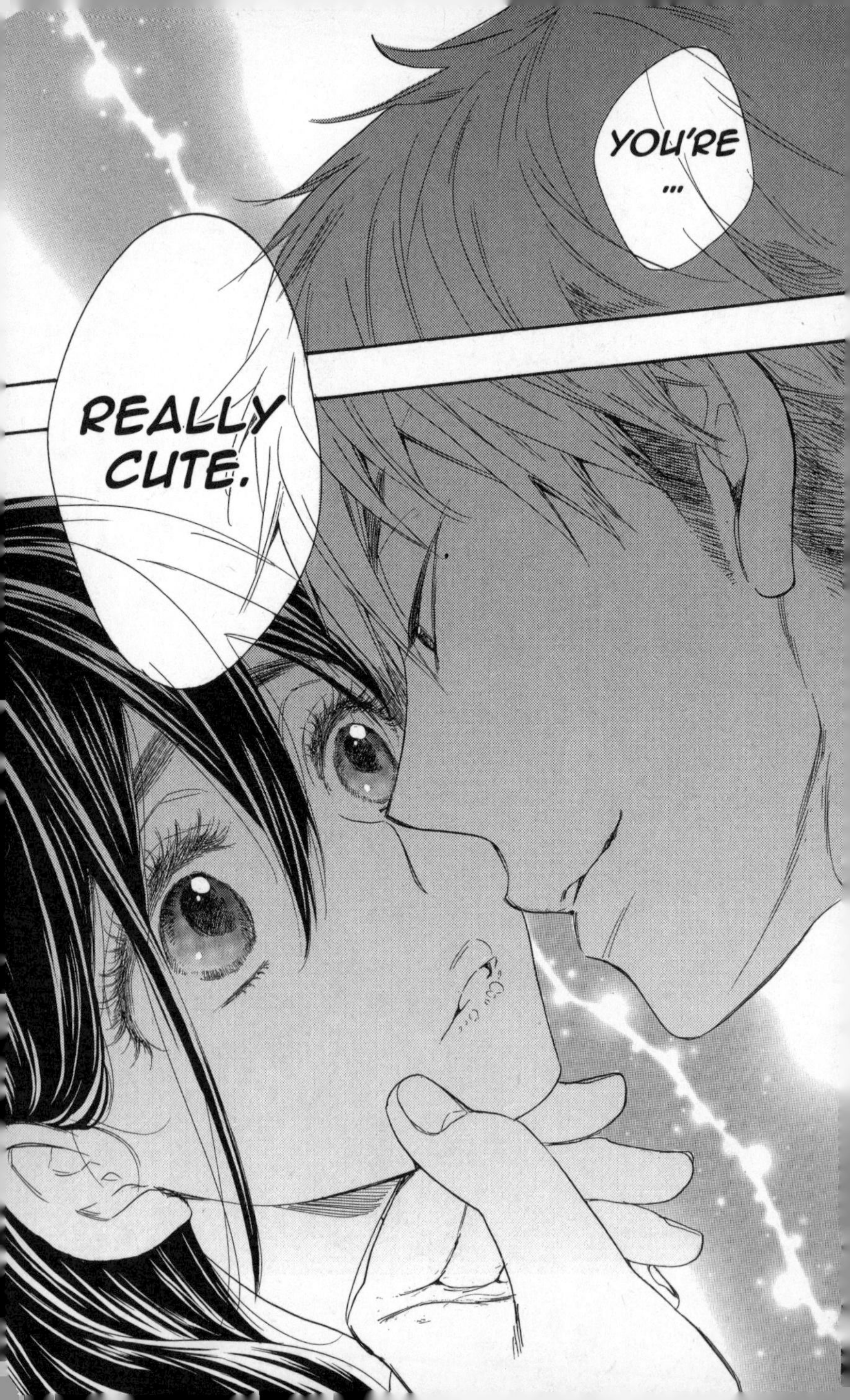
YOU'RE
...
REALLY CUTE.

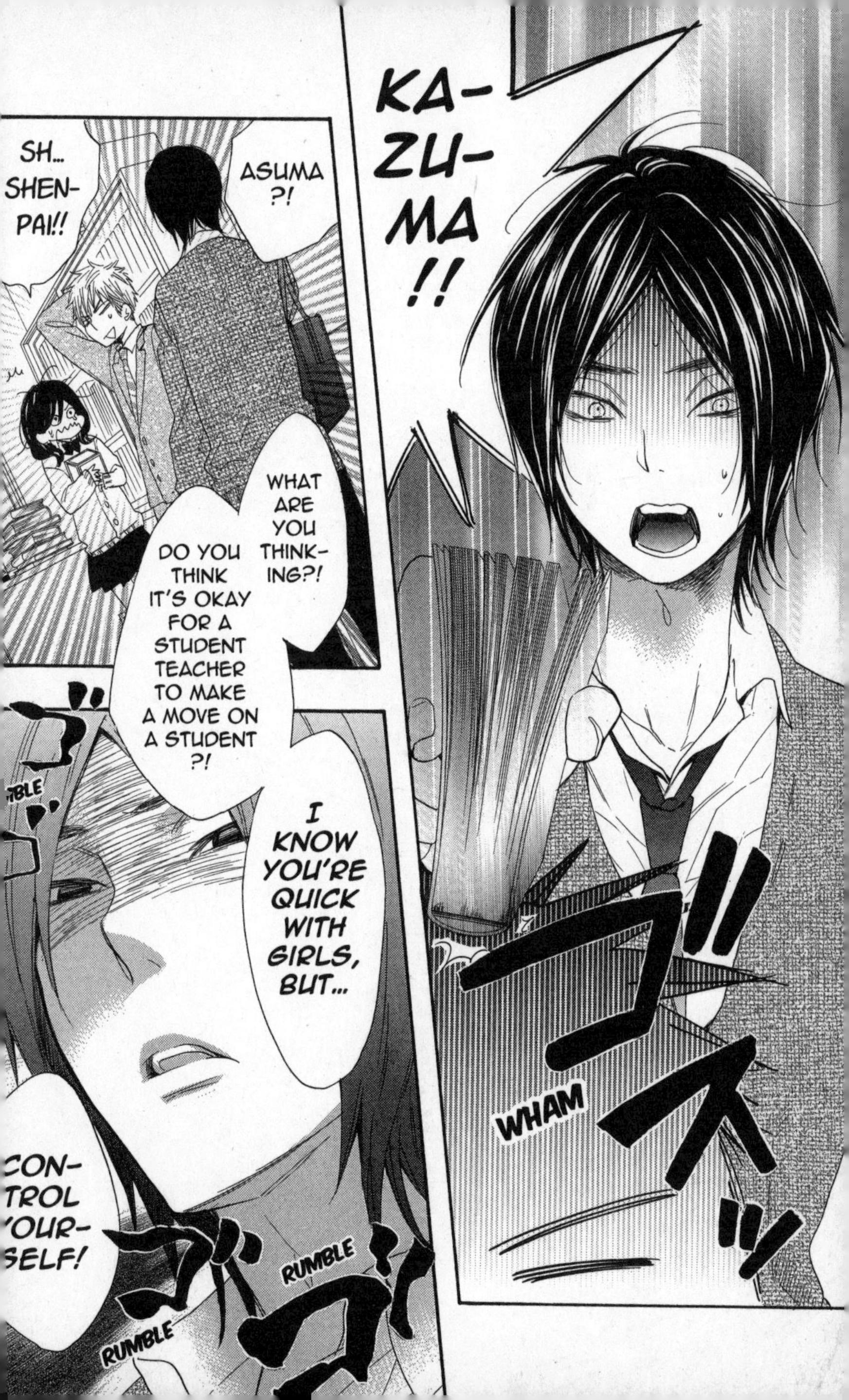
KA-ZU-MA!!
WHAM
ASUMA?!
SH... SHEN-PAI!!
WHAT ARE YOU THINKING?!
DO YOU THINK IT'S OKAY FOR A STUDENT TEACHER TO MAKE A MOVE ON A STUDENT?!
I KNOW YOU'RE QUICK WITH GIRLS, BUT...
CON-TROL YOUR-SELF!
RUMBLE
RUMBLE

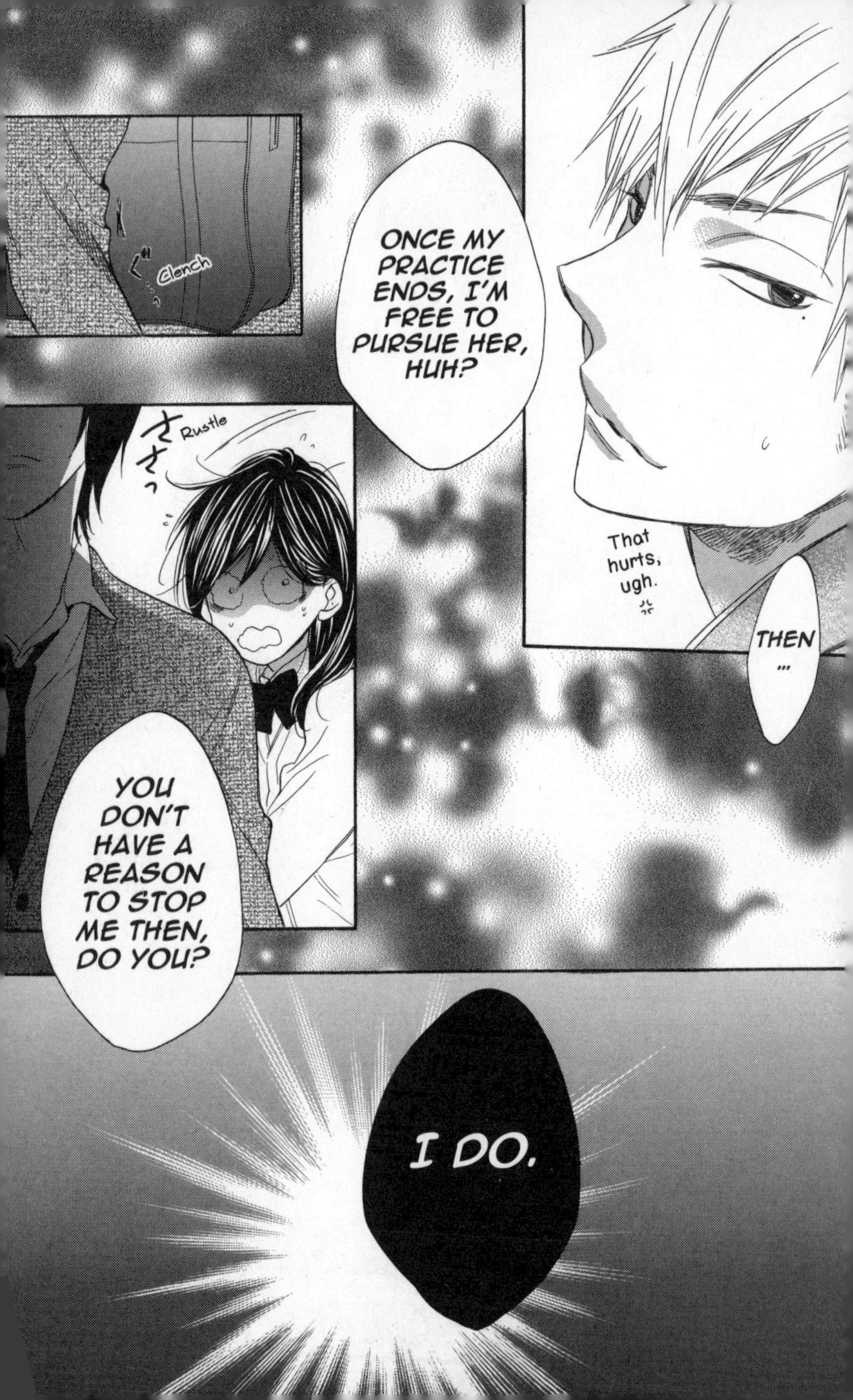
ONCE MY PRACTICE ENDS, I'M FREE TO PURSUE HER, HUH?
That hurts, ugh.
ぐっ Clench
さっ Rustle
THEN...
YOU DON'T HAVE A REASON TO STOP ME THEN, DO YOU?
I DO.

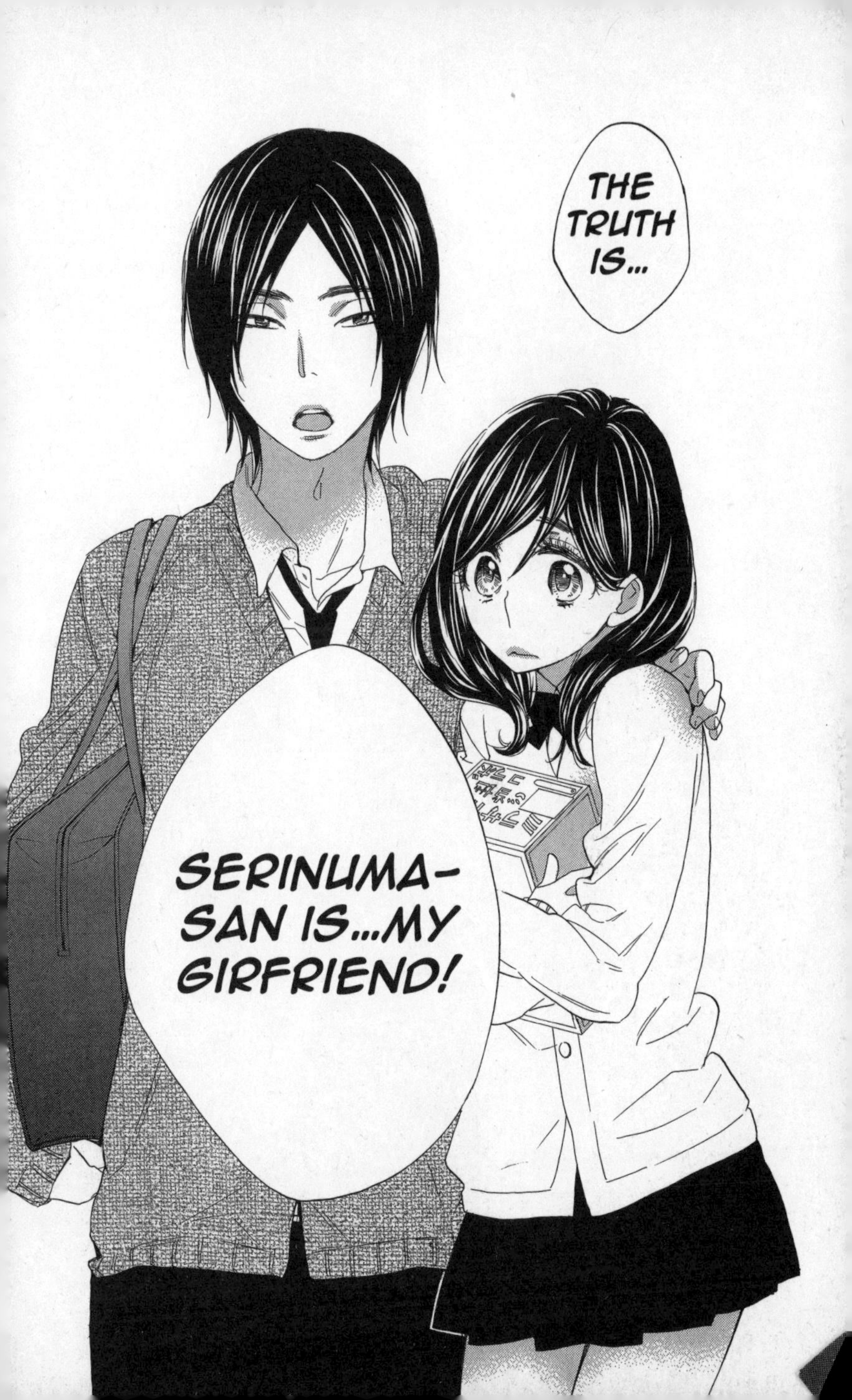
THE TRUTH IS...
SERINUMA-SAN IS...MY GIRFRIEND!

#19 BROTHER, UNRIVALED

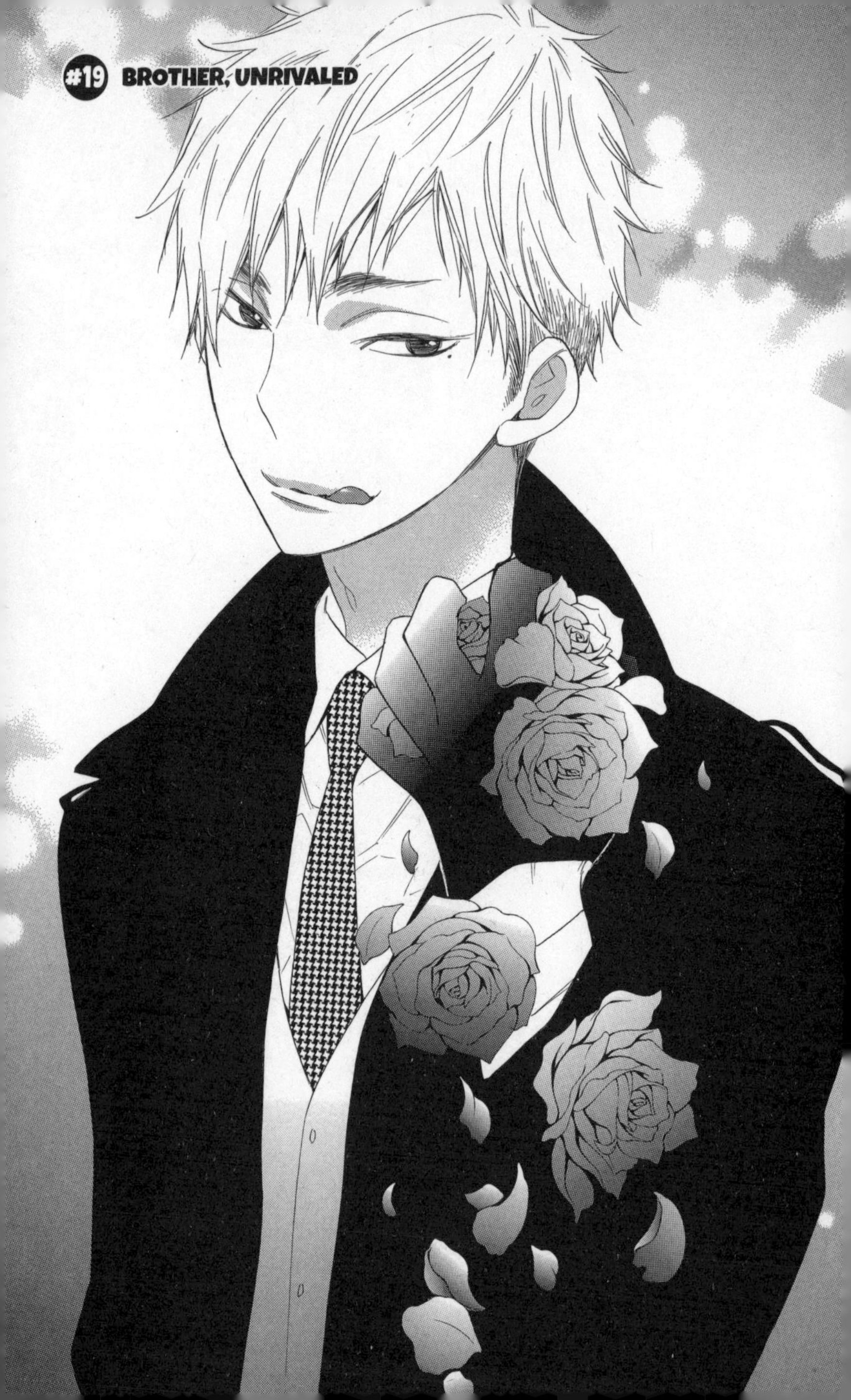

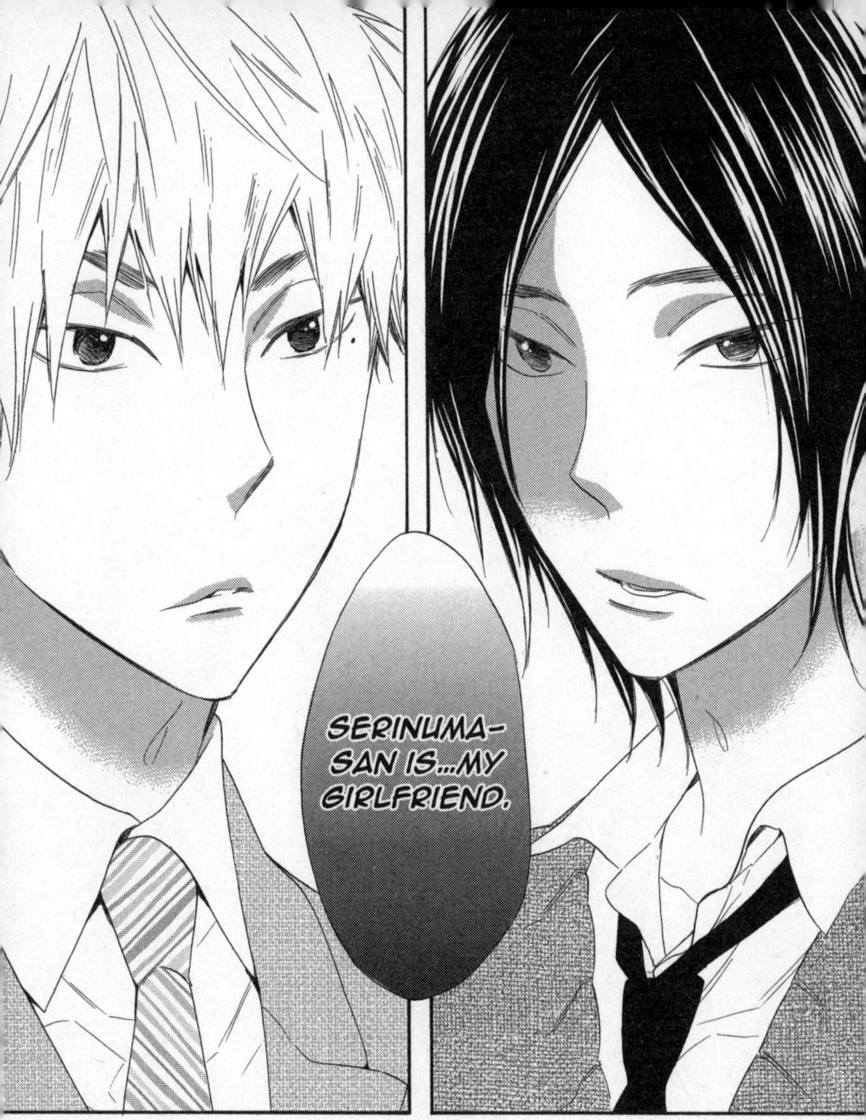
SERINUMA-SAN IS...MY GIRLFRIEND.

KiSS HiM, NOT ME!

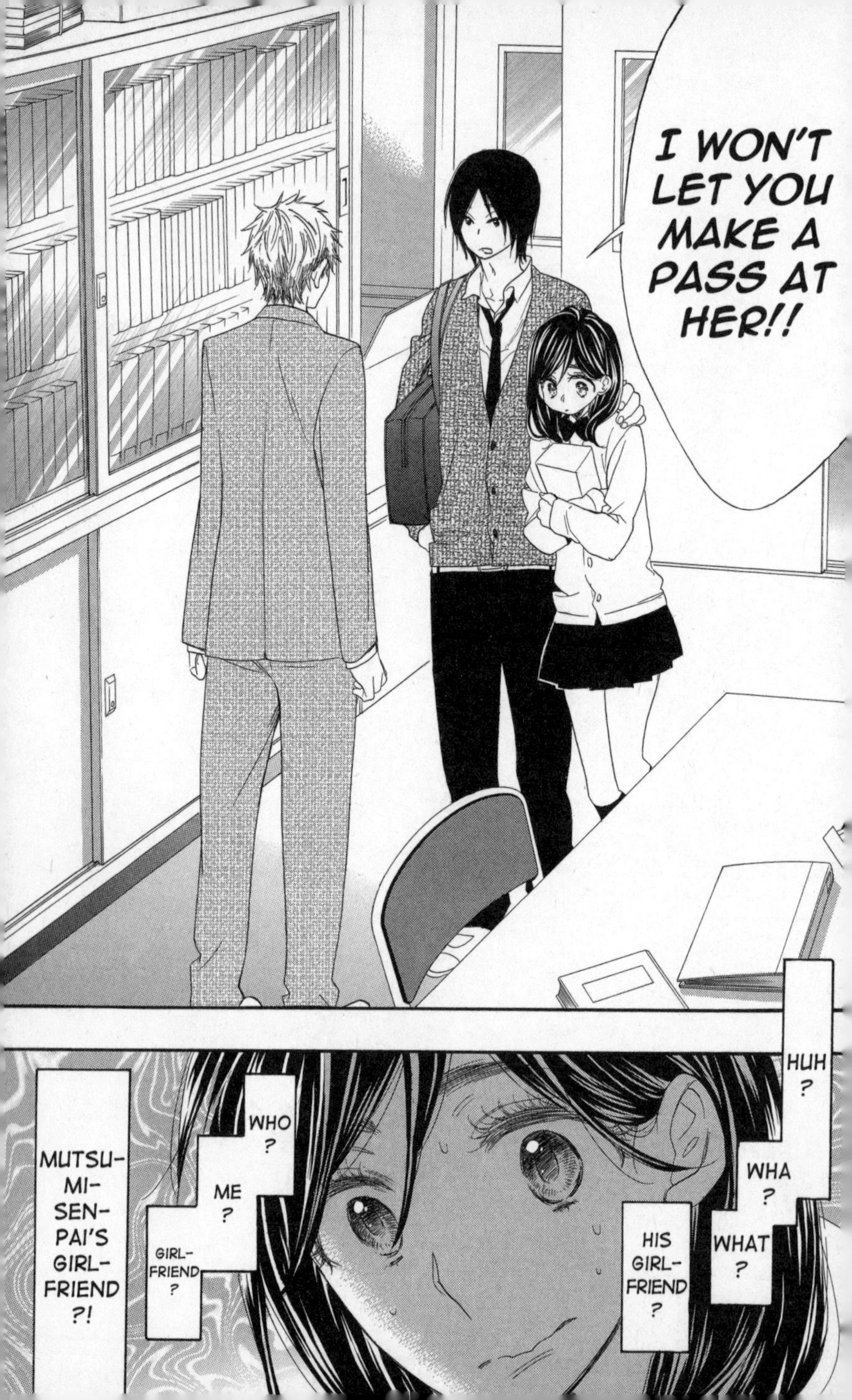
I WON'T LET YOU MAKE A PASS AT HER!!
HUH?
WHA?
WHAT?
HIS GIRL-FRIEND?
WHO?
ME?
GIRL-FRIEND?
MUTSU-MI-SEN-PAI'S GIRL-FRIEND?!

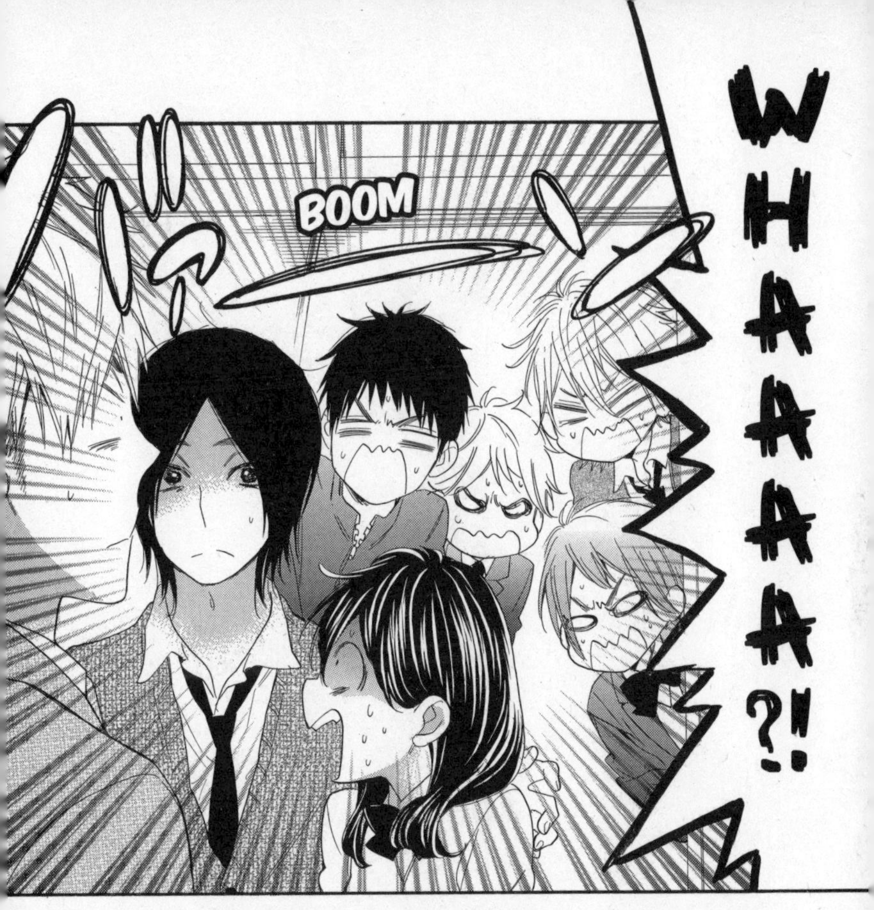
WHAAAAA?!
BOOM

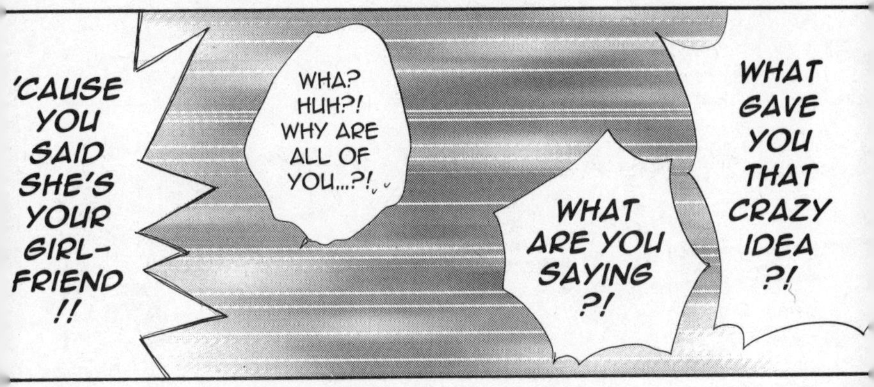
WHAT GAVE YOU THAT CRAZY IDEA?!
WHAT ARE YOU SAYING?!
WHA? HUH?! WHY ARE ALL OF YOU...?!
'CAUSE YOU SAID SHE'S YOUR GIRL-FRIEND!!

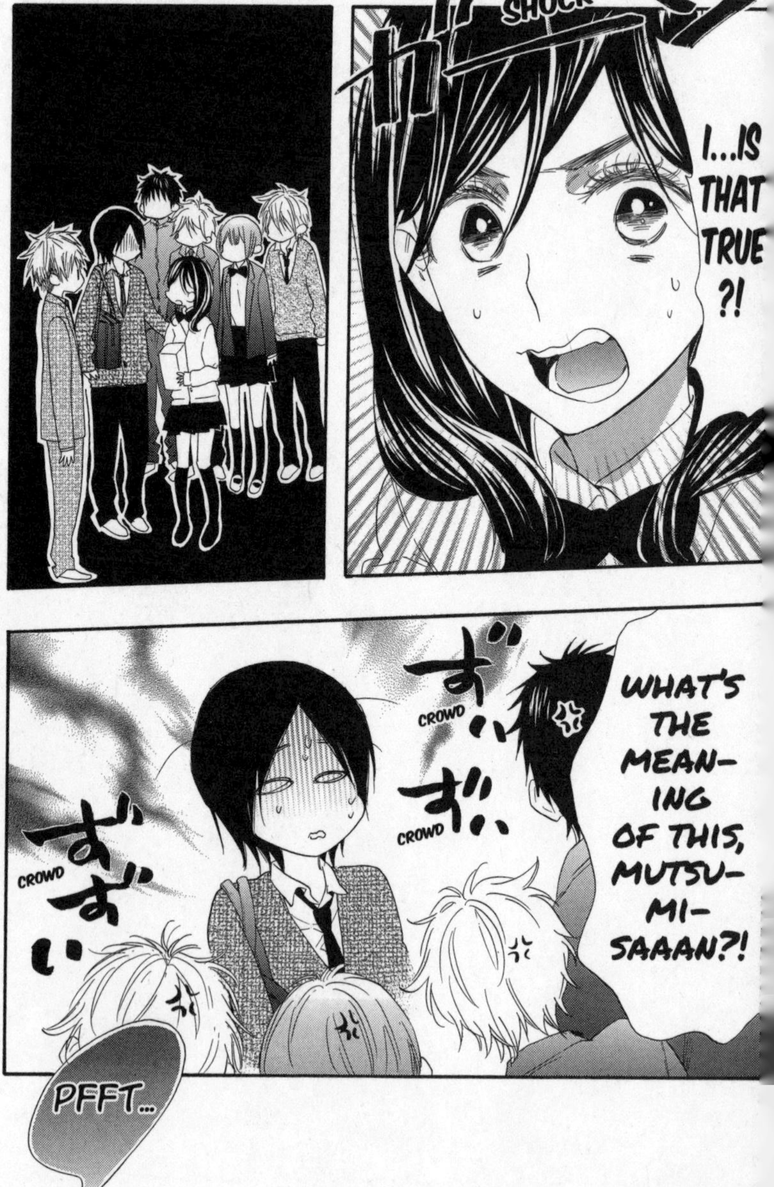
SHOCK
I...IS THAT TRUE?!
WHAT'S THE MEAN-ING OF THIS, MUTSU-MI-SAAAN?!
CROWD
CROWD
CROWD
PFFT...

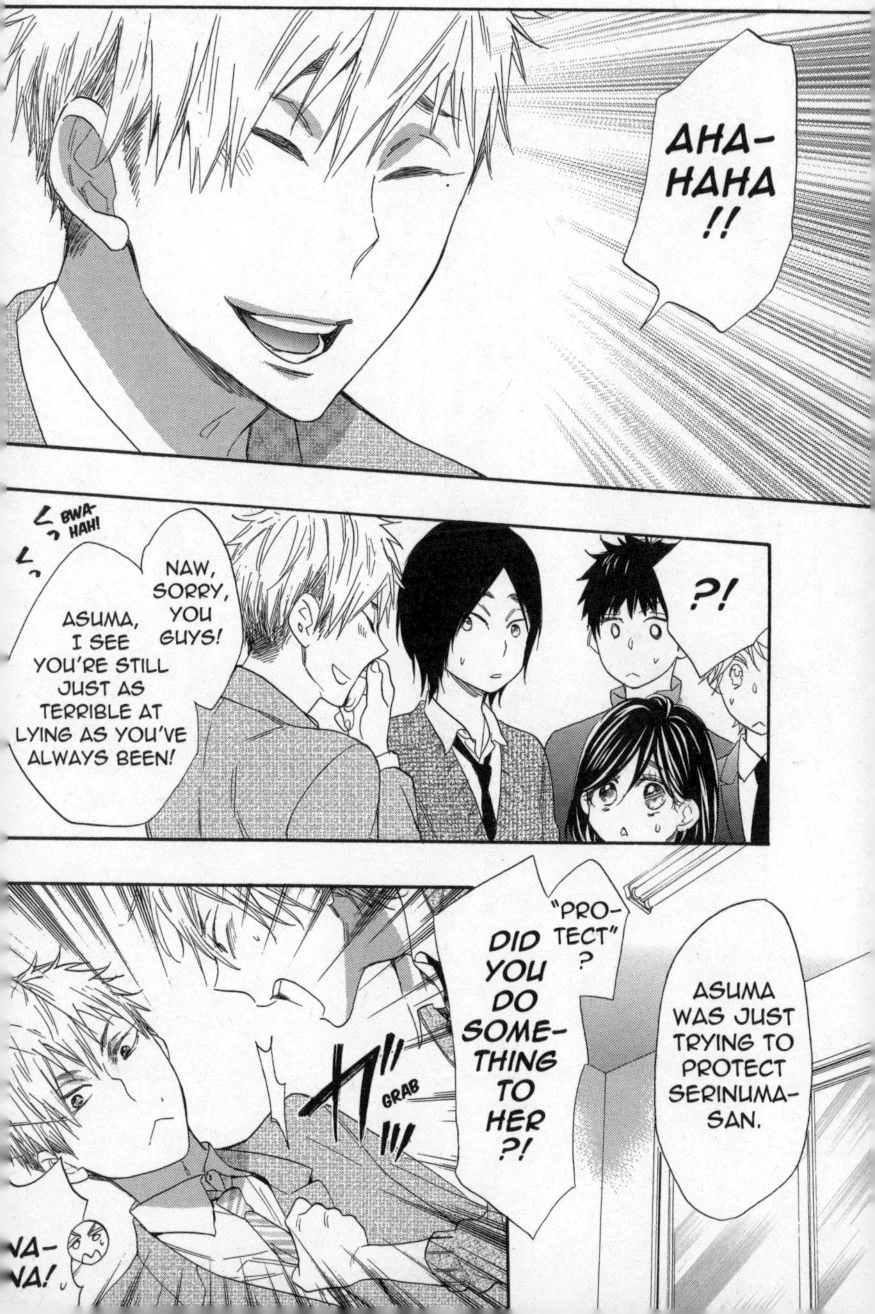
AHA-HAHA!!
?!
NAW, SORRY, YOU GUYS!
ASUMA, I SEE YOU'RE STILL JUST AS TERRIBLE AT LYING AS YOU'VE ALWAYS BEEN!
BWA HAH!
ASUMA WAS JUST TRYING TO PROTECT SERINUMA-SAN.
"PRO-TECT"?
DID YOU DO SOME-THING TO HER?!
GRAB
NA-NA!

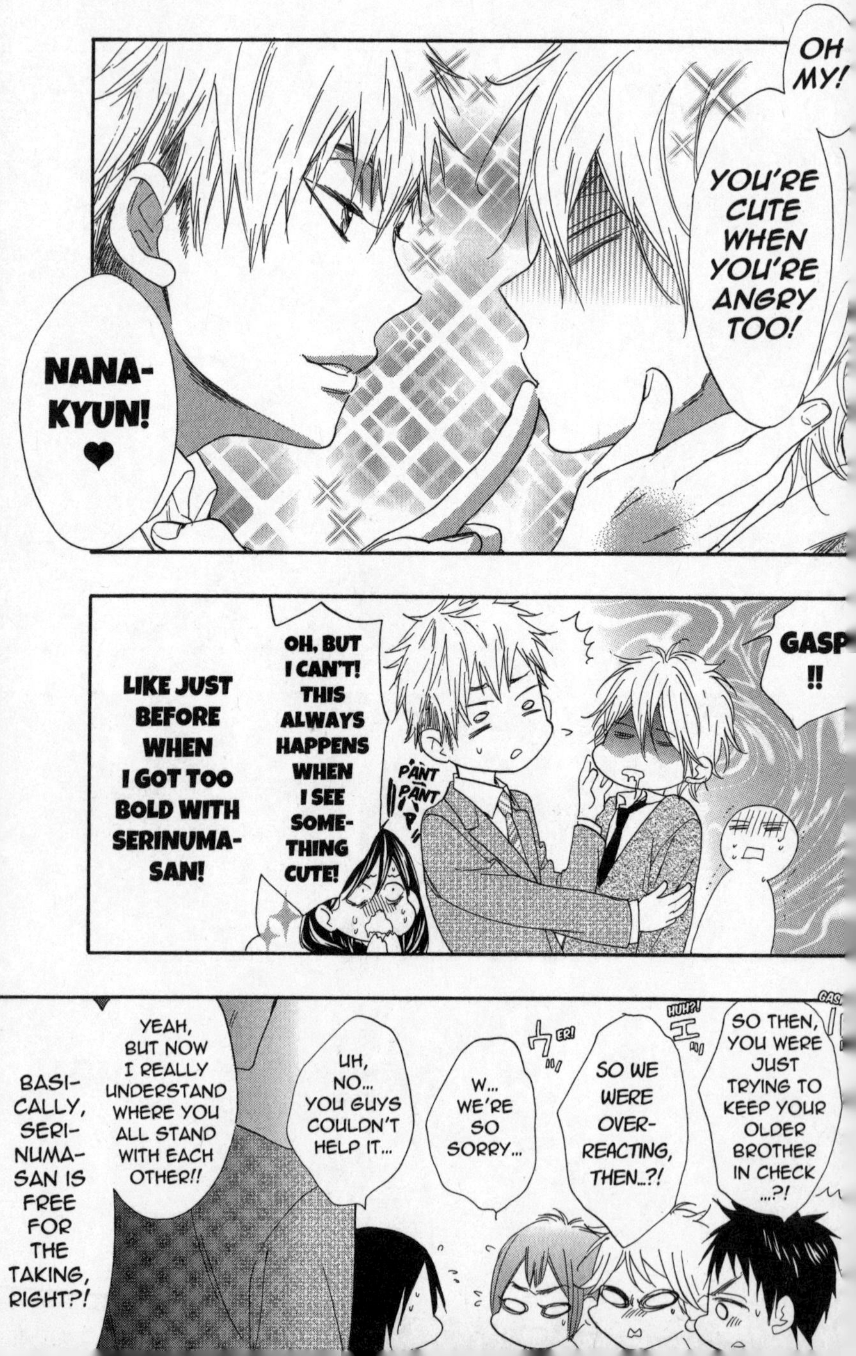
OH MY!
YOU'RE CUTE WHEN YOU'RE ANGRY TOO!
NANA-KYUN! ❤
GASP!!
OH, BUT I CAN'T! THIS ALWAYS HAPPENS WHEN I SEE SOMETHING CUTE!
LIKE JUST BEFORE WHEN I GOT TOO BOLD WITH SERINUMA-SAN!
PANT PANT
GASP
SO THEN, YOU WERE JUST TRYING TO KEEP YOUR OLDER BROTHER IN CHECK ...?!
HUH?!
SO WE WERE OVER-REACTING, THEN...?!
ER!
W... WE'RE SO SORRY...
UH, NO... YOU GUYS COULDN'T HELP IT...
YEAH, BUT NOW I REALLY UNDERSTAND WHERE YOU ALL STAND WITH EACH OTHER!!
BASICALLY, SERINUMA-SAN IS FREE FOR THE TAKING, RIGHT?!

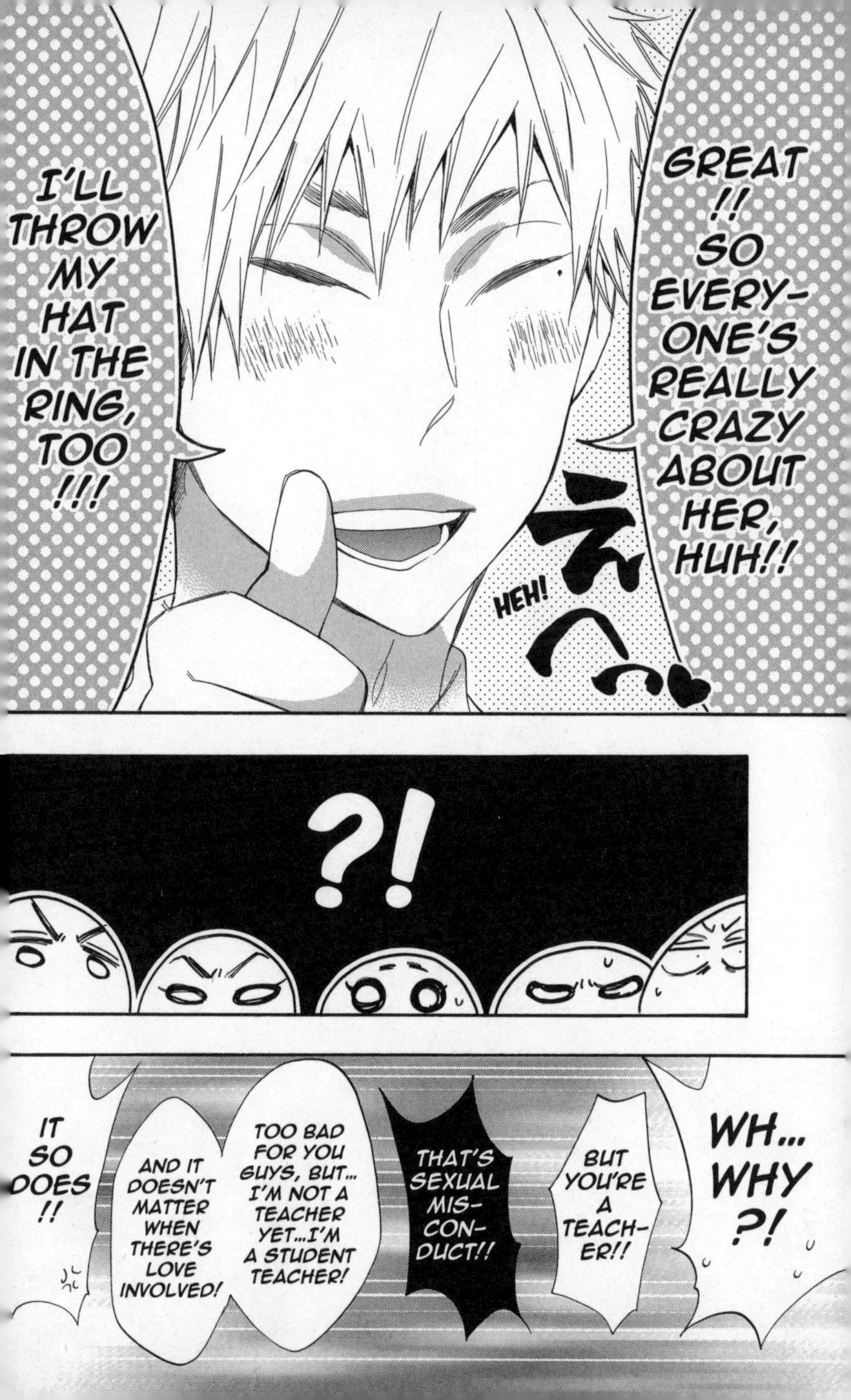
GREAT!! SO EVERYONE'S REALLY CRAZY ABOUT HER, HUH!!
HEH!
I'LL THROW MY HAT IN THE RING, TOO!!!
?!
WH... WHY?!
BUT YOU'RE A TEACHER!!
THAT'S SEXUAL MISCONDUCT!!
TOO BAD FOR YOU GUYS, BUT... I'M NOT A TEACHER YET...I'M A STUDENT TEACHER!
AND IT DOESN'T MATTER WHEN THERE'S LOVE INVOLVED!
IT SO DOES!!

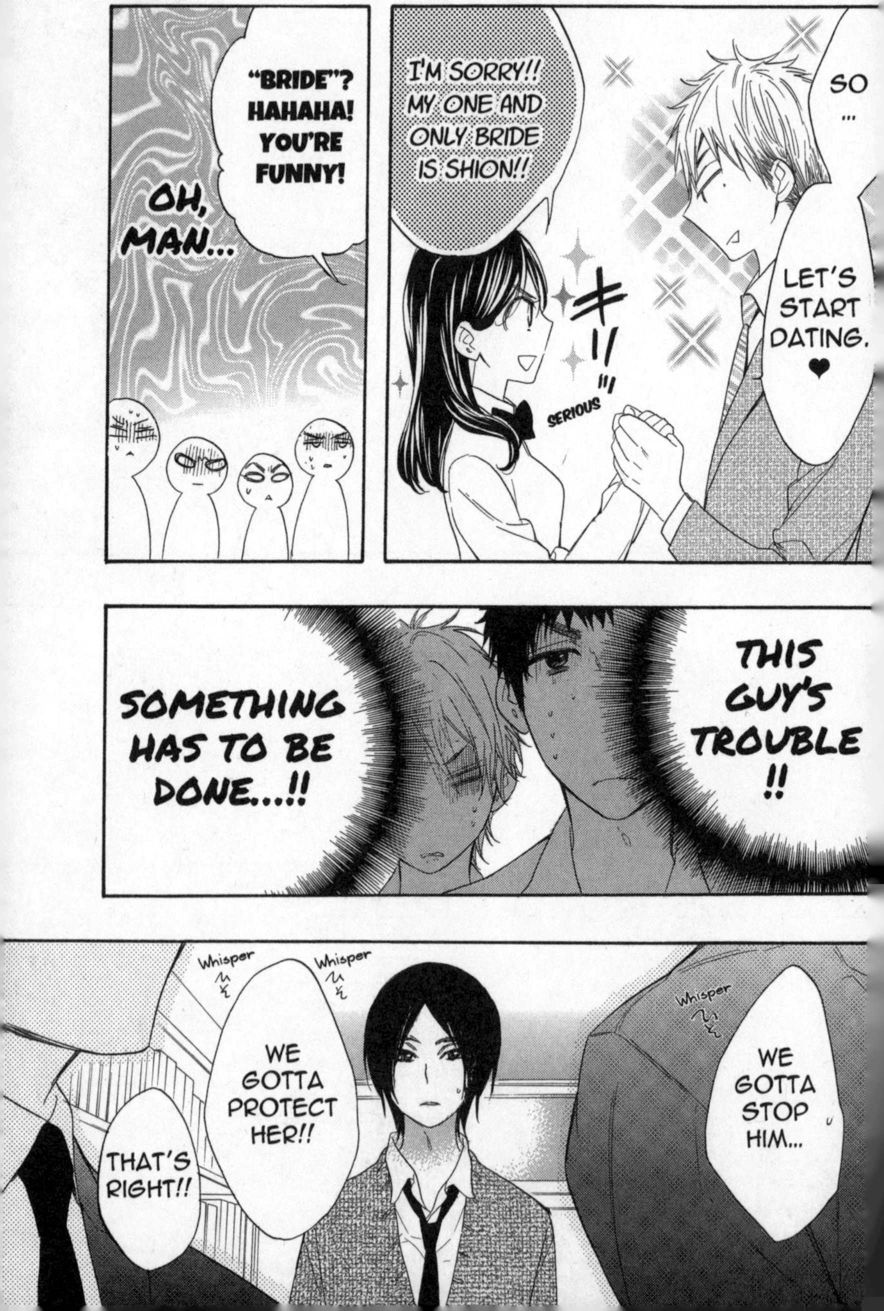
SO ...
LET'S START DATING. ❤
I'M SORRY!! MY ONE AND ONLY BRIDE IS SHION!!
SERIOUS
"BRIDE"? HAHAHA! YOU'RE FUNNY!
OH, MAN...
THIS GUY'S TROUBLE !!
SOMETHING HAS TO BE DONE...!!
Whisper
WE GOTTA STOP HIM...
Whisper
WE GOTTA PROTECT HER!!
Whisper
THAT'S RIGHT!!

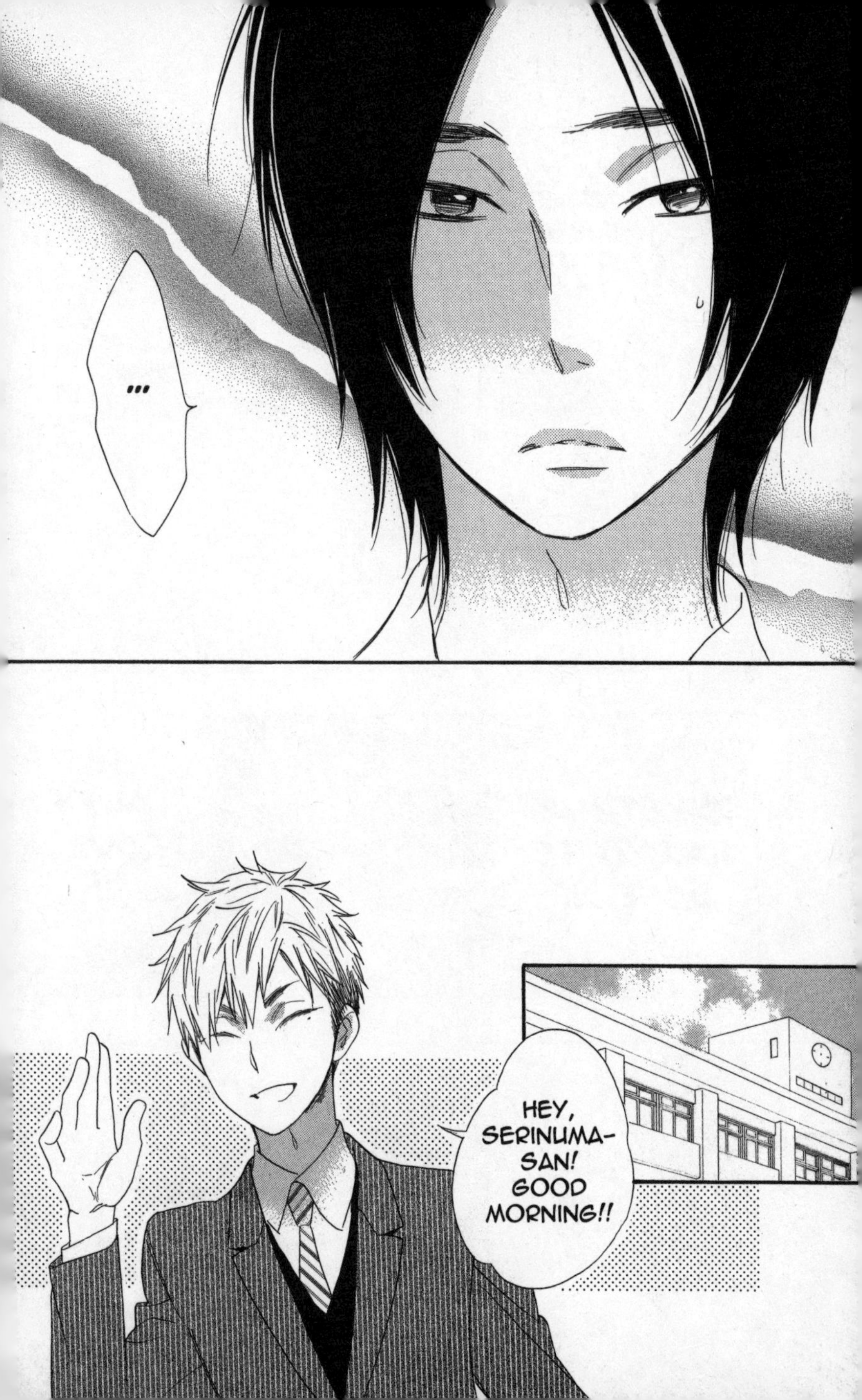
...
HEY, SERINUMA-SAN! GOOD MORNING!!

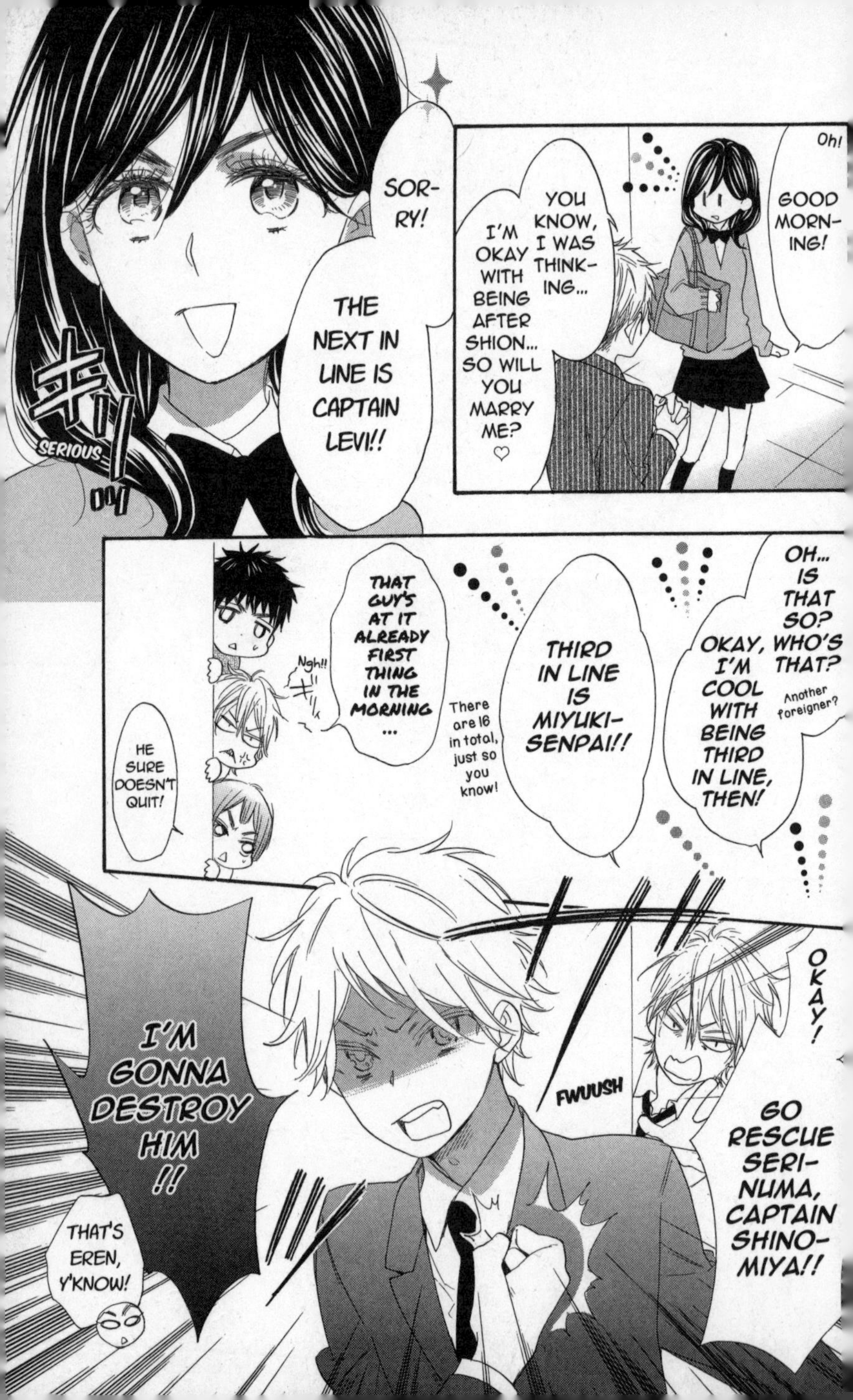
Oh!
GOOD MORNING!
YOU KNOW, I WAS THINKING...
I'M OKAY WITH BEING AFTER SHION... SO WILL YOU MARRY ME? ♡
SORRY!
THE NEXT IN LINE IS CAPTAIN LEVI!!
SERIOUS
OH... IS THAT SO? WHO'S THAT?
Another foreigner?
OKAY, I'M COOL WITH BEING THIRD IN LINE, THEN!
THIRD IN LINE IS MIYUKI-SENPAI!!
There are 16 in total, just so you know!
THAT GUY'S AT IT ALREADY FIRST THING IN THE MORNING...
Ngh!!
HE SURE DOESN'T QUIT!
OKAY!
GO RESCUE SERINUMA, CAPTAIN SHINOMIYA!!
FWUUSH
I'M GONNA DESTROY HIM!!
THAT'S EREN, Y'KNOW!

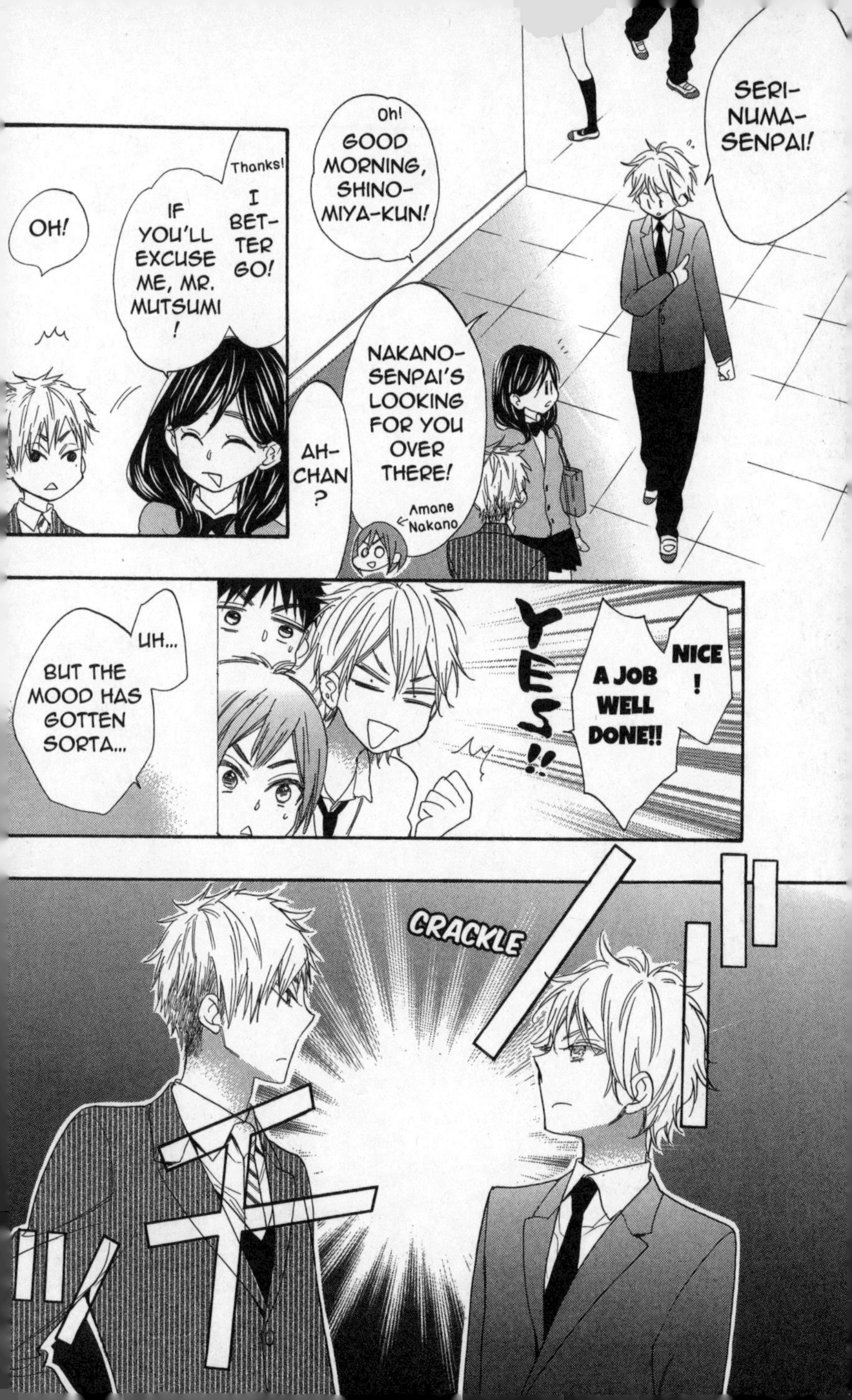
SERI-NUMA-SENPAI!
Oh! GOOD MORNING, SHINO-MIYA-KUN!
NAKANO-SENPAI'S LOOKING FOR YOU OVER THERE!
Amane Nakano
AH-CHAN?
Thanks!
I BET-TER GO!
IF YOU'LL EXCUSE ME, MR. MUTSUMI!
OH!
NICE!
A JOB WELL DONE!!
YES!!
UH... BUT THE MOOD HAS GOTTEN SORTA...
CRACKLE

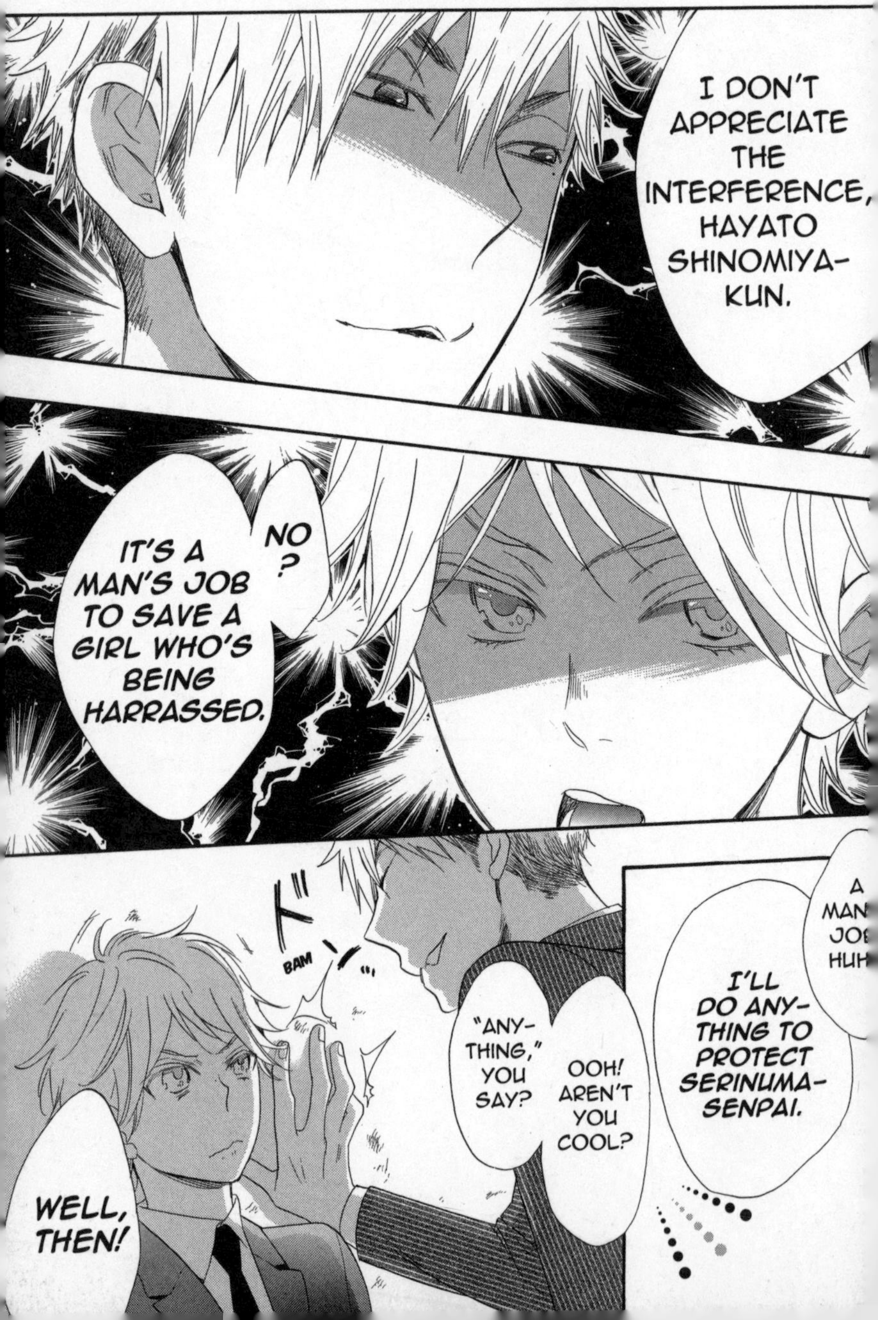
I DON'T APPRECIATE THE INTERFERENCE, HAYATO SHINOMIYA-KUN.
NO?
IT'S A MAN'S JOB TO SAVE A GIRL WHO'S BEING HARRASSED.
A MAN JOB HUH
I'LL DO ANYTHING TO PROTECT SERINUMA-SENPAI.
OOH! AREN'T YOU COOL?
"ANY-THING," YOU SAY?
BAM
WELL, THEN!

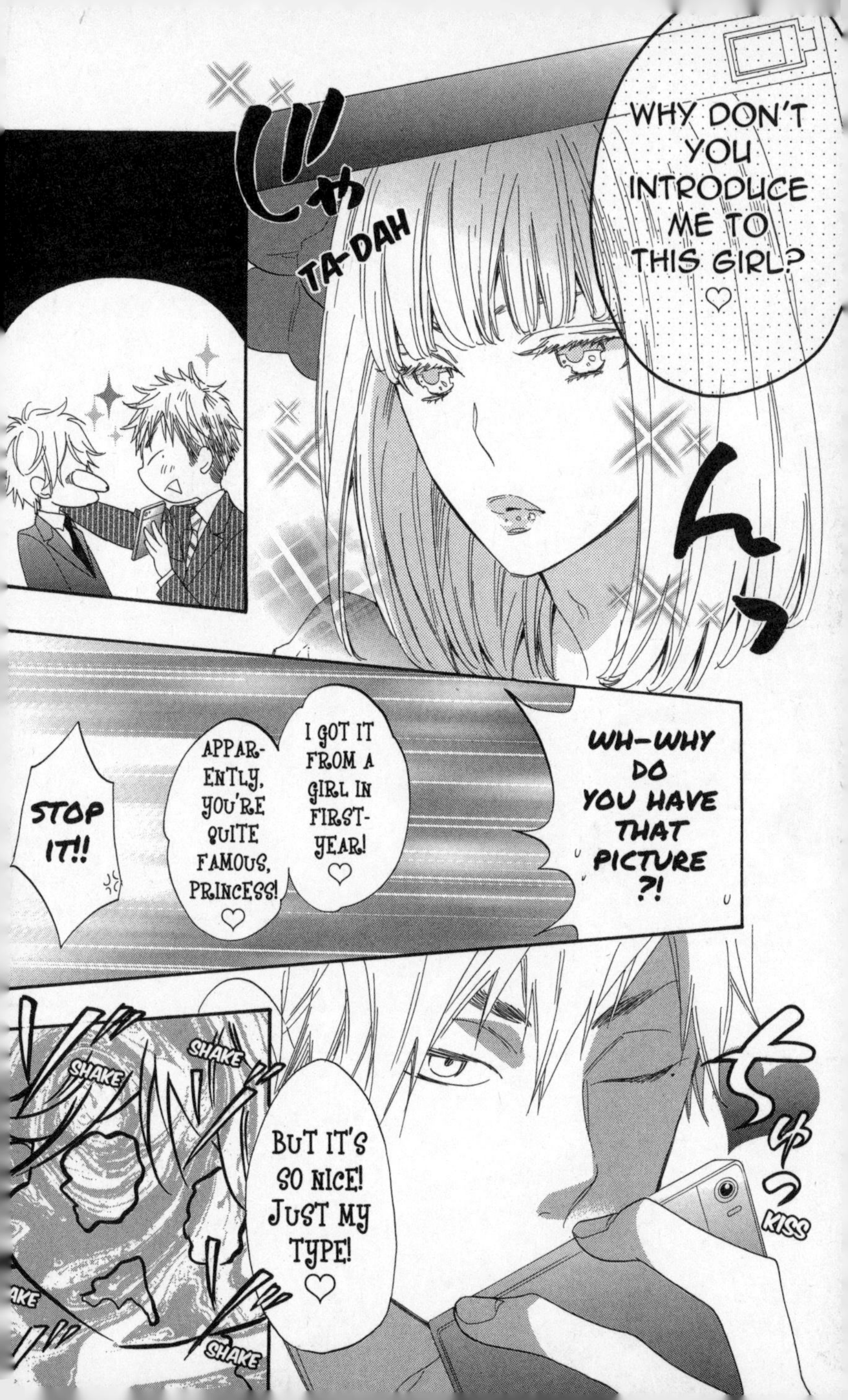
WHY DON'T YOU INTRODUCE ME TO THIS GIRL? ♡
TA-DAH
WH-WHY DO YOU HAVE THAT PICTURE ?!
I GOT IT FROM A GIRL IN FIRST-YEAR! ♡
APPARENTLY, YOU'RE QUITE FAMOUS, PRINCESS! ♡
STOP IT!!
KISS
BUT IT'S SO NICE! JUST MY TYPE! ♡
SHAKE
SHAKE
SHAKE

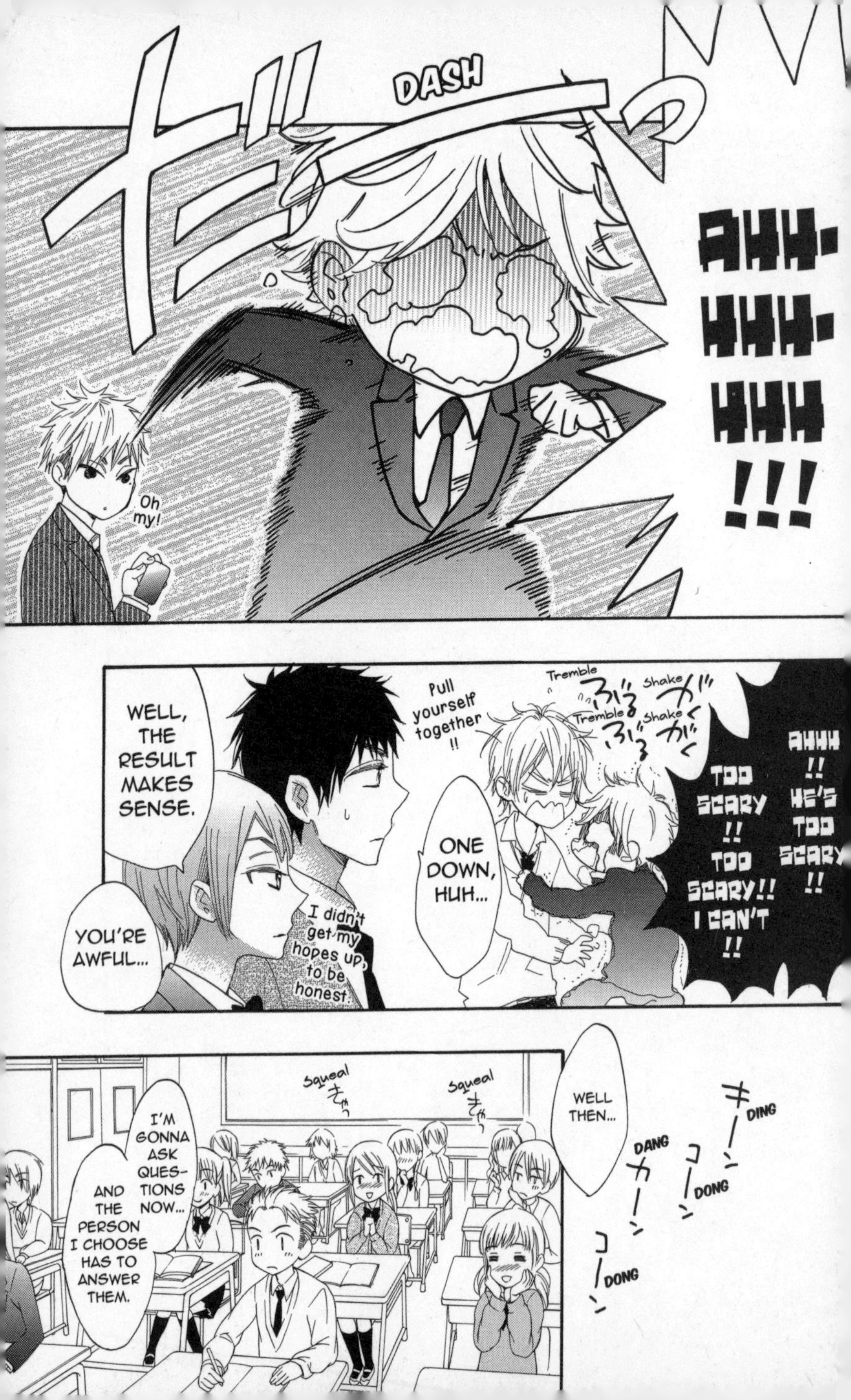

DASH
AHH-HHH-HHH!!!
Oh my!
AHHH!! HE'S TOO SCARY!!
TOO SCARY!! TOO SCARY!! I CAN'T!!
Shake Shake
Tremble Tremble
Pull yourself together!!
ONE DOWN, HUH...
WELL, THE RESULT MAKES SENSE.
I didn't get my hopes up, to be honest.
YOU'RE AWFUL...
DING DONG
DANG DONG
WELL THEN...
Squeal
Squeal
I'M GONNA ASK QUESTIONS NOW...
AND THE PERSON I CHOOSE HAS TO ANSWER THEM.

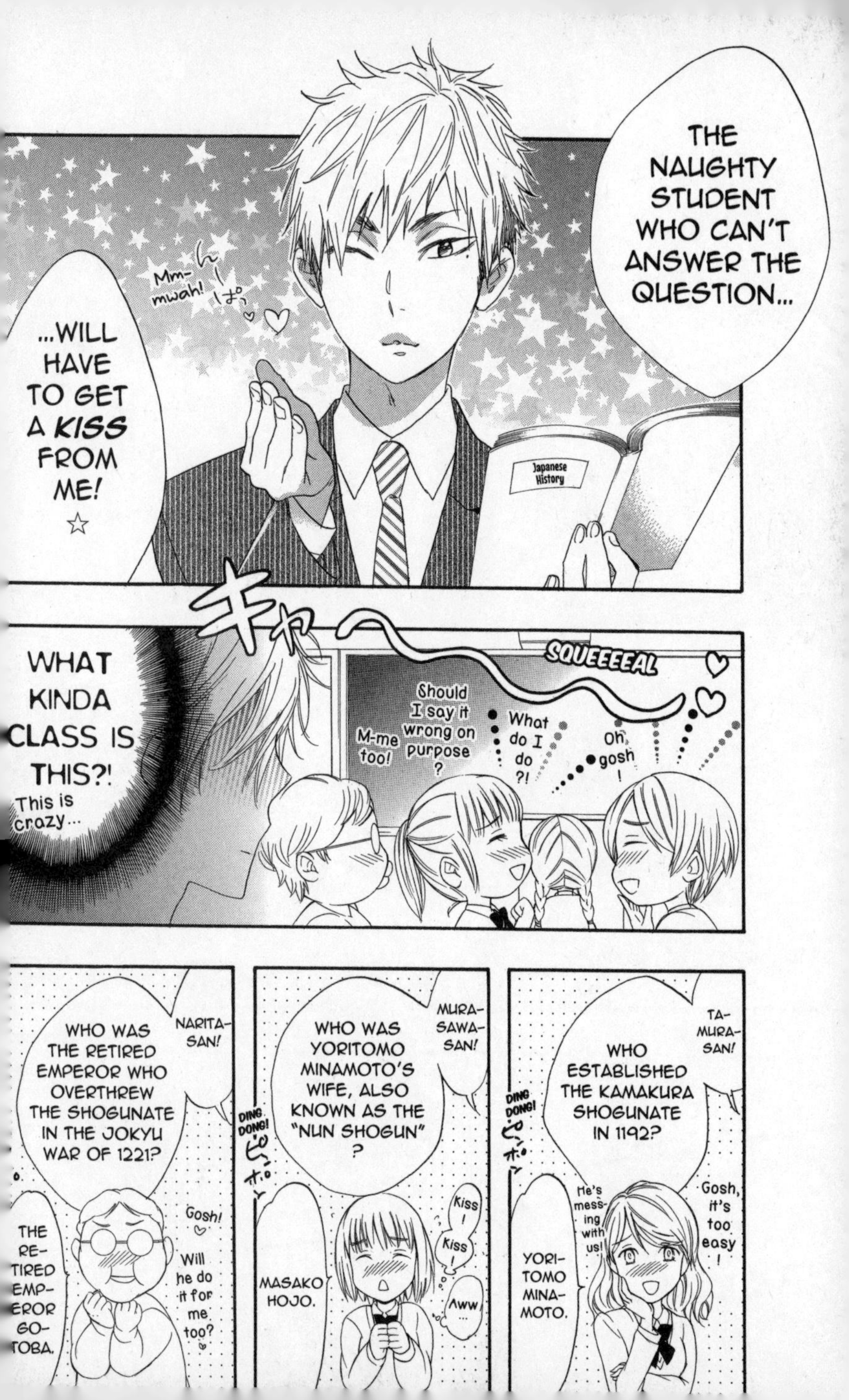
THE NAUGHTY STUDENT WHO CAN'T ANSWER THE QUESTION...
Mm-mwah!
...WILL HAVE TO GET A KISS FROM ME! ☆
Japanese History
SQUEEEEAL
Oh gosh!
What do I do?!
Should I say it wrong on purpose?
M-me too!
WHAT KINDA CLASS IS THIS?!
This is crazy...
TA-MURA-SAN!
WHO ESTABLISHED THE KAMAKURA SHOGUNATE IN 1192?
DING DONG!
Gosh, it's too easy!
He's messing with us!
YORITOMO MINAMOTO.
MURA-SAWA-SAN!
WHO WAS YORITOMO MINAMOTO'S WIFE, ALSO KNOWN AS THE "NUN SHOGUN"?
DING DONG!
Kiss! Kiss!
Aww...
MASAKO HOJO.
NARITA-SAN!
WHO WAS THE RETIRED EMPEROR WHO OVERTHREW THE SHOGUNATE IN THE JOKYU WAR OF 1221?
Gosh! ♡
Will he do it for me too?
THE RETIRED EMPEROR GO-TOBA.

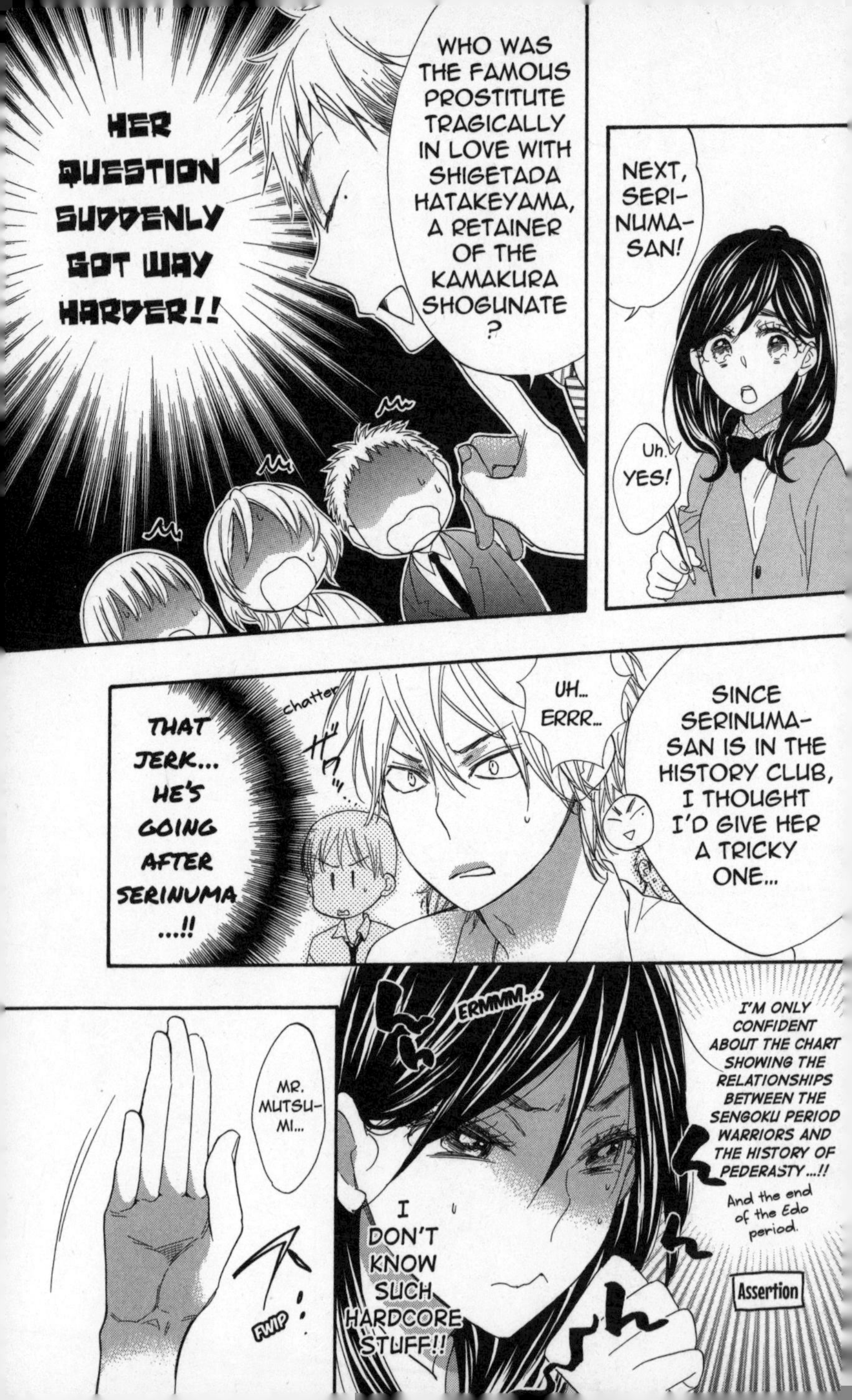
NEXT, SERI-NUMA-SAN!
Uh. YES!
WHO WAS THE FAMOUS PROSTITUTE TRAGICALLY IN LOVE WITH SHIGETADA HATAKEYAMA, A RETAINER OF THE KAMAKURA SHOGUNATE?
HER QUESTION SUDDENLY GOT WAY HARDER!!
SINCE SERINUMA-SAN IS IN THE HISTORY CLUB, I THOUGHT I'D GIVE HER A TRICKY ONE...
UH... ERRR...
chatter
THAT JERK... HE'S GOING AFTER SERINUMA...!!
ERMMM...
I'M ONLY CONFIDENT ABOUT THE CHART SHOWING THE RELATIONSHIPS BETWEEN THE SENGOKU PERIOD WARRIORS AND THE HISTORY OF PEDERASTY...!!
And the end of the Edo period.
Assertion
I DON'T KNOW SUCH HARDCORE STUFF!!
MR. MUTSUMI...
FWIP

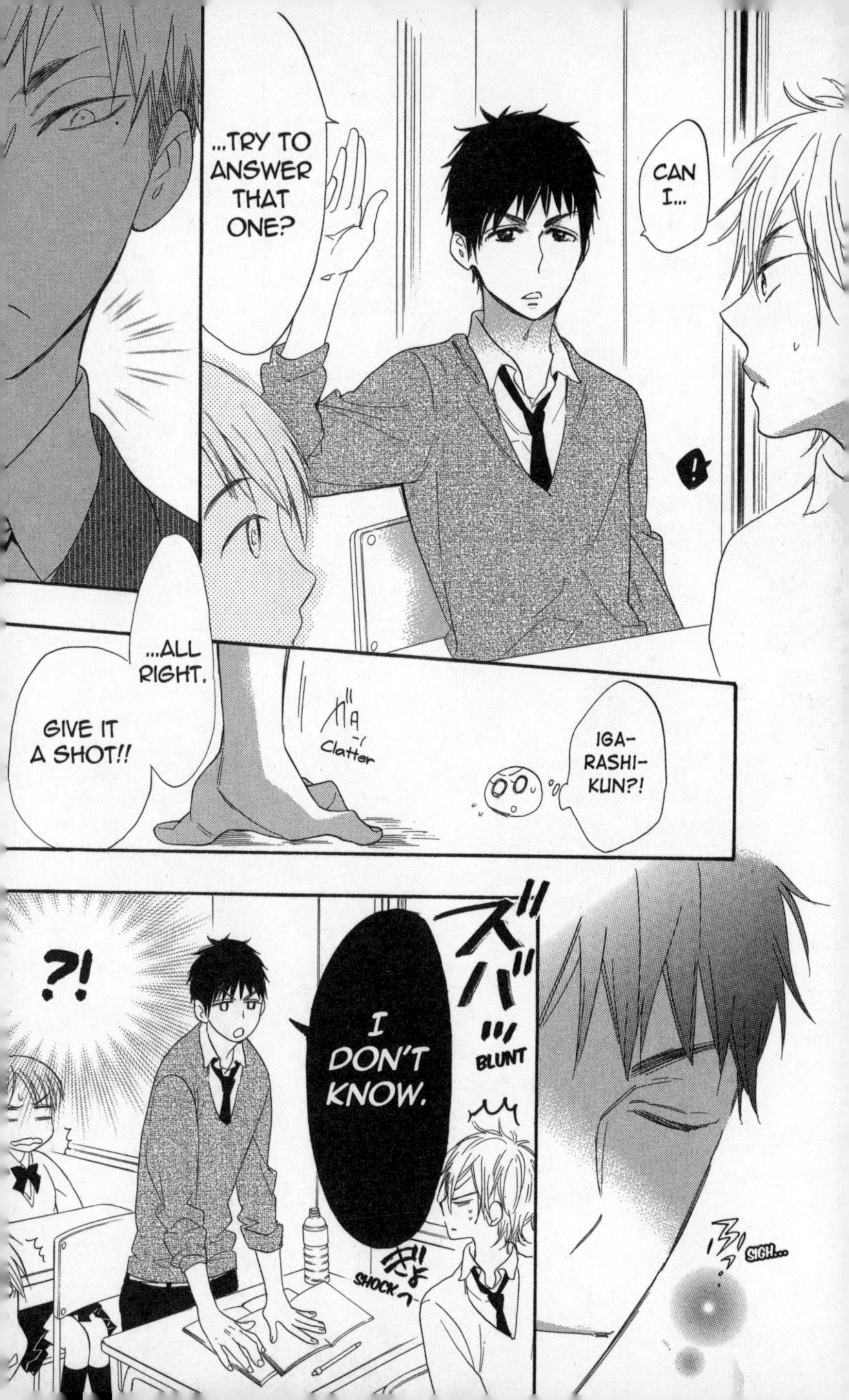
CAN I...
...TRY TO ANSWER THAT ONE?
!
IGA-RASHI-KUN?!
Clatter
...ALL RIGHT.
GIVE IT A SHOT!!
SIGH...
BLUNT
I DON'T KNOW.
SHOCK
?!

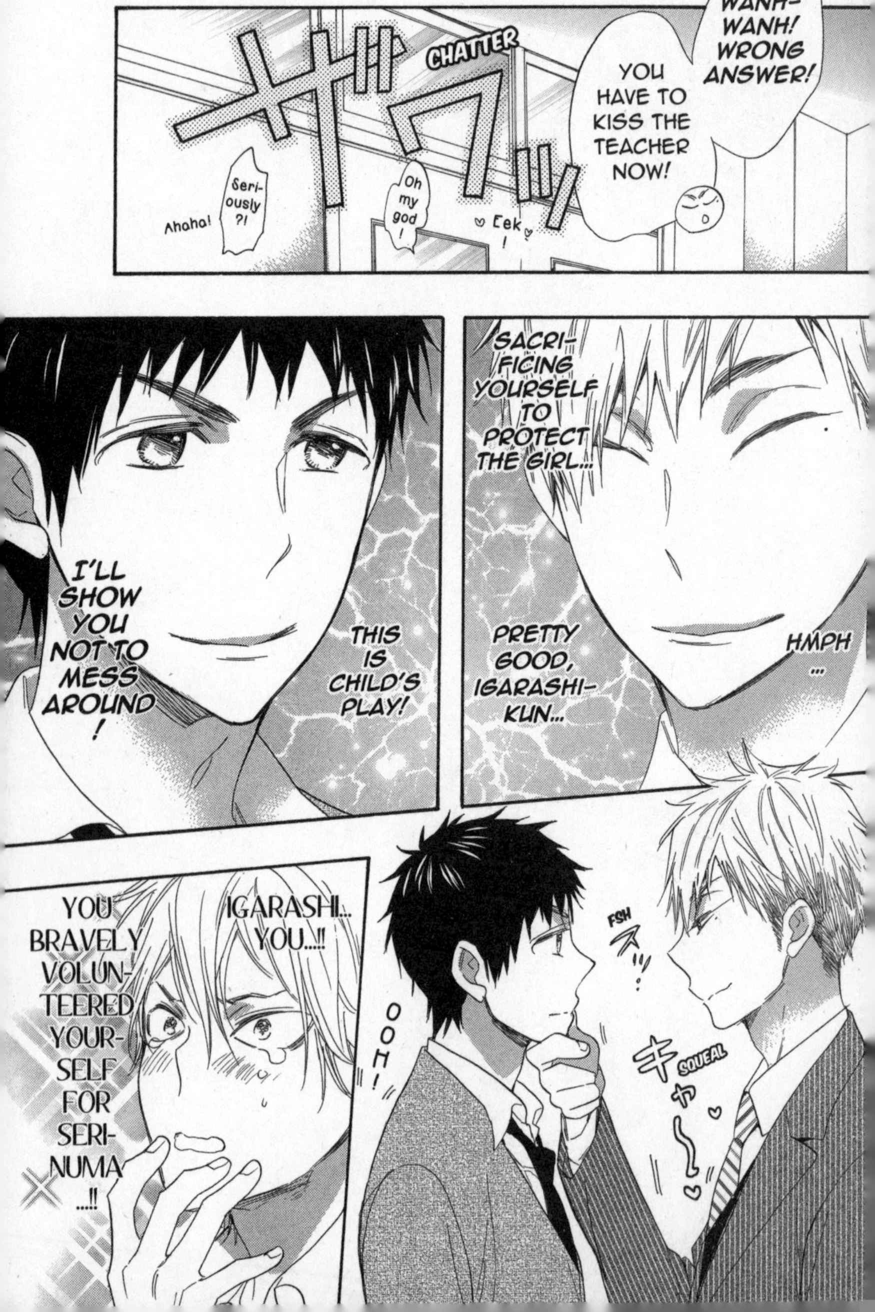
WANH-WANH! WRONG ANSWER!
YOU HAVE TO KISS THE TEACHER NOW!
CHATTER
Eek!
Oh my god!
Seri-ously?!
Ahaha!
SACRI-FICING YOURSELF TO PROTECT THE GIRL...
HMPH...
PRETTY GOOD, IGARASHI-KUN...
THIS IS CHILD'S PLAY!
I'LL SHOW YOU NOT TO MESS AROUND!
FSH
SQUEAL
OOH!
IGARASHI... YOU...!!
YOU BRAVELY VOLUN-TEERED YOUR-SELF FOR SERI-NUMA...!!

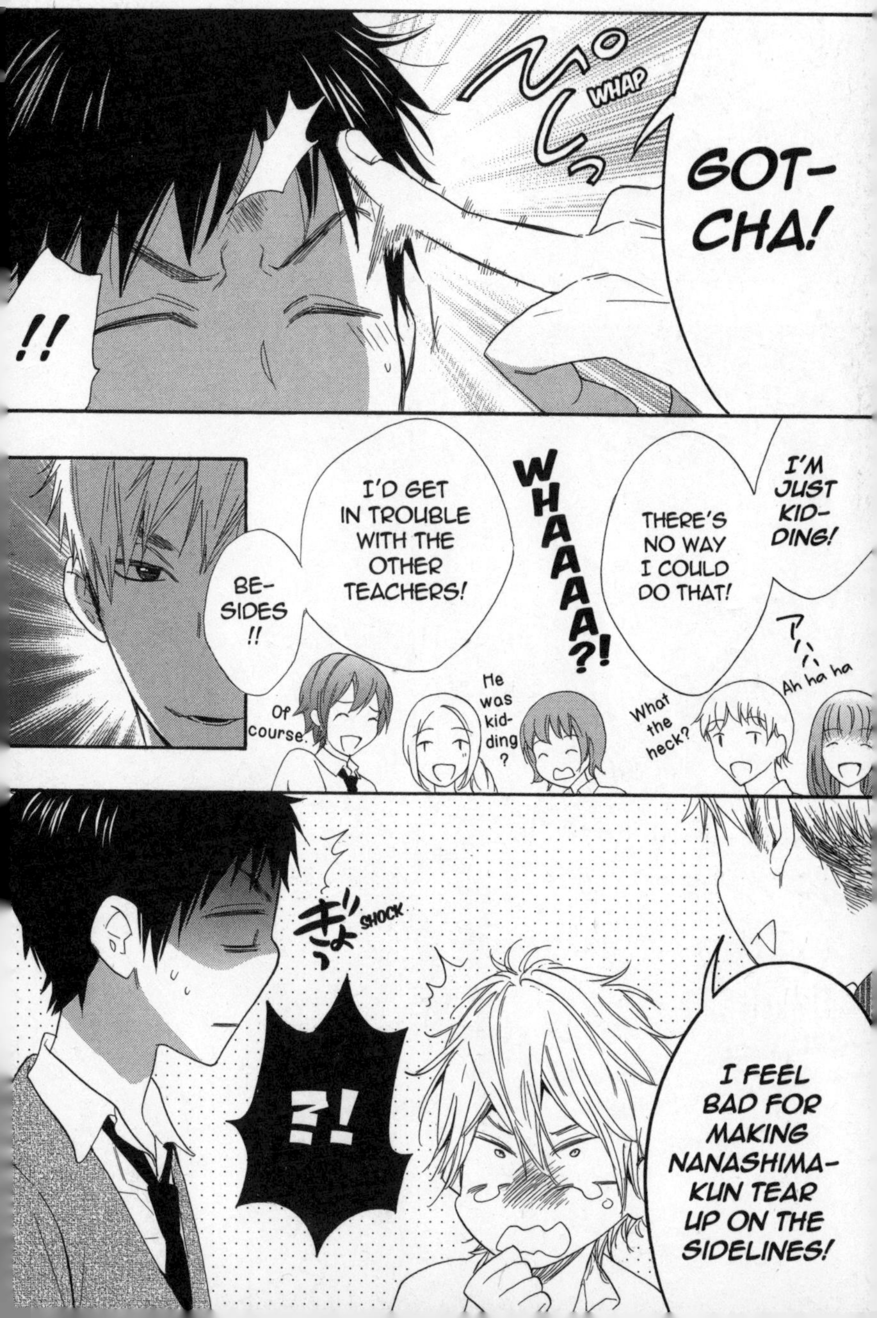
GOT-CHA!
WHAP
!!
I'M JUST KID-DING!
THERE'S NO WAY I COULD DO THAT!
WHAAAA?!
I'D GET IN TROUBLE WITH THE OTHER TEACHERS!
BE-SIDES !!
Ah ha ha
What the heck?
He was kid-ding?
Of course.
I FEEL BAD FOR MAKING NANASHIMA-KUN TEAR UP ON THE SIDELINES!
?!
SHOCK

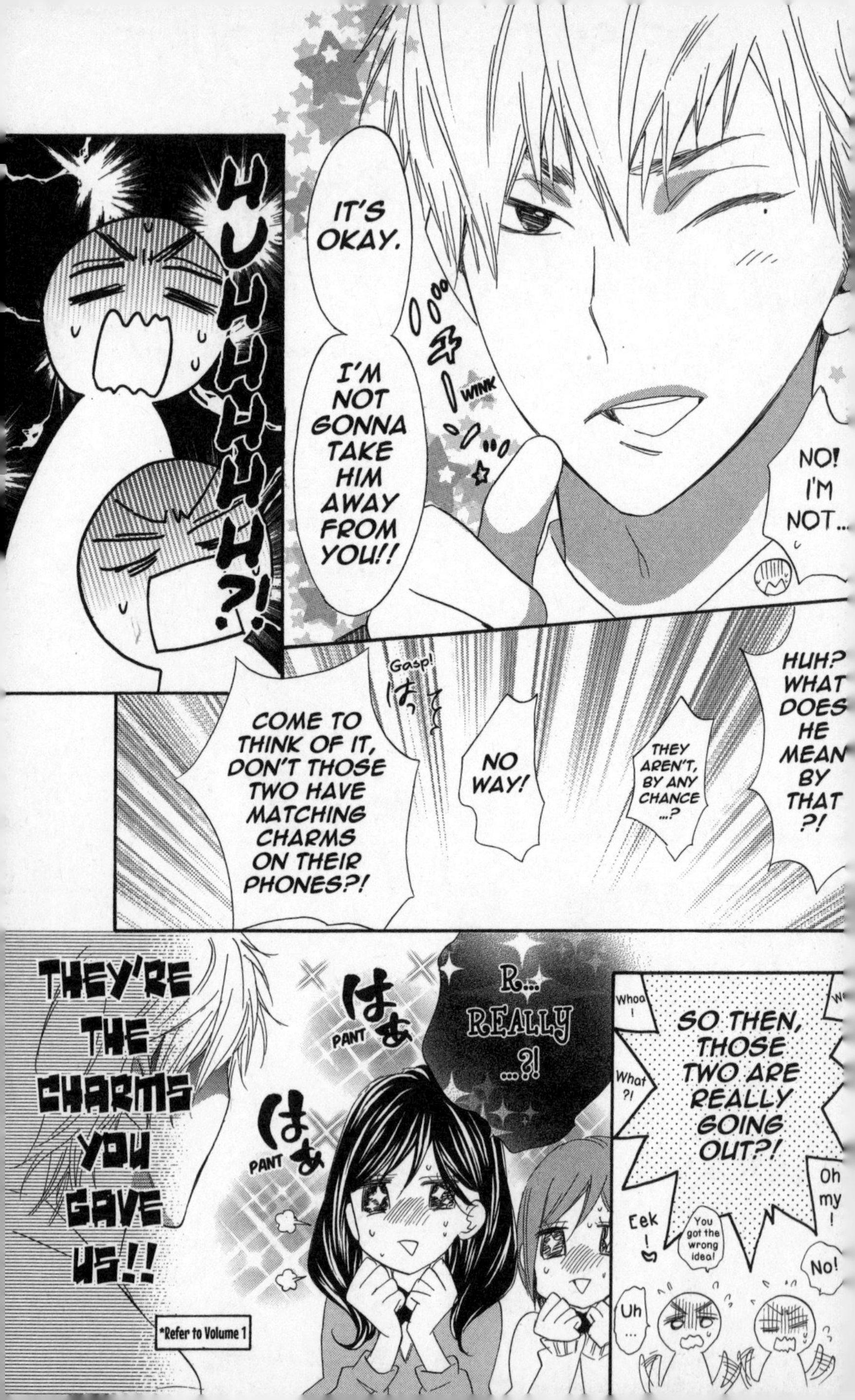
IT'S OKAY.
I'M NOT GONNA TAKE HIM AWAY FROM YOU!!
WINK
NO! I'M NOT...
HUHHHHH?!!
HUH? WHAT DOES HE MEAN BY THAT?!
THEY AREN'T, BY ANY CHANCE ...?
NO WAY!
Gasp!
はっ
COME TO THINK OF IT, DON'T THOSE TWO HAVE MATCHING CHARMS ON THEIR PHONES?!
Whoa!
What?!
SO THEN, THOSE TWO ARE REALLY GOING OUT?!
Oh my!
Eek!
You got the wrong idea!
No!
Uh ...
R... REALLY ...?!
はぁ
PANT
はぁ
PANT
THEY'RE THE CHARMS YOU GAVE US!!
*Refer to Volume 1

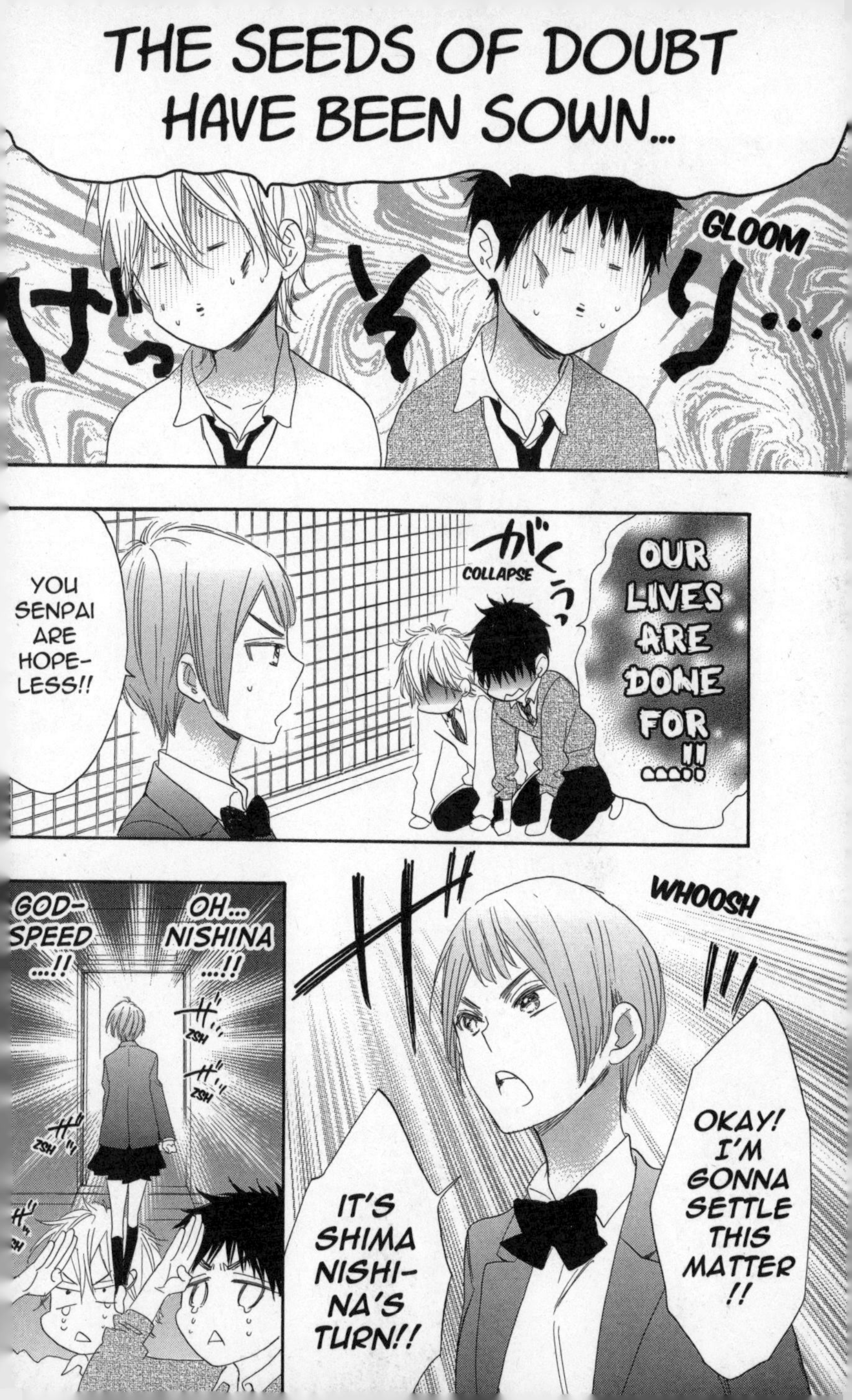
THE SEEDS OF DOUBT HAVE BEEN SOWN...
げっそり…
GLOOM
OUR LIVES ARE DONE FOR .....!!
がくっ
COLLAPSE
YOU SENPAI ARE HOPE-LESS!!
WHOOSH
OKAY! I'M GONNA SETTLE THIS MATTER !!
IT'S SHIMA NISHI-NA'S TURN!!
OH... NISHINA ...!!
GOD-SPEED ...!!
ZSH
ZSH
ZSH

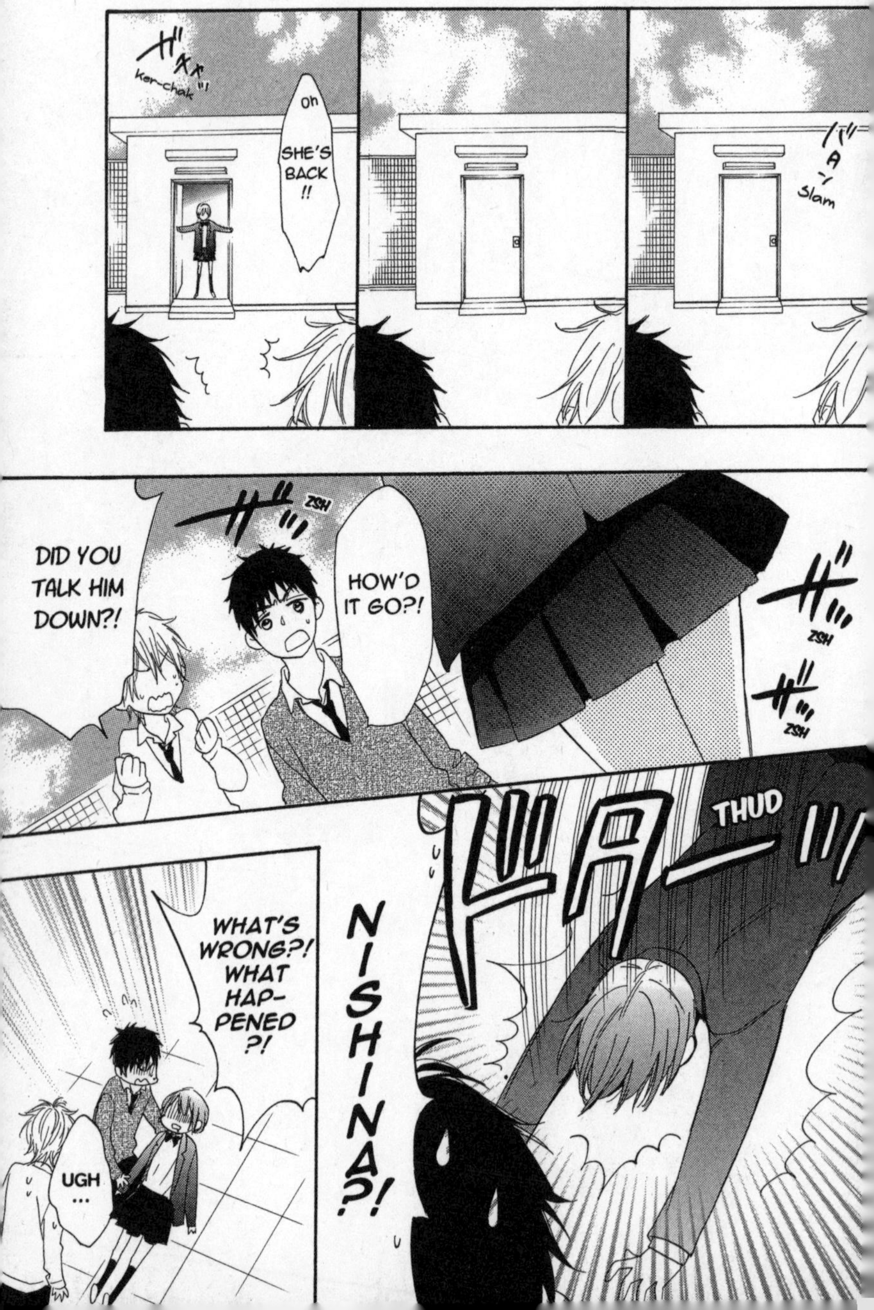
Slam
Ker-chak
Oh SHE'S BACK!!
ZSH
ZSH
ZSH
HOW'D IT GO?!
DID YOU TALK HIM DOWN?!
THUD
NISHINA?!
WHAT'S WRONG?! WHAT HAP-PENED?!
UGH...

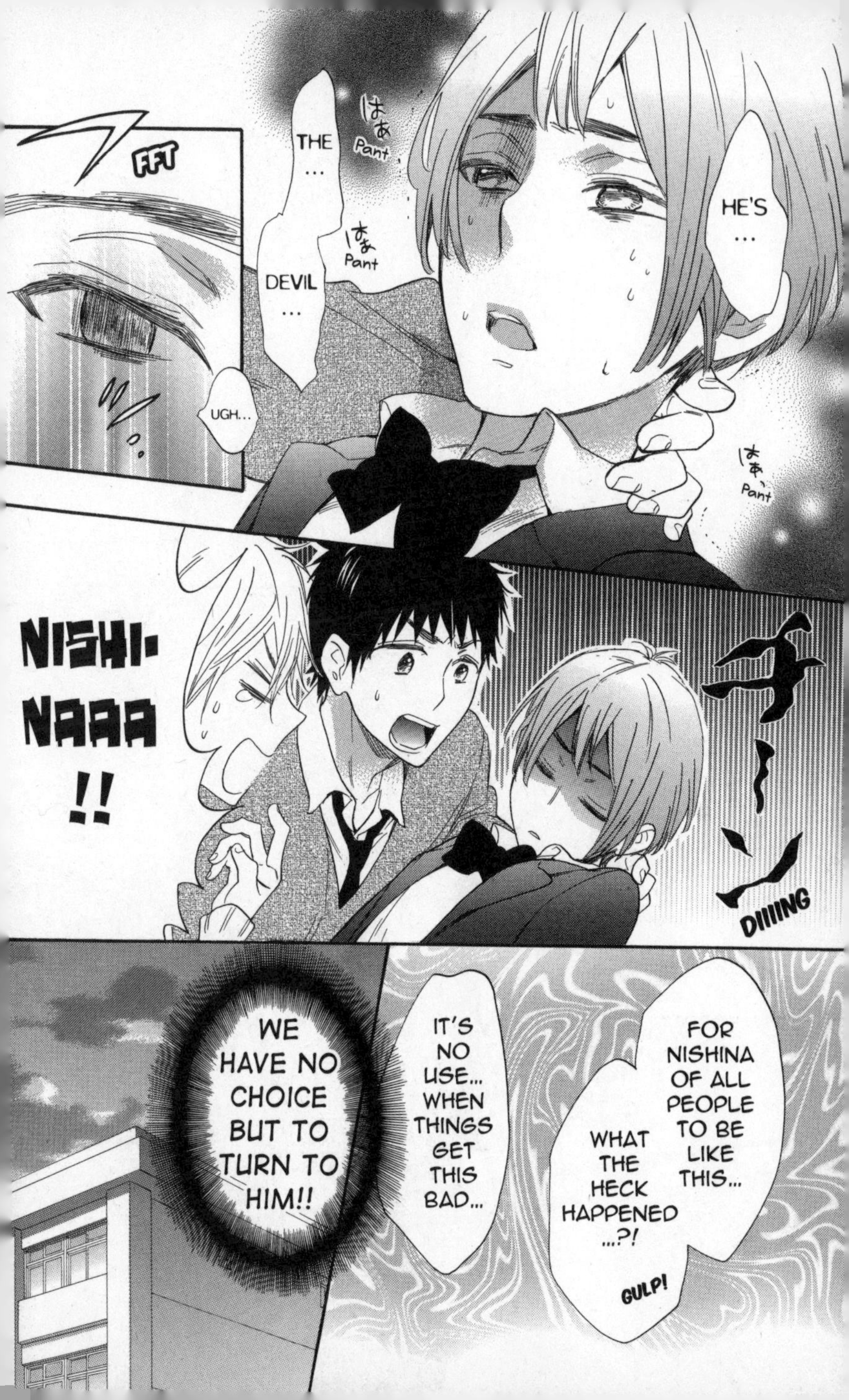
HE'S …
はぁ Pant
THE …
はぁ Pant
DEVIL …
はぁ Pant
FFT
UGH…
チーン
DIIIING
NISHI-NAAA!!
FOR NISHINA OF ALL PEOPLE TO BE LIKE THIS…
WHAT THE HECK HAPPENED …?!
GULP!
IT'S NO USE… WHEN THINGS GET THIS BAD…
WE HAVE NO CHOICE BUT TO TURN TO HIM!!

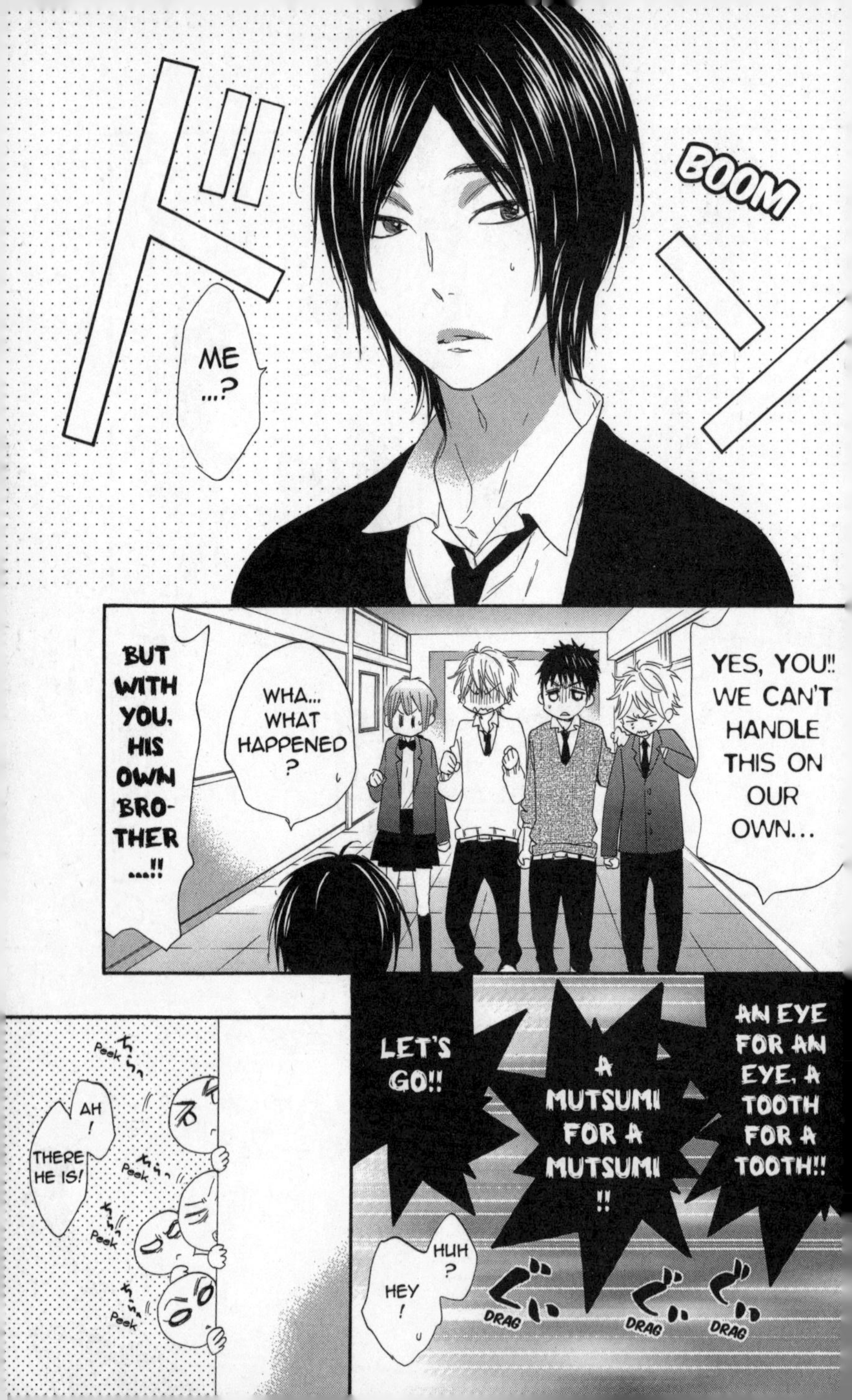
BOOM
ME ...?
YES, YOU!! WE CAN'T HANDLE THIS ON OUR OWN...
WHA... WHAT HAPPENED?
BUT WITH YOU, HIS OWN BROTHER ...!!
AN EYE FOR AN EYE, A TOOTH FOR A TOOTH!!
A MUTSUMI FOR A MUTSUMI!!
LET'S GO!!
HUH?
HEY!
DRAG
DRAG
DRAG
Peek
AH!
THERE HE IS!
Peek
Peek
Peek

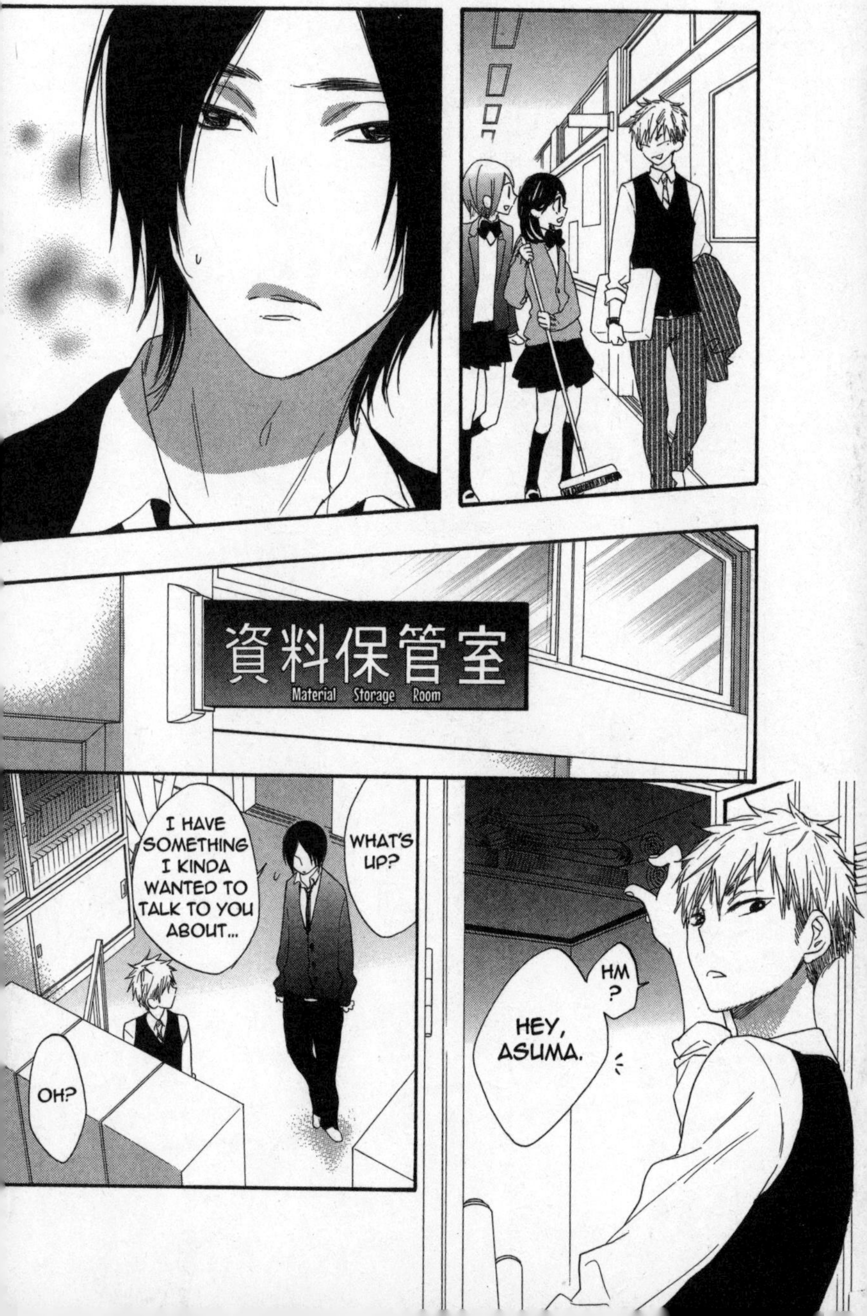
資料保管室
Material Storage Room
HM ?
HEY, ASUMA.
WHAT'S UP?
I HAVE SOMETHING I KINDA WANTED TO TALK TO YOU ABOUT...
OH?

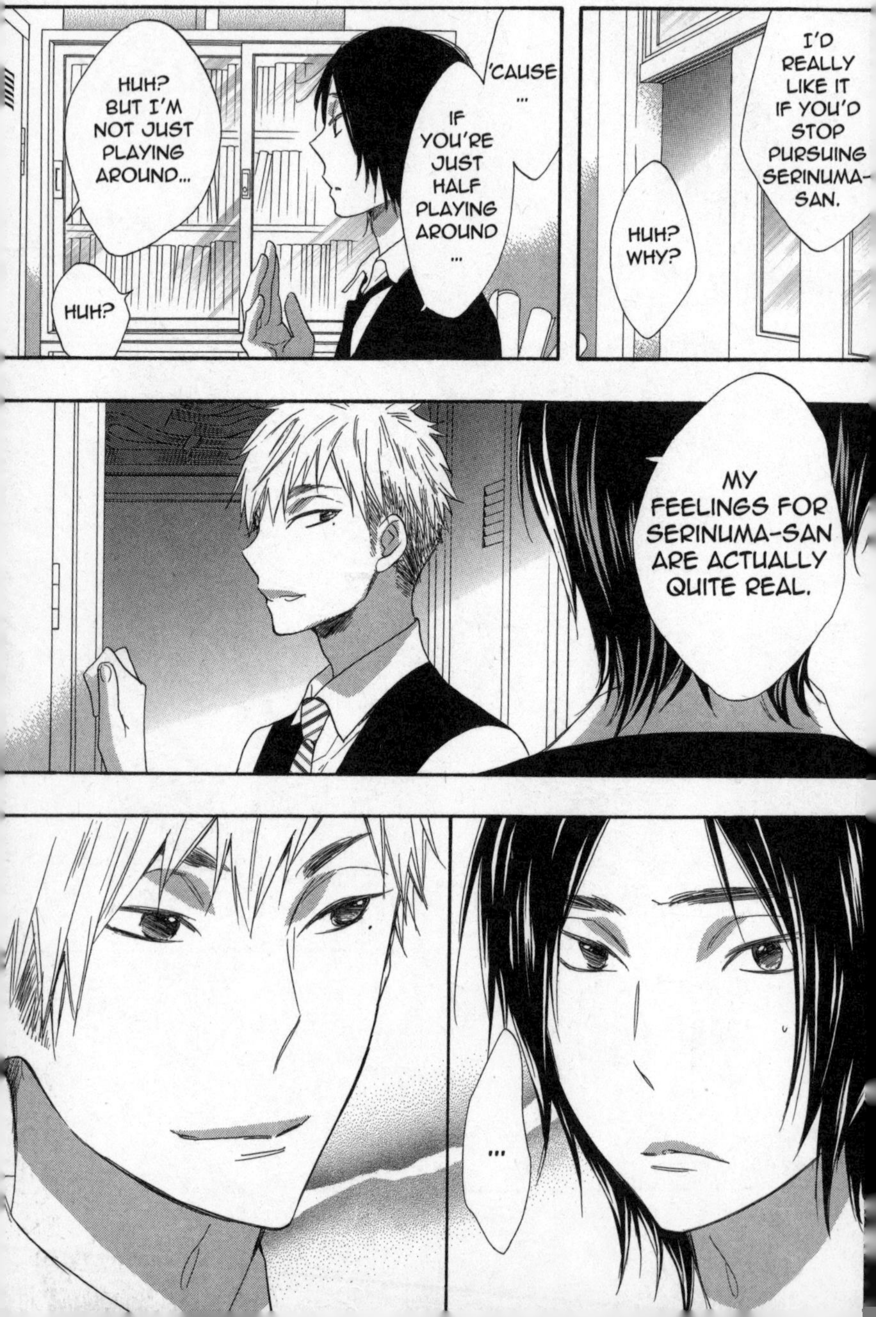
I'D REALLY LIKE IT IF YOU'D STOP PURSUING SERINUMA-SAN.
HUH? WHY?
'CAUSE ...
IF YOU'RE JUST HALF PLAYING AROUND ...
HUH? BUT I'M NOT JUST PLAYING AROUND...
HUH?
MY FEELINGS FOR SERINUMA-SAN ARE ACTUALLY QUITE REAL.
...

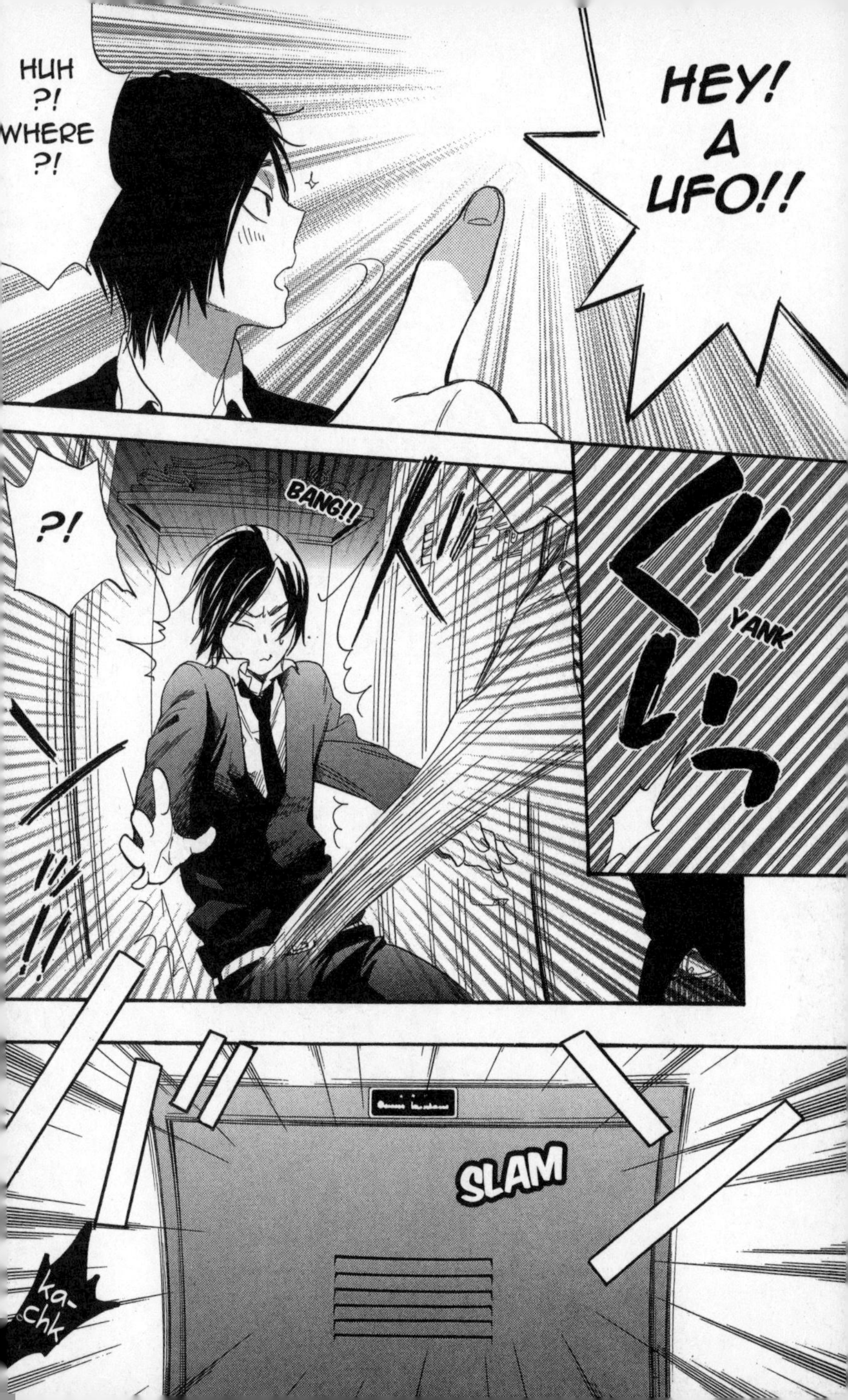
HEY! A UFO!!
HUH?! WHERE?!
YANK
BANG!!
?!
SLAM
ka-chk

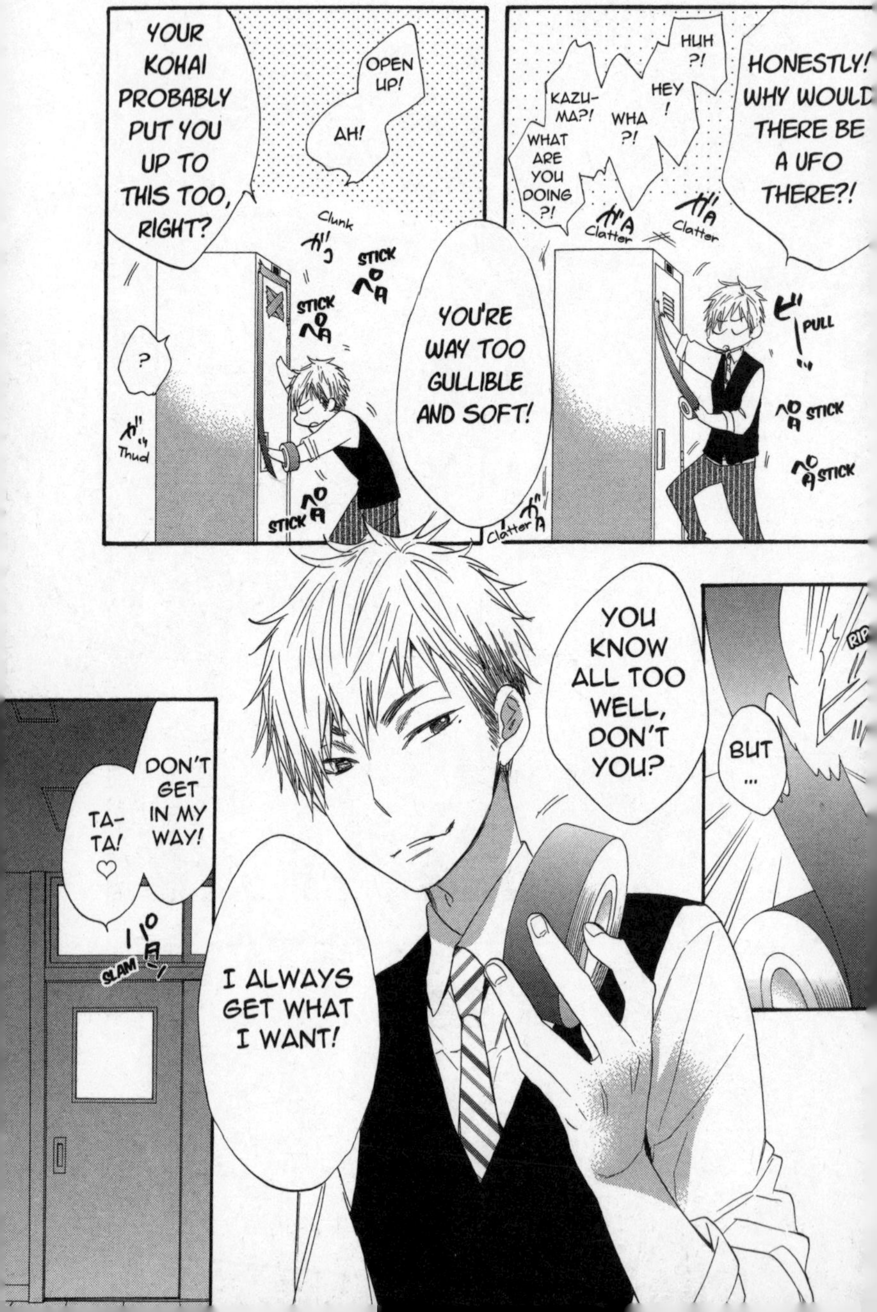
HONESTLY! WHY WOULD THERE BE A UFO THERE?!
HUH?!
HEY!
WHA?!
KAZUMA?! WHAT ARE YOU DOING?!
Clatter
Clatter
PULL
STICK
STICK
Clatter
OPEN UP!
AH!
YOUR KOHAI PROBABLY PUT YOU UP TO THIS TOO, RIGHT?
Clunk
STICK
STICK
STICK
?
Thud
YOU'RE WAY TOO GULLIBLE AND SOFT!
RIP
BUT ...
YOU KNOW ALL TOO WELL, DON'T YOU?
I ALWAYS GET WHAT I WANT!
DON'T GET IN MY WAY!
TA-TA! ♡
SLAM

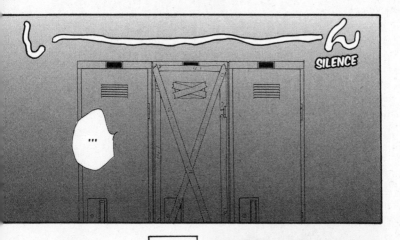

SILENCE

...

IT'S PITCH BLACK AND I CAN'T SEE ANYTHING.

I CAN'T MOVE...

IT'S THE SAME AS THAT TIME...

THAT TIME...

S...SO DARK...

SHUDDER

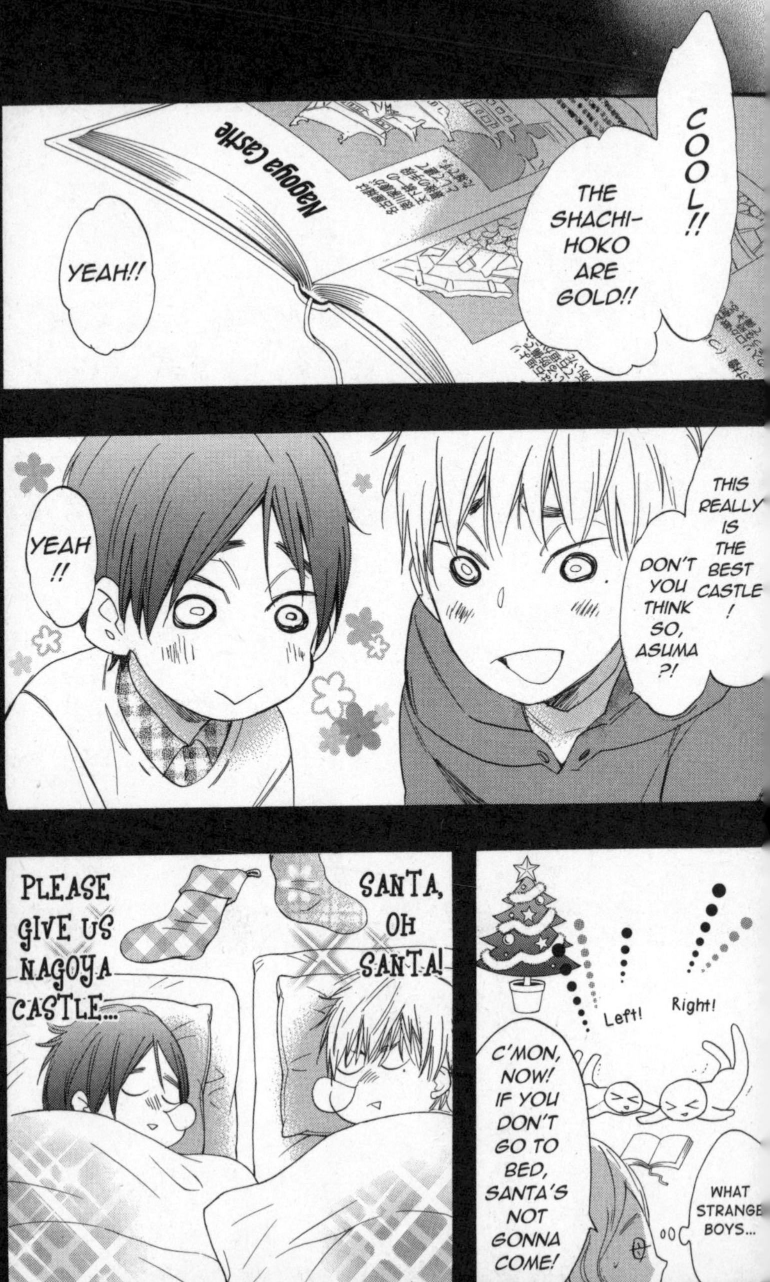
COOL!!
THE SHACHI-HOKO ARE GOLD!!
Nagoya Castle
YEAH!!
THIS REALLY IS THE BEST CASTLE!
DON'T YOU THINK SO, ASUMA?!
YEAH!!
Right!
Left!
C'MON, NOW! IF YOU DON'T GO TO BED, SANTA'S NOT GONNA COME!
WHAT STRANGE BOYS...
SANTA, OH SANTA!
PLEASE GIVE US NAGOYA CASTLE...

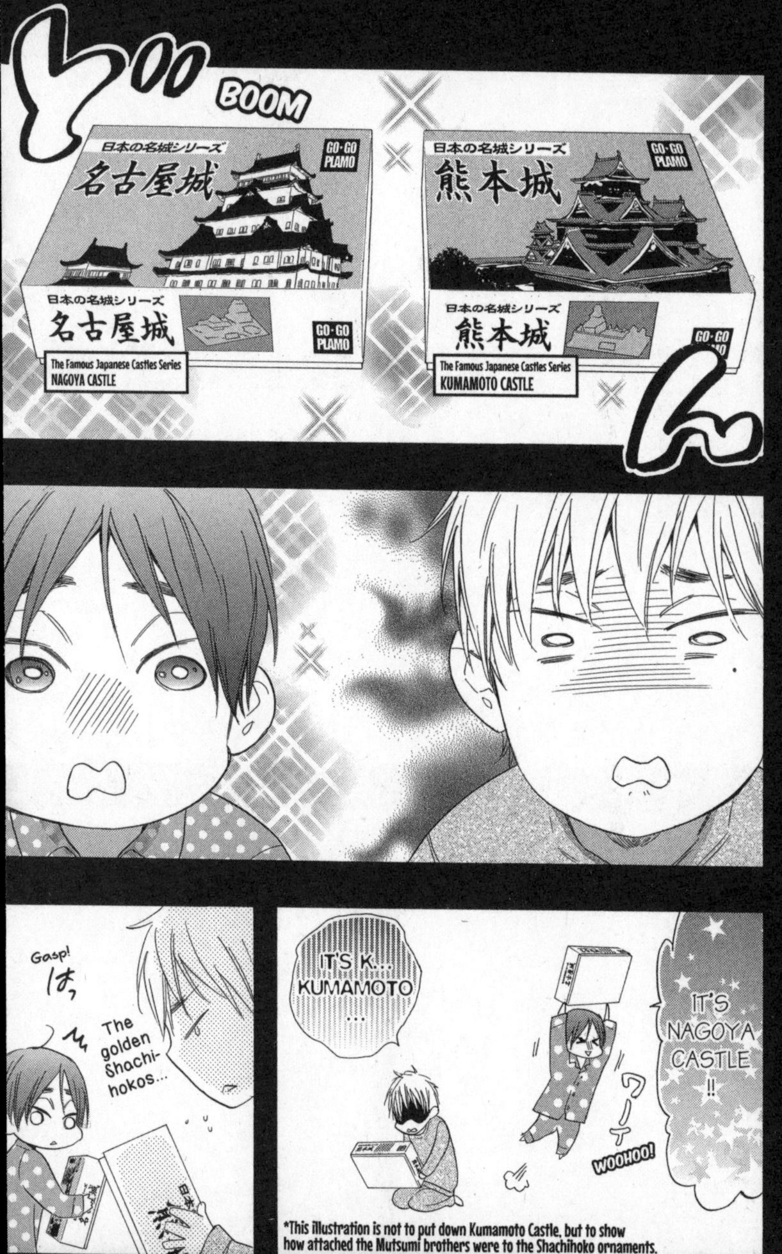
BOOM
日本の名城シリーズ
熊本城
GO·GO PLAMO
The Famous Japanese Castles Series
KUMAMOTO CASTLE
日本の名城シリーズ
名古屋城
GO·GO PLAMO
The Famous Japanese Castles Series
NAGOYA CASTLE
IT'S NAGOYA CASTLE !!
WOOHOO!
IT'S K... KUMAMOTO ...
Gasp!
The golden Shachi-hokos...
*This illustration is not to put down Kumamoto Castle, but to show how attached the Mutsumi brothers were to the Shachihoko ornaments.

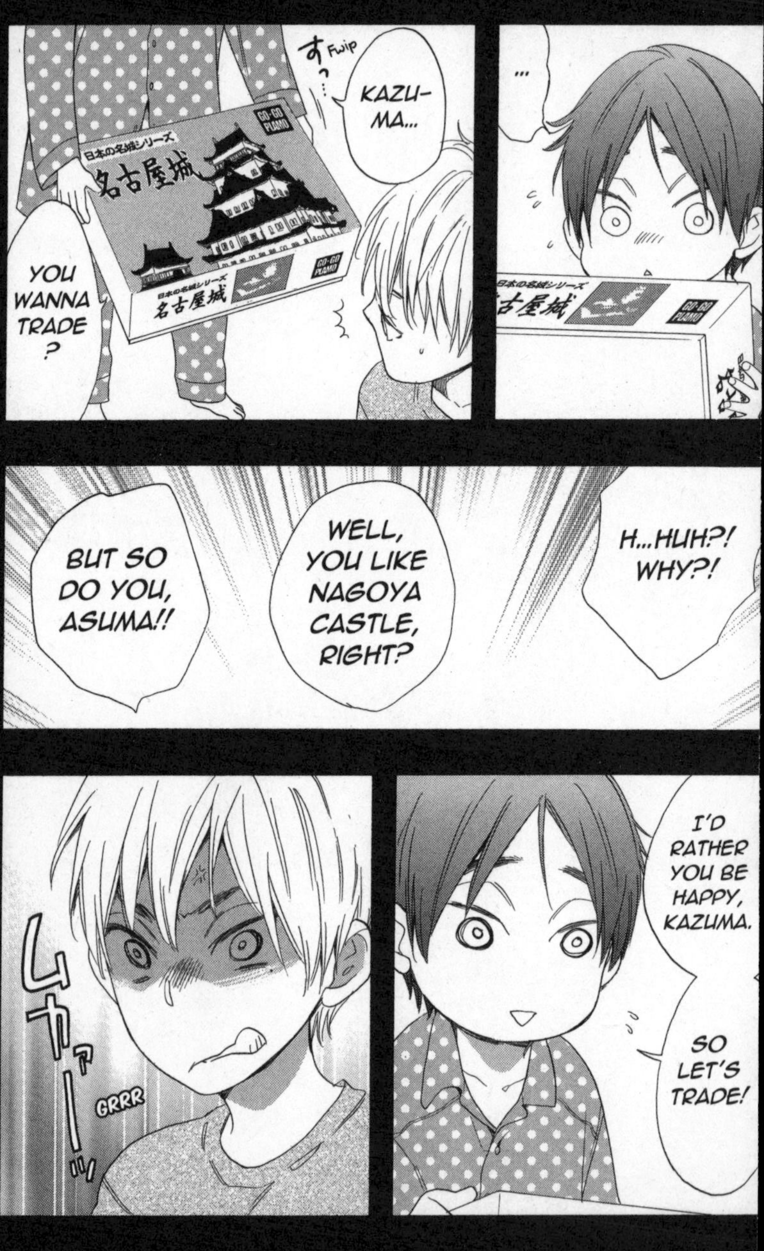
...
日本の名城シリーズ
名古屋城
GO-GO PLAMO
す Fwip
KAZU-MA...
日本の名城シリーズ
名古屋城
GO-GO PLAMO
YOU WANNA TRADE?
H...HUH?! WHY?!
WELL, YOU LIKE NAGOYA CASTLE, RIGHT?
BUT SO DO YOU, ASUMA!!
I'D RATHER YOU BE HAPPY, KAZUMA.
SO LET'S TRADE!
ムカァー
GRRR

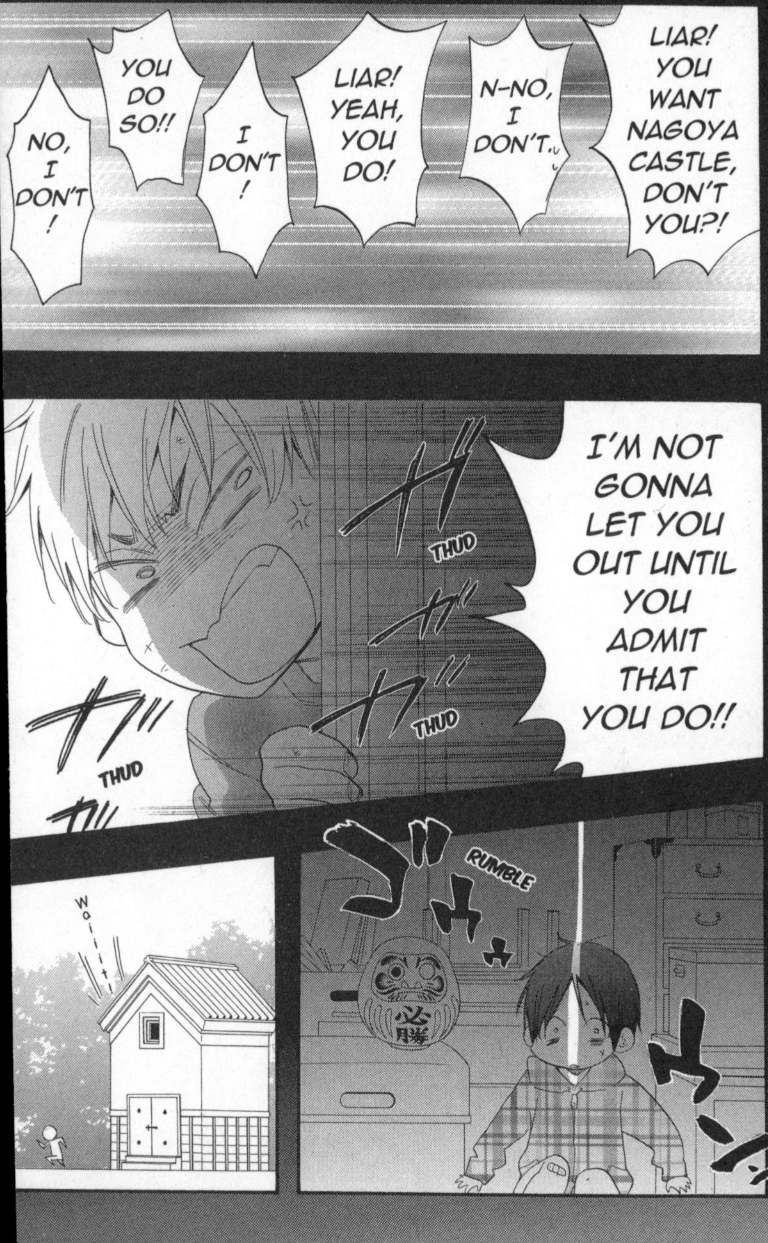
LIAR! YOU WANT NAGOYA CASTLE, DON'T YOU?!
N-NO, I DON'T.
LIAR! YEAH, YOU DO!
I DON'T!
YOU DO SO!!
NO, I DON'T!
I'M NOT GONNA LET YOU OUT UNTIL YOU ADMIT THAT YOU DO!!
THUD
THUD
THUD
RUMBLE
Waiiit!

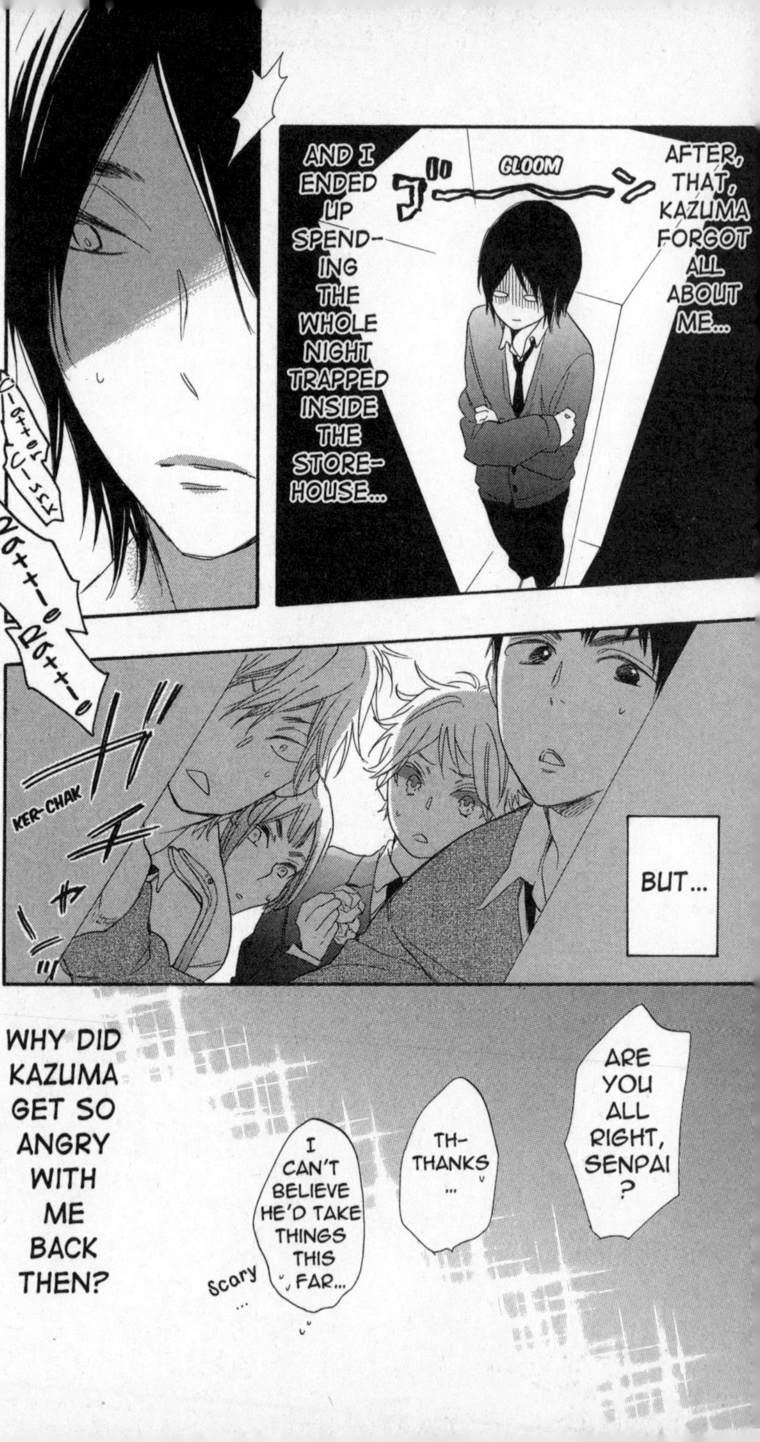
AFTER, THAT, KAZUMA FORGOT ALL ABOUT ME...
GLOOM
AND I ENDED UP SPENDING THE WHOLE NIGHT TRAPPED INSIDE THE STOREHOUSE...
Clatter Clunk
Rattle Rattle
BUT...
KER-CHAK
ARE YOU ALL RIGHT, SENPAI?
TH-THANKS...
I CAN'T BELIEVE HE'D TAKE THINGS THIS FAR...
Scary...
WHY DID KAZUMA GET SO ANGRY WITH ME BACK THEN?

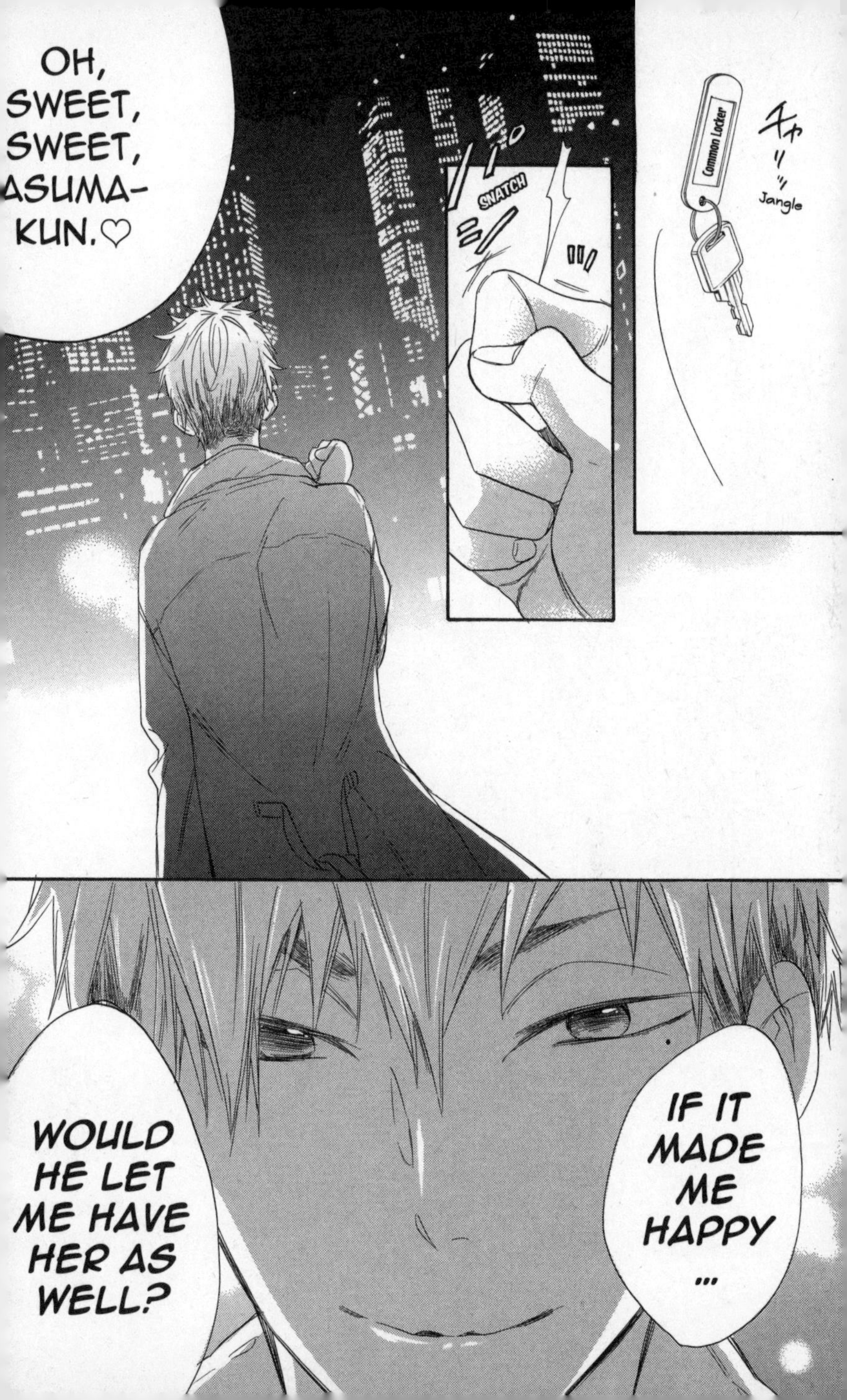
Common Locker
チャリッ
Jangle
SNATCH
OH, SWEET, SWEET, ASUMA-KUN.♡
IF IT MADE ME HAPPY...
WOULD HE LET ME HAVE HER AS WELL?

#20 DUEL BETWEEN BROTHERS

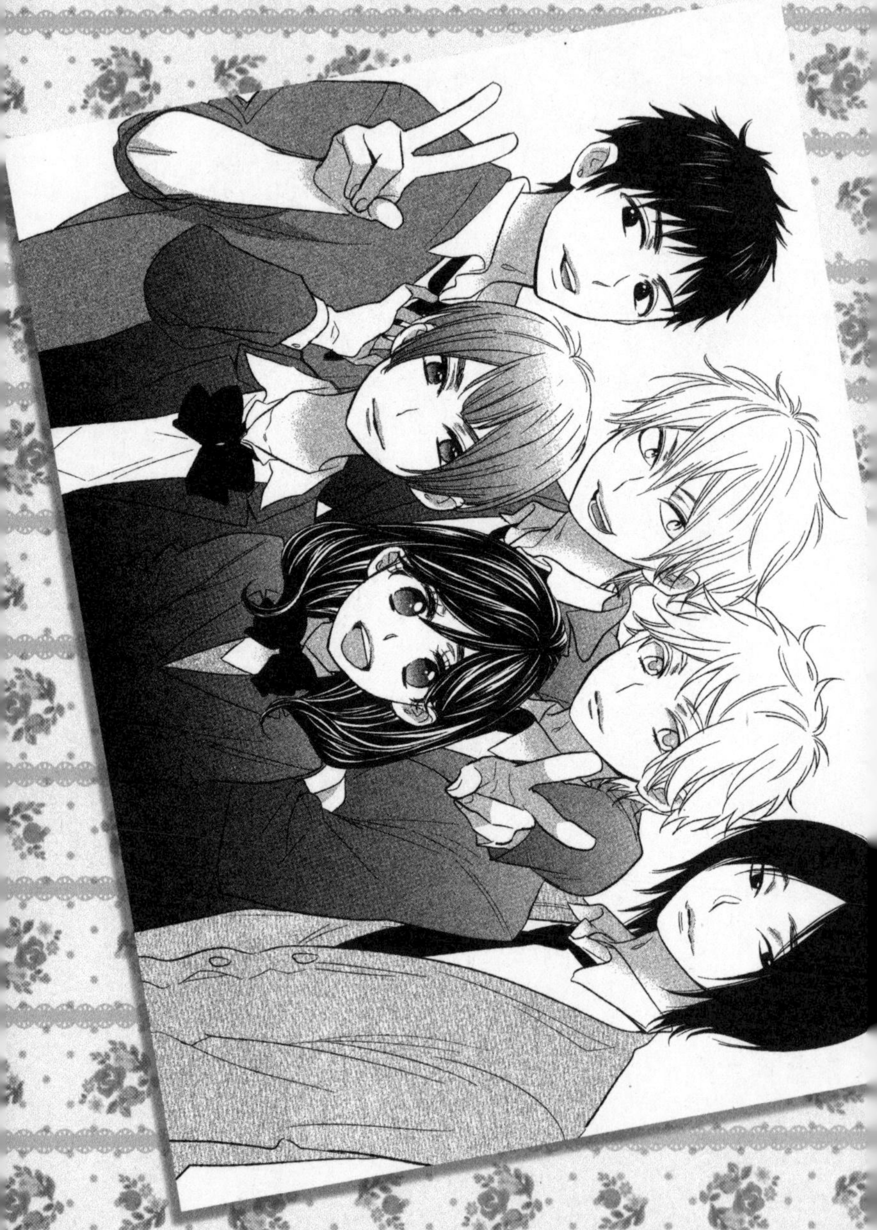

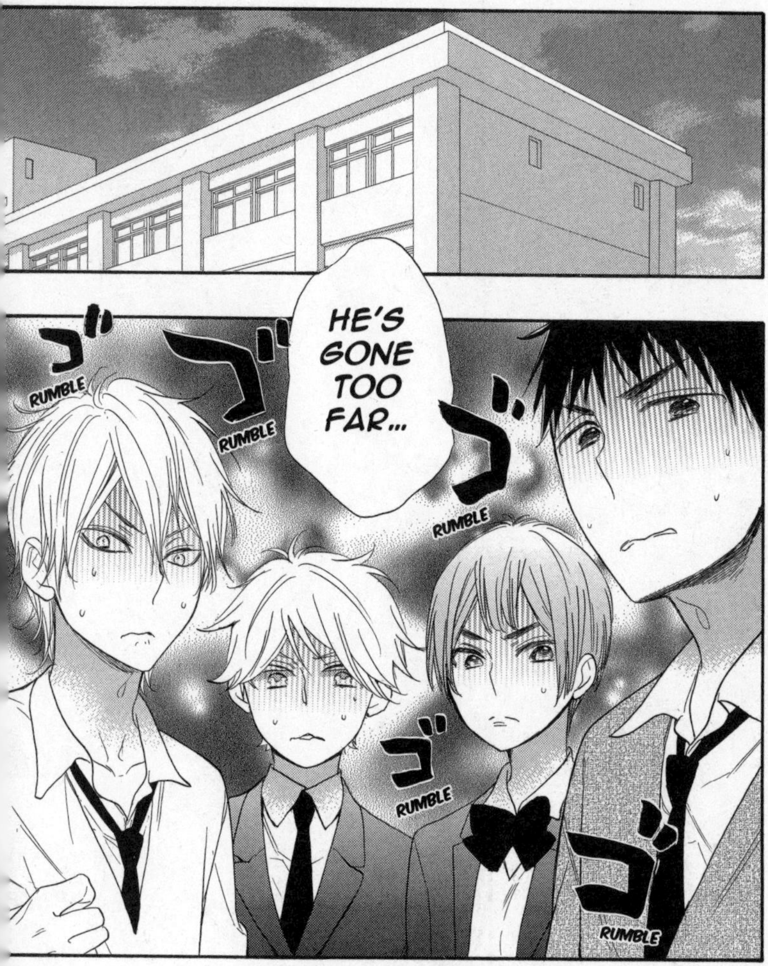
ゴ
RUMBLE
HE'S GONE TOO FAR...
ゴ
RUMBLE
ゴ
RUMBLE
ゴ
RUMBLE
ゴ
RUMBLE

KiSS HiM, NOT ME!

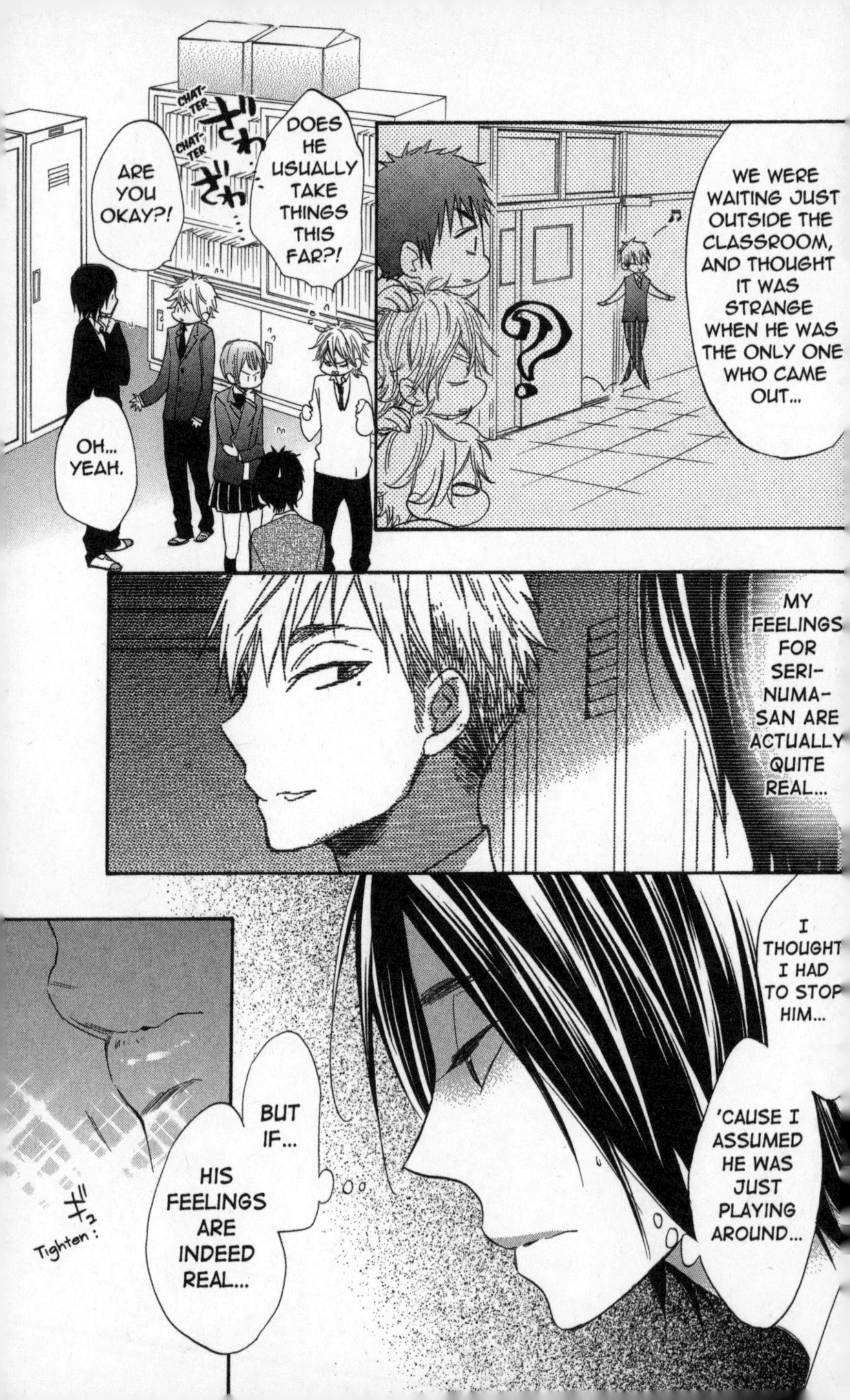
WE WERE WAITING JUST OUTSIDE THE CLASSROOM, AND THOUGHT IT WAS STRANGE WHEN HE WAS THE ONLY ONE WHO CAME OUT...
DOES HE USUALLY TAKE THINGS THIS FAR?!
ざわ ざわ
CHAT-TER CHAT-TER
ARE YOU OKAY?!
OH... YEAH.
MY FEELINGS FOR SERI-NUMA-SAN ARE ACTUALLY QUITE REAL...
I THOUGHT I HAD TO STOP HIM...
'CAUSE I ASSUMED HE WAS JUST PLAYING AROUND...
BUT IF...
HIS FEELINGS ARE INDEED REAL...
Tighten

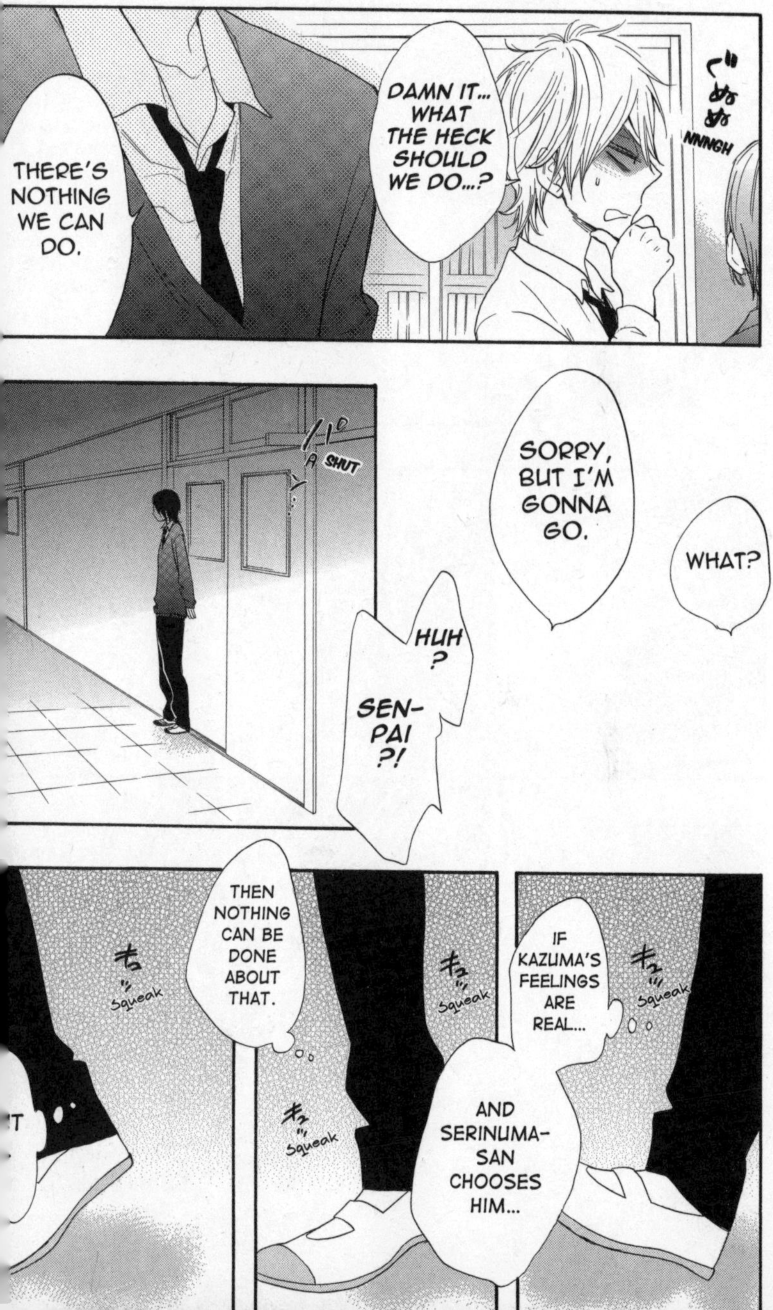
ぐぬぬ
NNNGH
DAMN IT... WHAT THE HECK SHOULD WE DO...?
THERE'S NOTHING WE CAN DO.
WHAT?
SORRY, BUT I'M GONNA GO.
SHUT
HUH?
SEN-PAI?!
Squeak
IF KAZUMA'S FEELINGS ARE REAL...
AND SERINUMA-SAN CHOOSES HIM...
Squeak
THEN NOTHING CAN BE DONE ABOUT THAT.
Squeak
Squeak

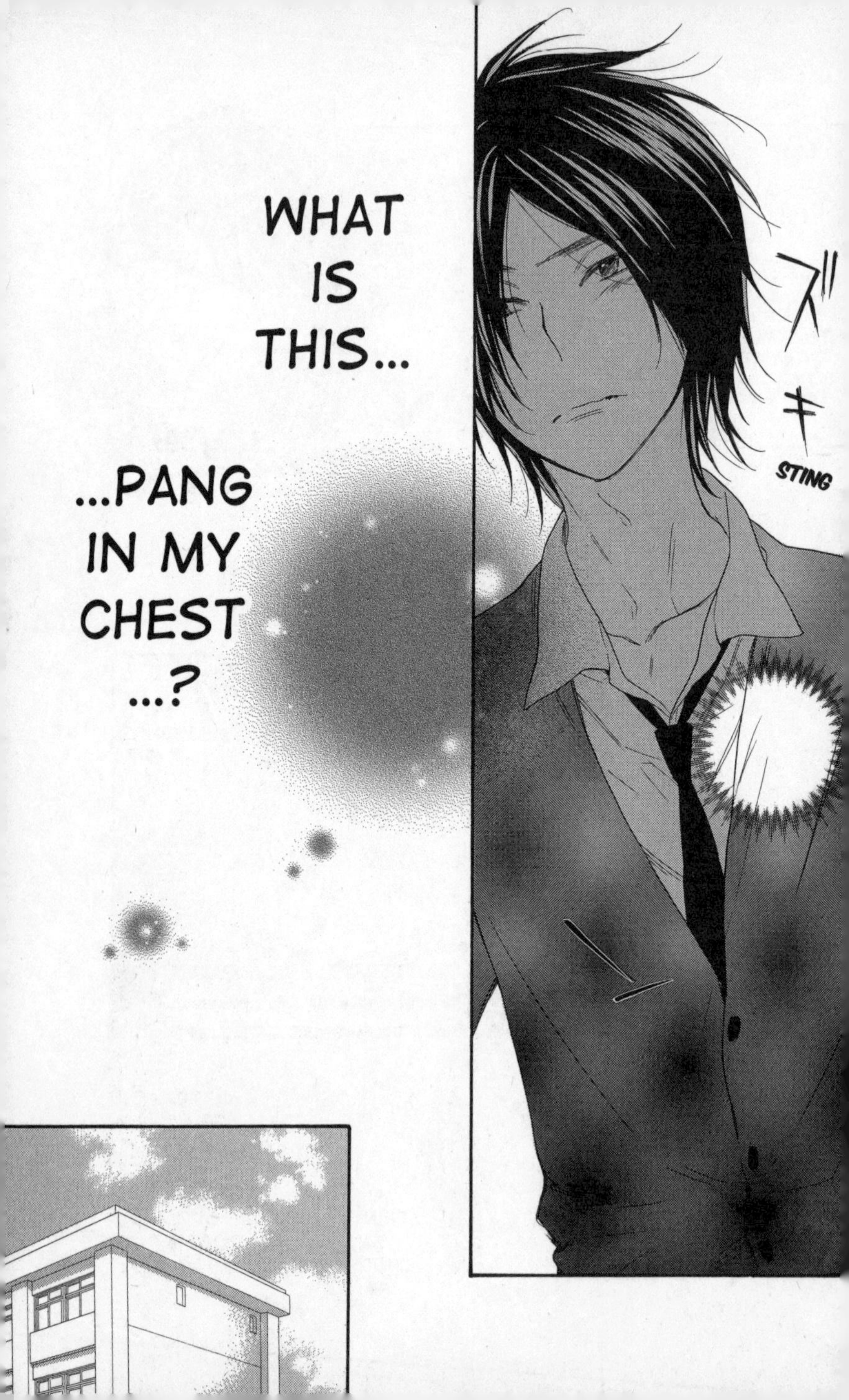
ズキ
STING
WHAT IS THIS...
...PANG IN MY CHEST ...?

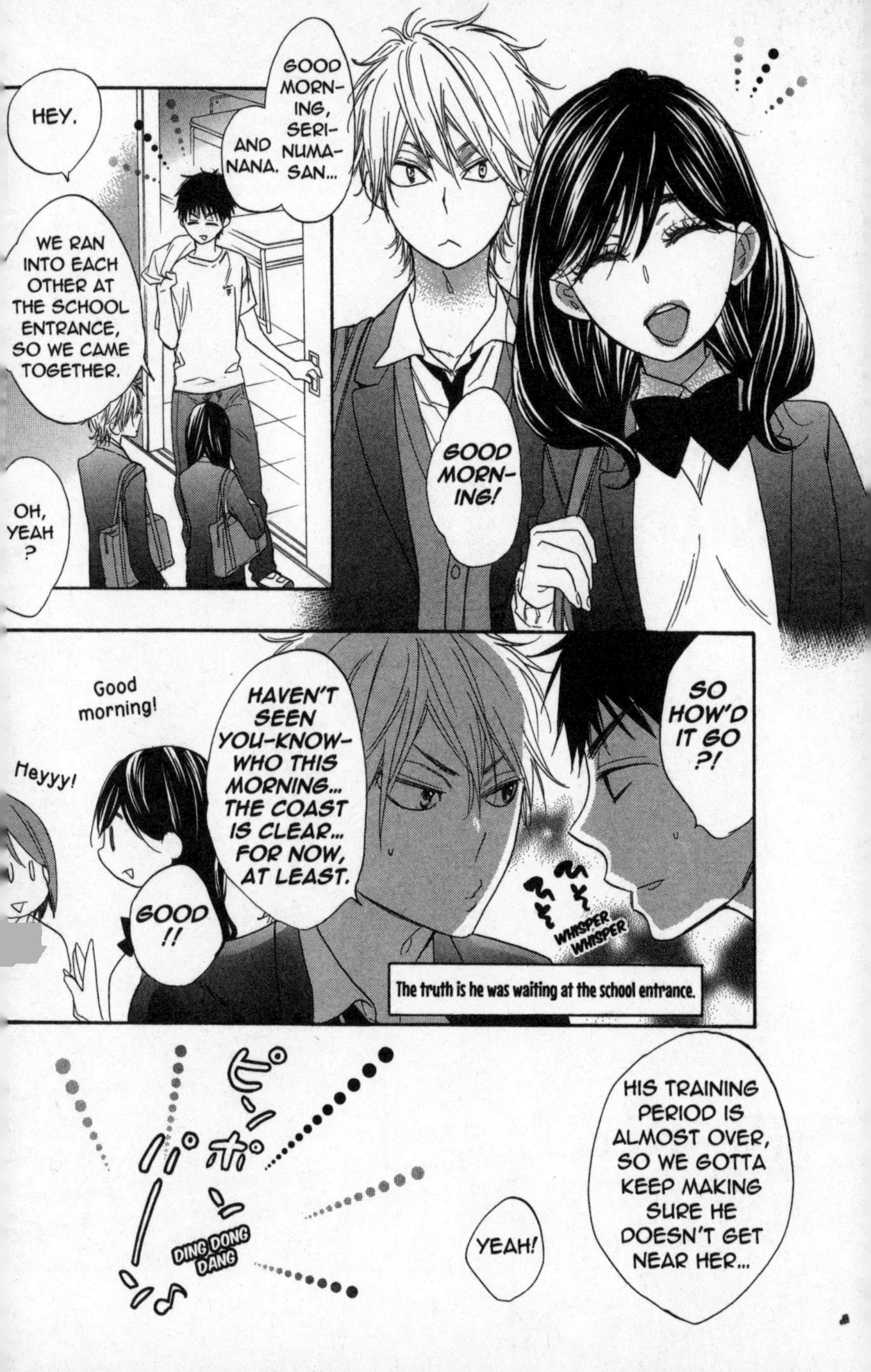
GOOD MORNING, SERINUMA-SAN...
AND NANA.
GOOD MORNING!
HEY.
WE RAN INTO EACH OTHER AT THE SCHOOL ENTRANCE, SO WE CAME TOGETHER.
OH, YEAH?
SO HOW'D IT GO?!
HAVEN'T SEEN YOU-KNOW-WHO THIS MORNING... THE COAST IS CLEAR... FOR NOW, AT LEAST.
WHISPER WHISPER
Good morning!
Heyyy!
GOOD!!
The truth is he was waiting at the school entrance.
HIS TRAINING PERIOD IS ALMOST OVER, SO WE GOTTA KEEP MAKING SURE HE DOESN'T GET NEAR HER...
YEAH!
DING DONG DANG

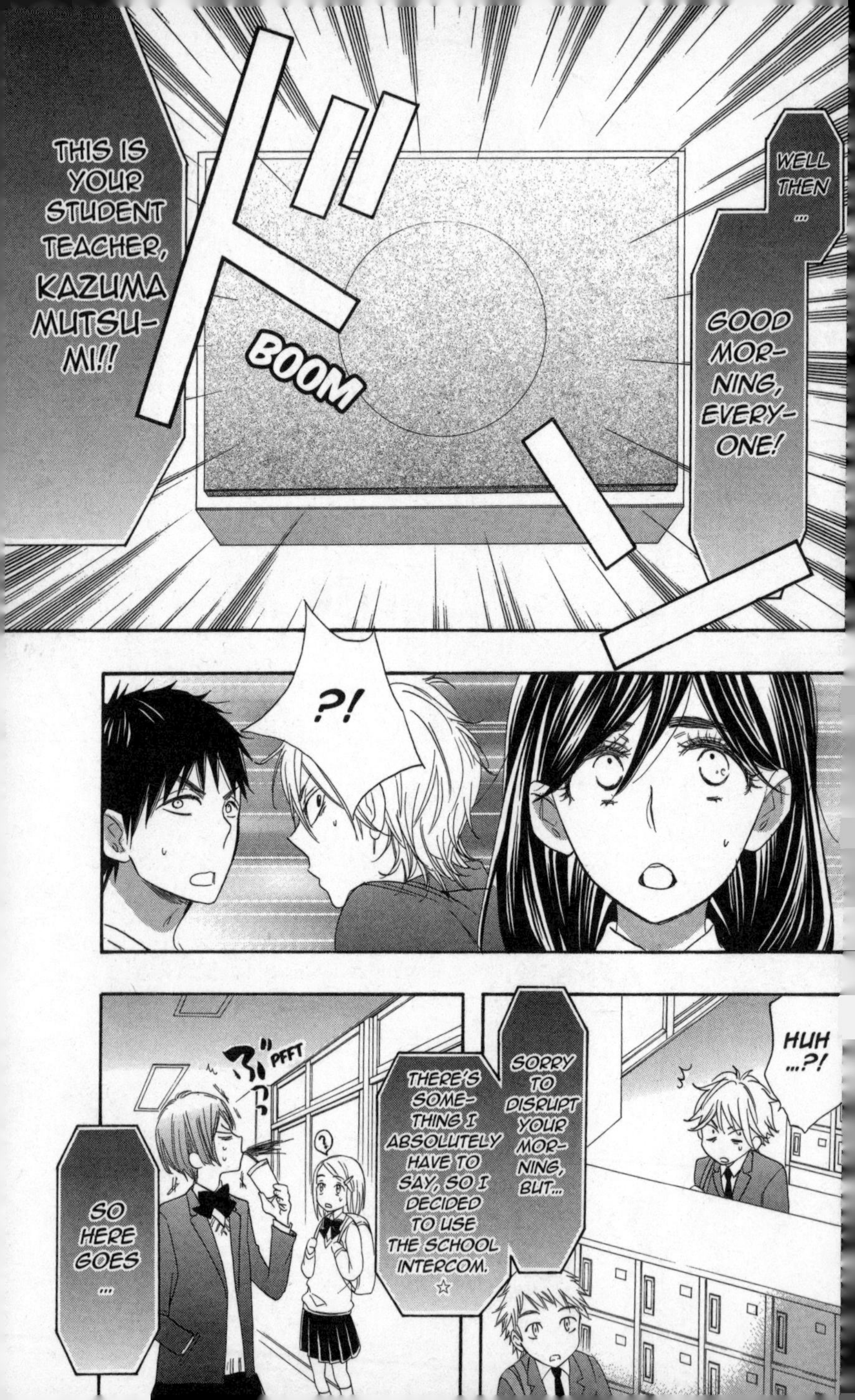
WELL THEN ...
GOOD MORNING, EVERYONE!
BOOM
THIS IS YOUR STUDENT TEACHER, KAZUMA MUTSUMI!!
?!
HUH ...?!
SORRY TO DISRUPT YOUR MORNING, BUT...
THERE'S SOMETHING I ABSOLUTELY HAVE TO SAY, SO I DECIDED TO USE THE SCHOOL INTERCOM. ☆
PFFT
?
SO HERE GOES ...

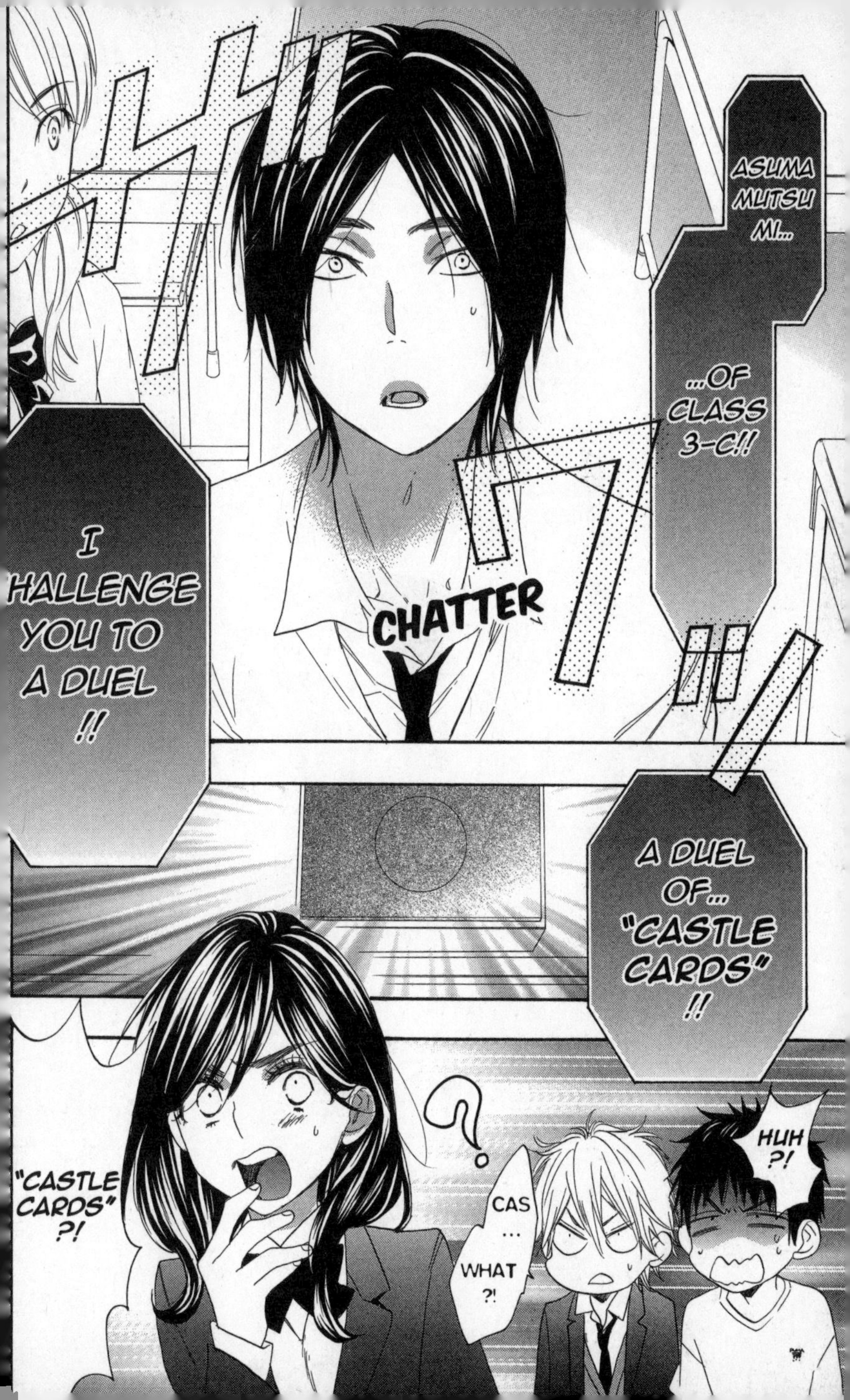

ASUMA MUTSUMI...
...OF CLASS 3-C!!
I HALLENGE YOU TO A DUEL !!
CHATTER
A DUEL OF... "CASTLE CARDS" !!
HUH ?!
CAS ... WHAT ?!
"CASTLE CARDS" ?!

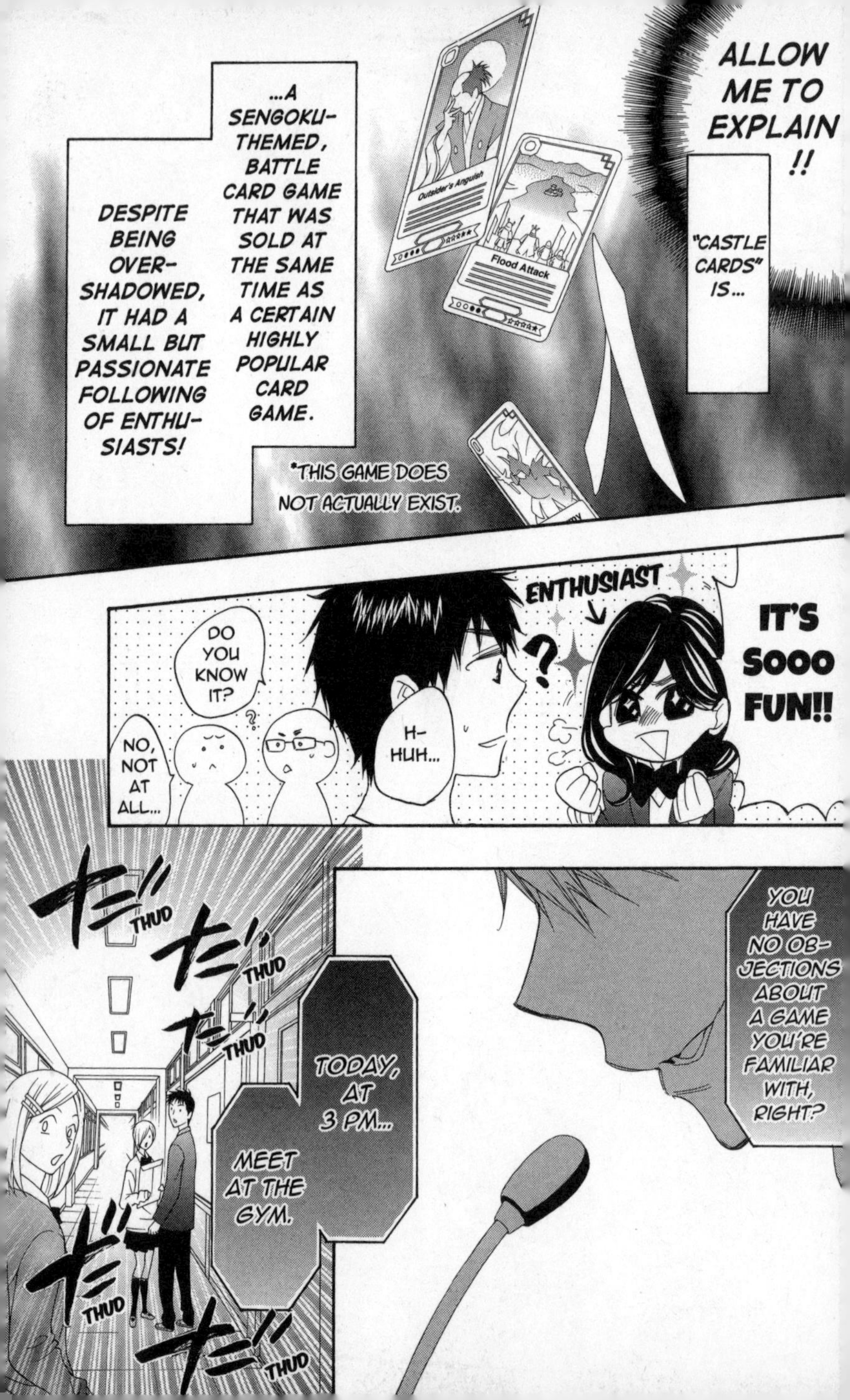
ALLOW ME TO EXPLAIN !!
"CASTLE CARDS" IS...
Outsider's Anguish
Flood Attack
...A SENGOKU-THEMED, BATTLE CARD GAME THAT WAS SOLD AT THE SAME TIME AS A CERTAIN HIGHLY POPULAR CARD GAME.
DESPITE BEING OVER-SHADOWED, IT HAD A SMALL BUT PASSIONATE FOLLOWING OF ENTHUSIASTS!
*THIS GAME DOES NOT ACTUALLY EXIST.
IT'S SOOO FUN!!
ENTHUSIAST
H-HUH...
DO YOU KNOW IT?
NO, NOT AT ALL...
YOU HAVE NO OB-JECTIONS ABOUT A GAME YOU'RE FAMILIAR WITH, RIGHT?
TODAY, AT 3 PM...
MEET AT THE GYM.
THUD
THUD
THUD
THUD
THUD

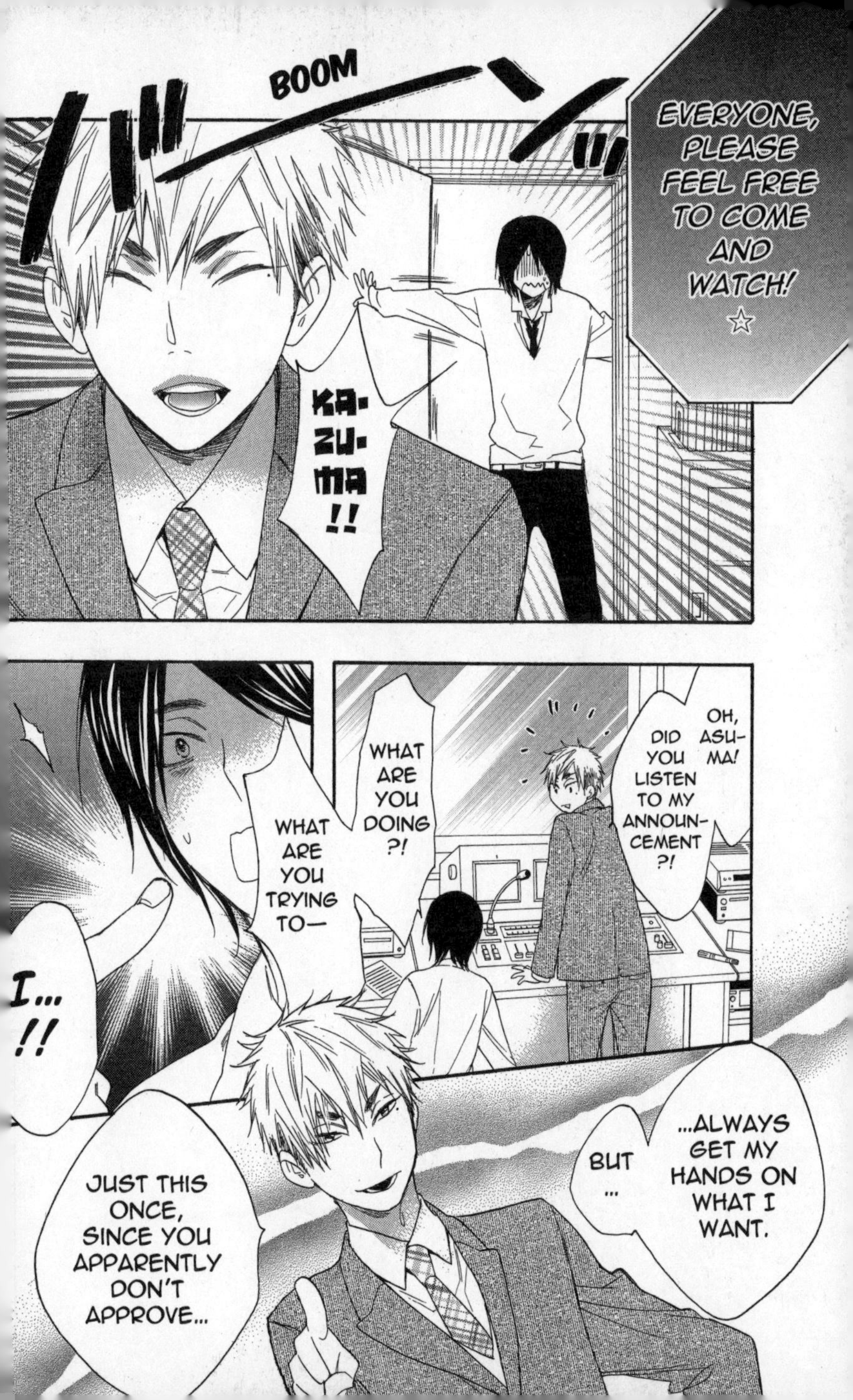
EVERYONE, PLEASE FEEL FREE TO COME AND WATCH! ☆
BOOM
KA-ZU-MA!!
OH, ASUMA!
DID YOU LISTEN TO MY ANNOUNCEMENT?!
WHAT ARE YOU DOING?!
WHAT ARE YOU TRYING TO—
I...!!
...ALWAYS GET MY HANDS ON WHAT I WANT.
BUT...
JUST THIS ONCE, SINCE YOU APPARENTLY DON'T APPROVE...

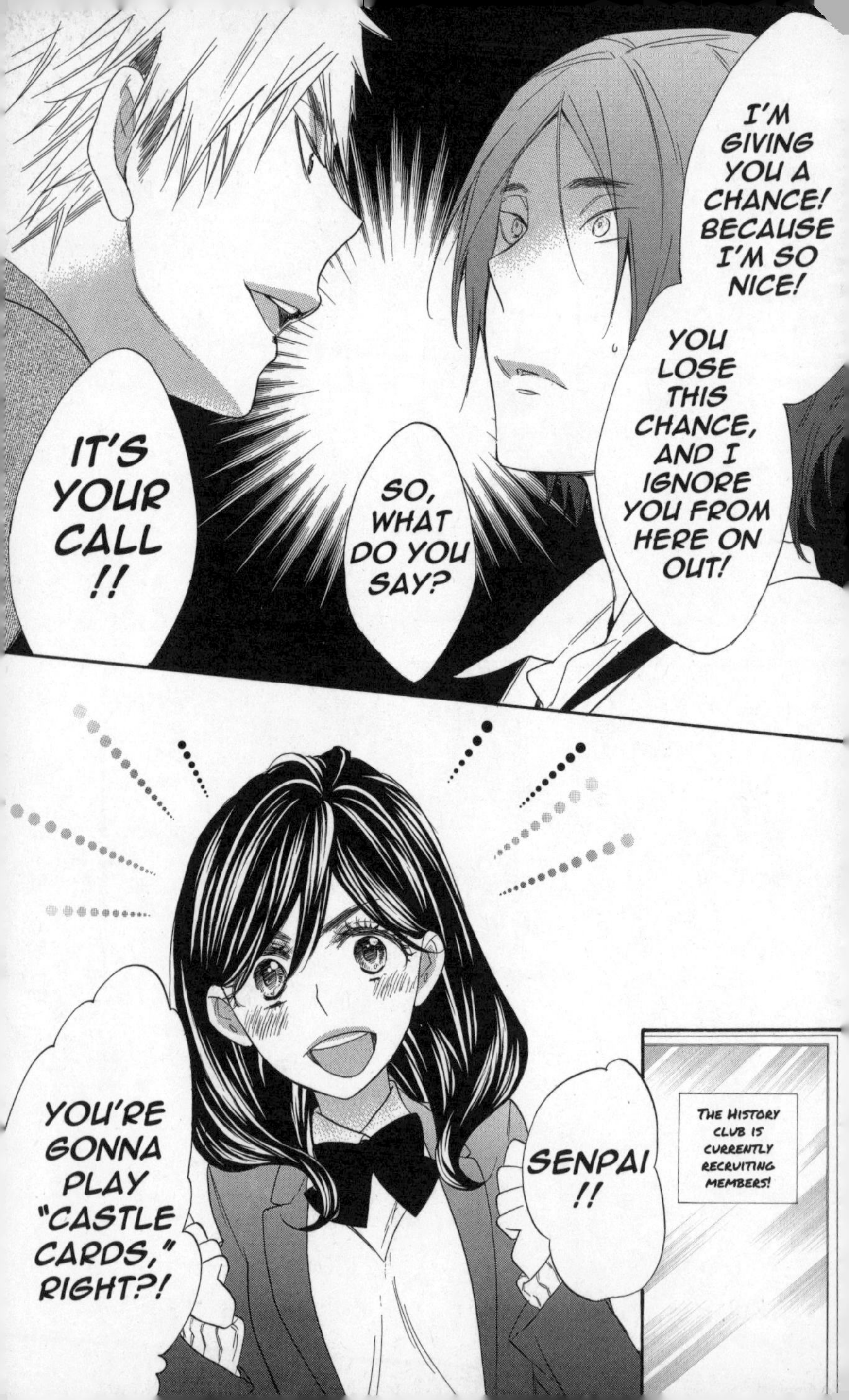
I'M GIVING YOU A CHANCE! BECAUSE I'M SO NICE!
YOU LOSE THIS CHANCE, AND I IGNORE YOU FROM HERE ON OUT!
SO, WHAT DO YOU SAY?
IT'S YOUR CALL!!
The History club is currently recruiting members!
SENPAI!!
YOU'RE GONNA PLAY "CASTLE CARDS," RIGHT?!

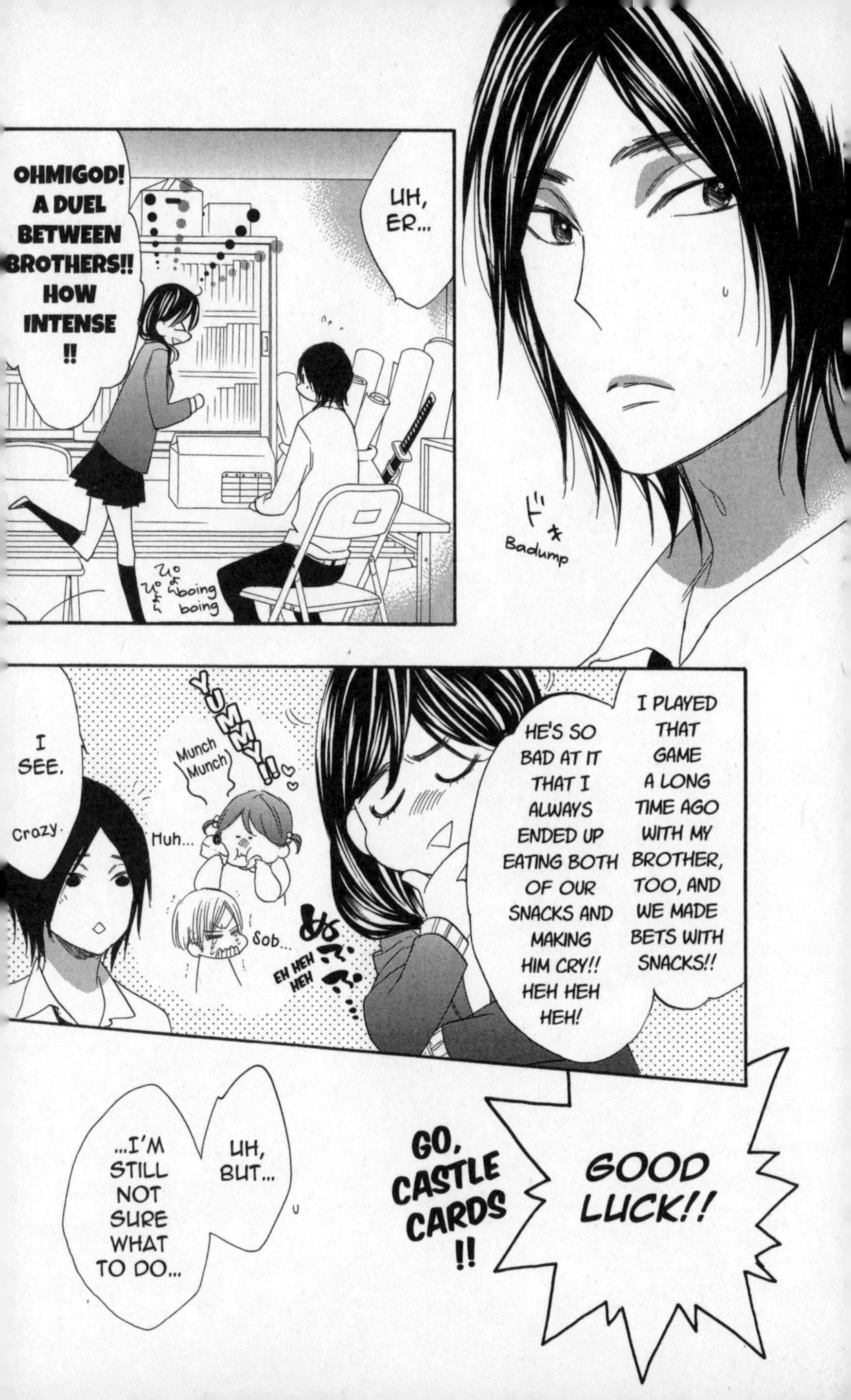
Badump
UH, ER...
OHMIGOD! A DUEL BETWEEN BROTHERS!! HOW INTENSE !!
boing boing
I PLAYED THAT GAME A LONG TIME AGO WITH MY BROTHER, TOO, AND WE MADE BETS WITH SNACKS!!
HE'S SO BAD AT IT THAT I ALWAYS ENDED UP EATING BOTH OF OUR SNACKS AND MAKING HIM CRY!! HEH HEH HEH!
EH HEH HEH
YUMMY!!
Munch Munch
Huh...
Sob...
I SEE.
Crazy.
GOOD LUCK!!
GO, CASTLE CARDS !!
UH, BUT...
...I'M STILL NOT SURE WHAT TO DO...

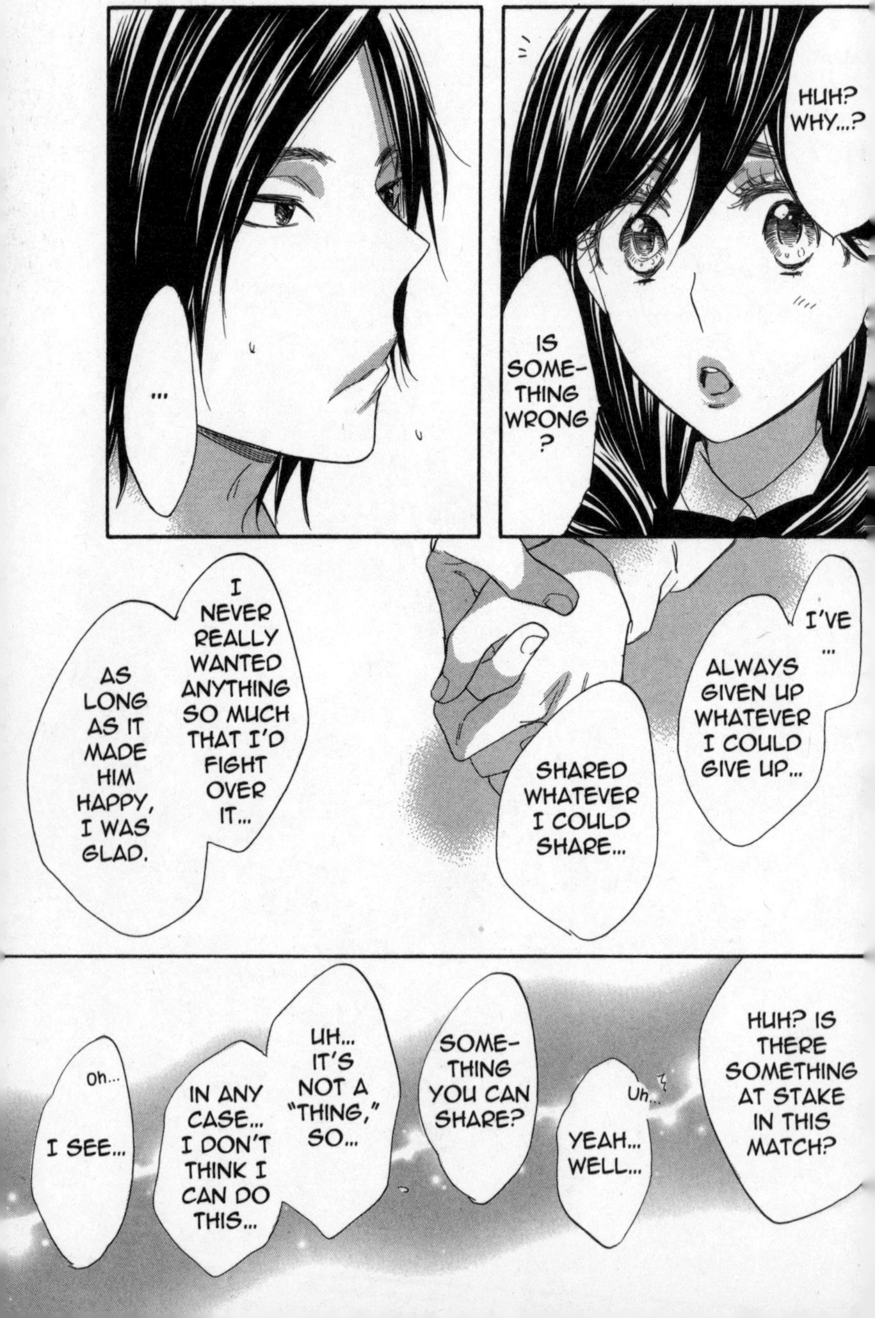
HUH? WHY...?
IS SOMETHING WRONG?
...
I'VE ... ALWAYS GIVEN UP WHATEVER I COULD GIVE UP...
SHARED WHATEVER I COULD SHARE...
I NEVER REALLY WANTED ANYTHING SO MUCH THAT I'D FIGHT OVER IT...
AS LONG AS IT MADE HIM HAPPY, I WAS GLAD.
HUH? IS THERE SOMETHING AT STAKE IN THIS MATCH?
Uh...
YEAH... WELL...
SOMETHING YOU CAN SHARE?
UH... IT'S NOT A "THING," SO...
IN ANY CASE... I DON'T THINK I CAN DO THIS...
Oh...
I SEE...

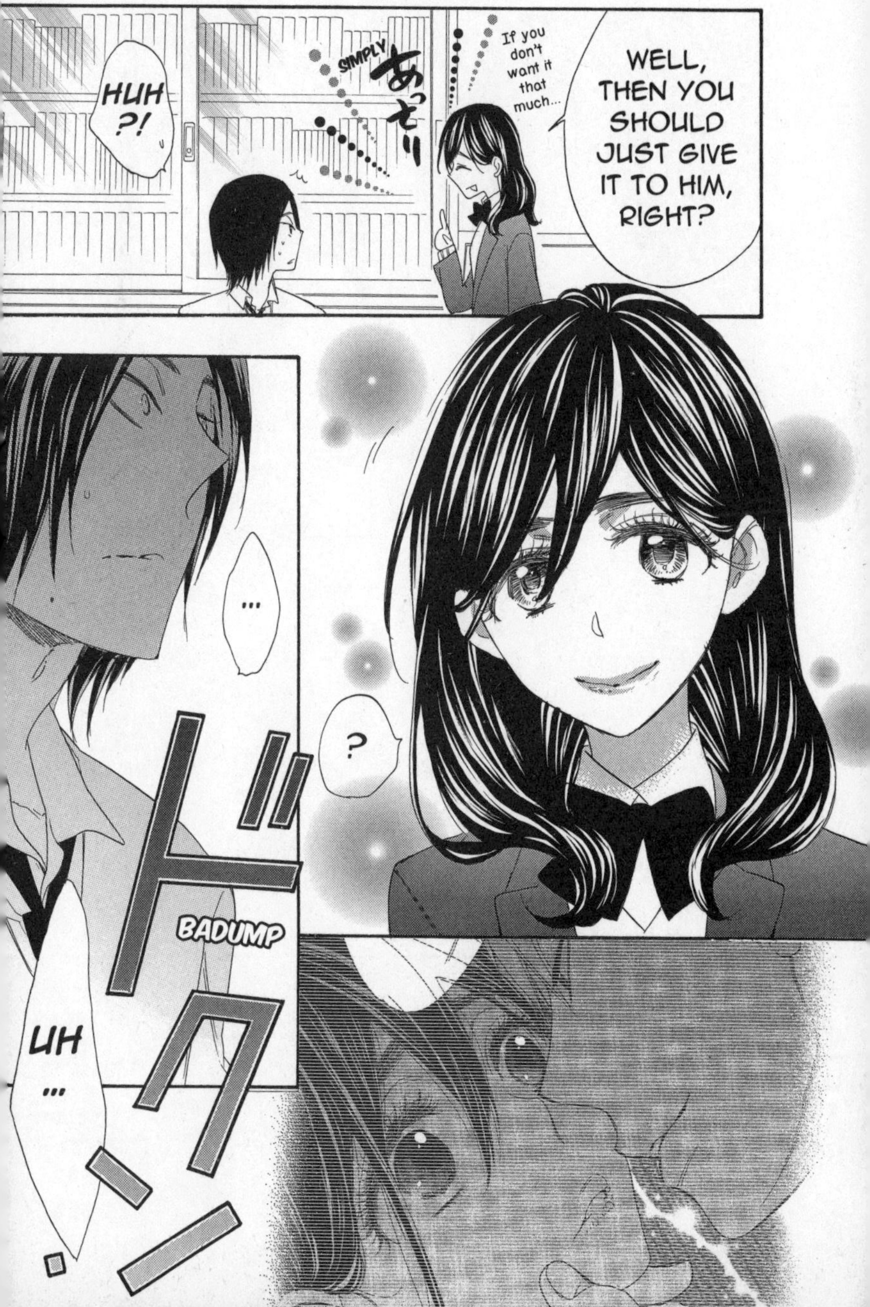
WELL, THEN YOU SHOULD JUST GIVE IT TO HIM, RIGHT?
If you don't want it that much...
SIMPLY
あっさり
HUH ?!
?
...
ドクン
BADUMP
UH ...

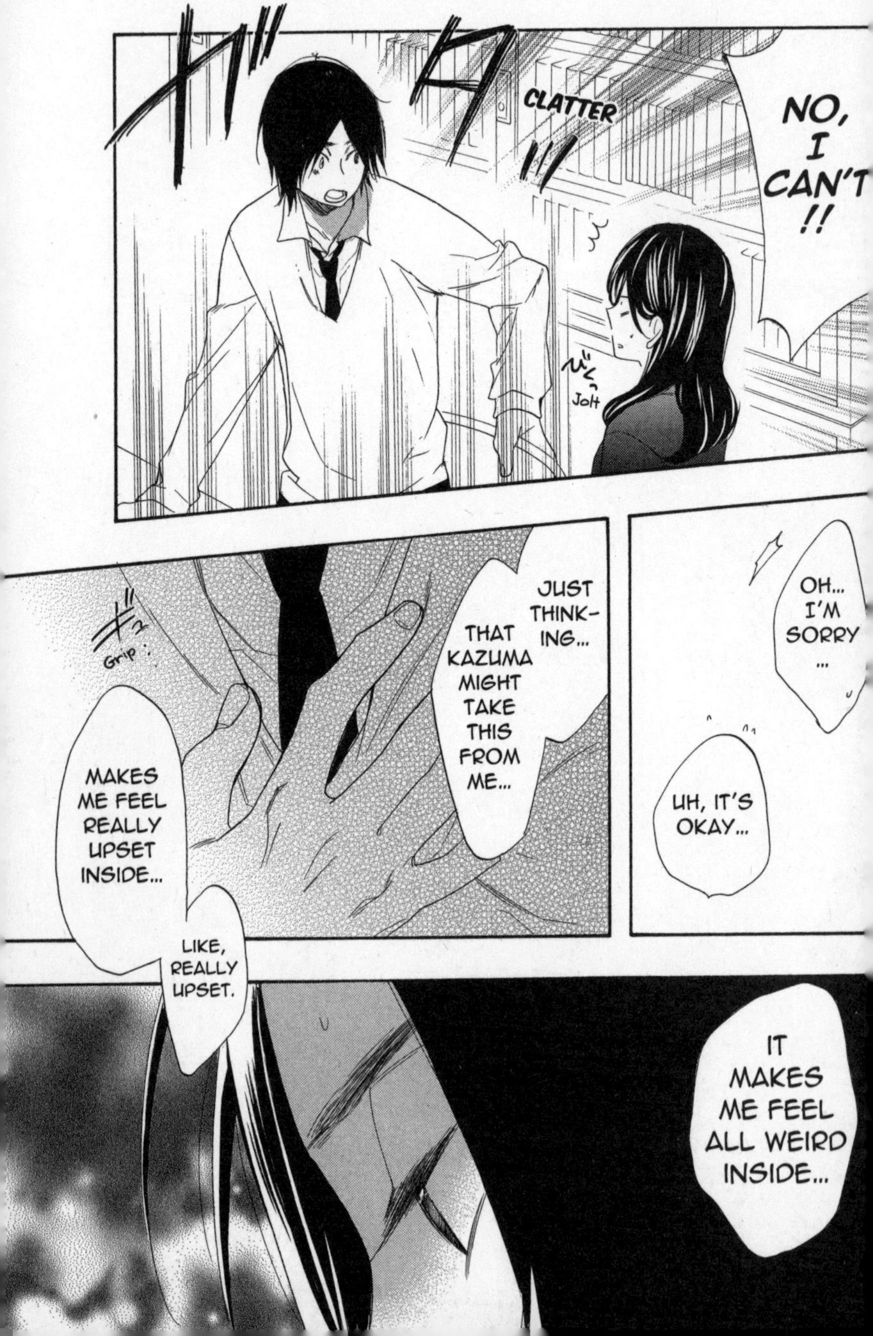
NO, I CAN'T!!
CLATTER
Jolt
OH... I'M SORRY ...
UH, IT'S OKAY...
JUST THINKING...
THAT KAZUMA MIGHT TAKE THIS FROM ME...
Grip
MAKES ME FEEL REALLY UPSET INSIDE...
LIKE, REALLY UPSET.
IT MAKES ME FEEL ALL WEIRD INSIDE...

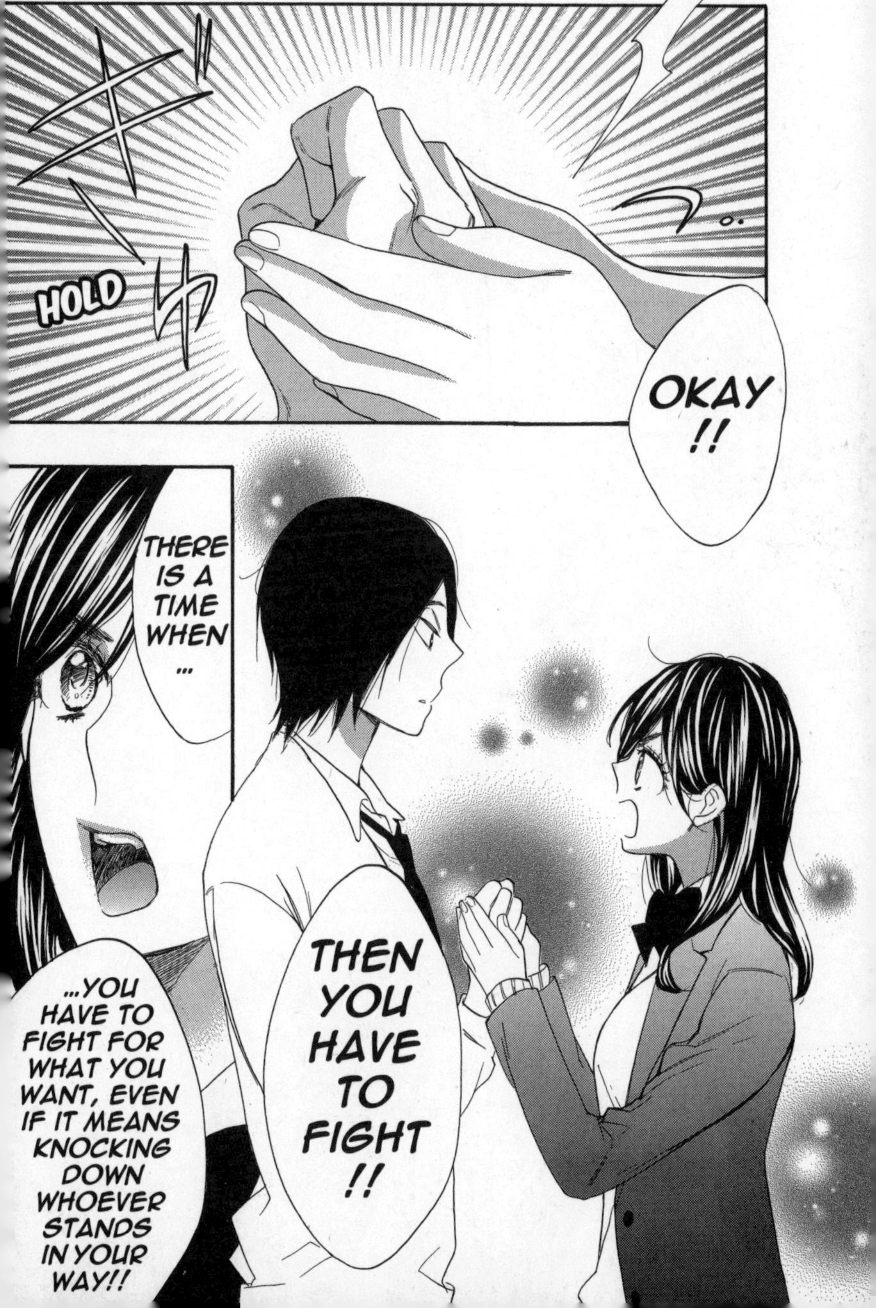
OKAY !!
HOLD
THERE IS A TIME WHEN ...
...YOU HAVE TO FIGHT FOR WHAT YOU WANT, EVEN IF IT MEANS KNOCKING DOWN WHOEVER STANDS IN YOUR WAY!!
THEN YOU HAVE TO FIGHT !!

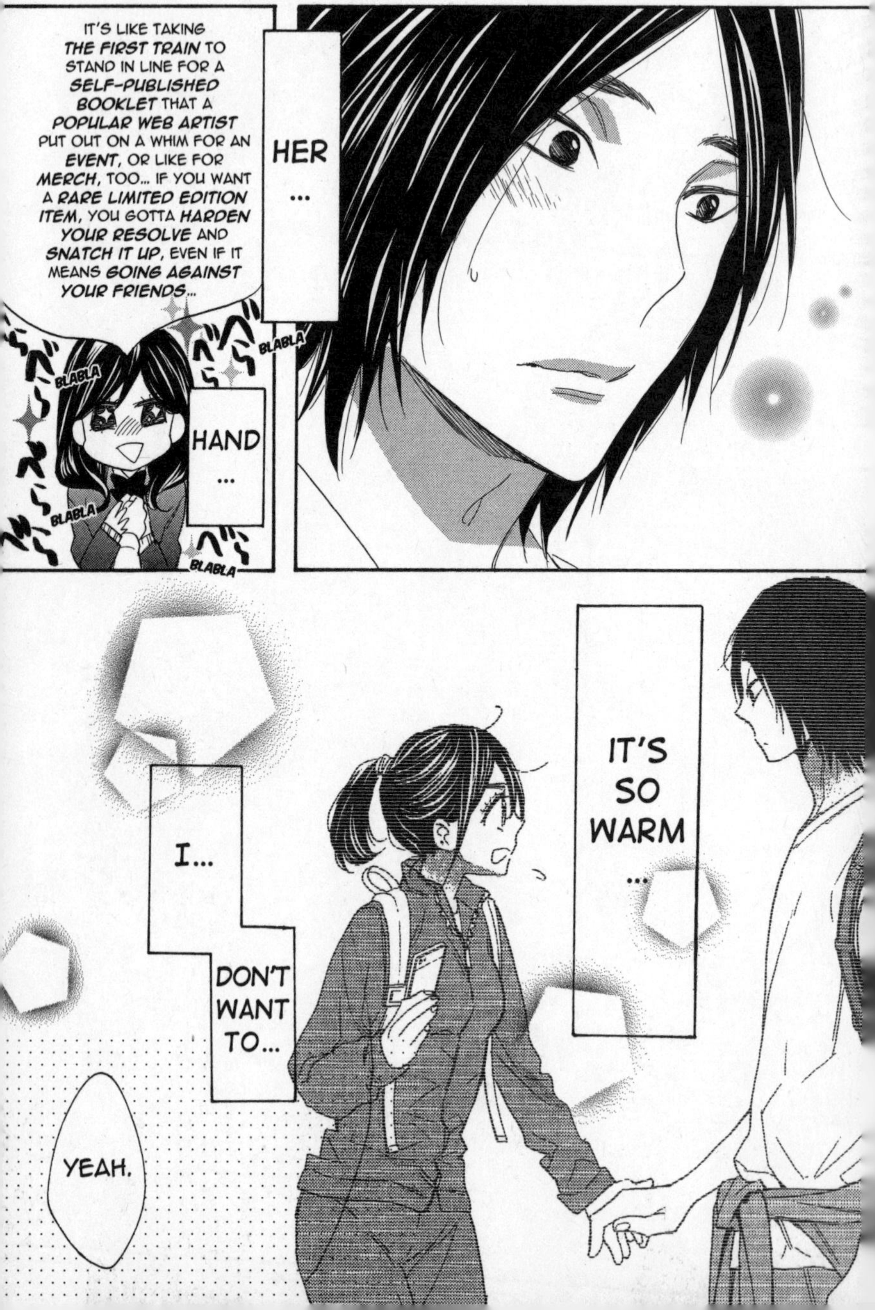
HER ...
IT'S LIKE TAKING THE FIRST TRAIN TO STAND IN LINE FOR A SELF-PUBLISHED BOOKLET THAT A POPULAR WEB ARTIST PUT OUT ON A WHIM FOR AN EVENT, OR LIKE FOR MERCH, TOO... IF YOU WANT A RARE LIMITED EDITION ITEM, YOU GOTTA HARDEN YOUR RESOLVE AND SNATCH IT UP, EVEN IF IT MEANS GOING AGAINST YOUR FRIENDS...
BLABLA
BLABLA
BLABLA
BLABLA
HAND ...
IT'S SO WARM ...
I...
DON'T WANT TO...
YEAH.

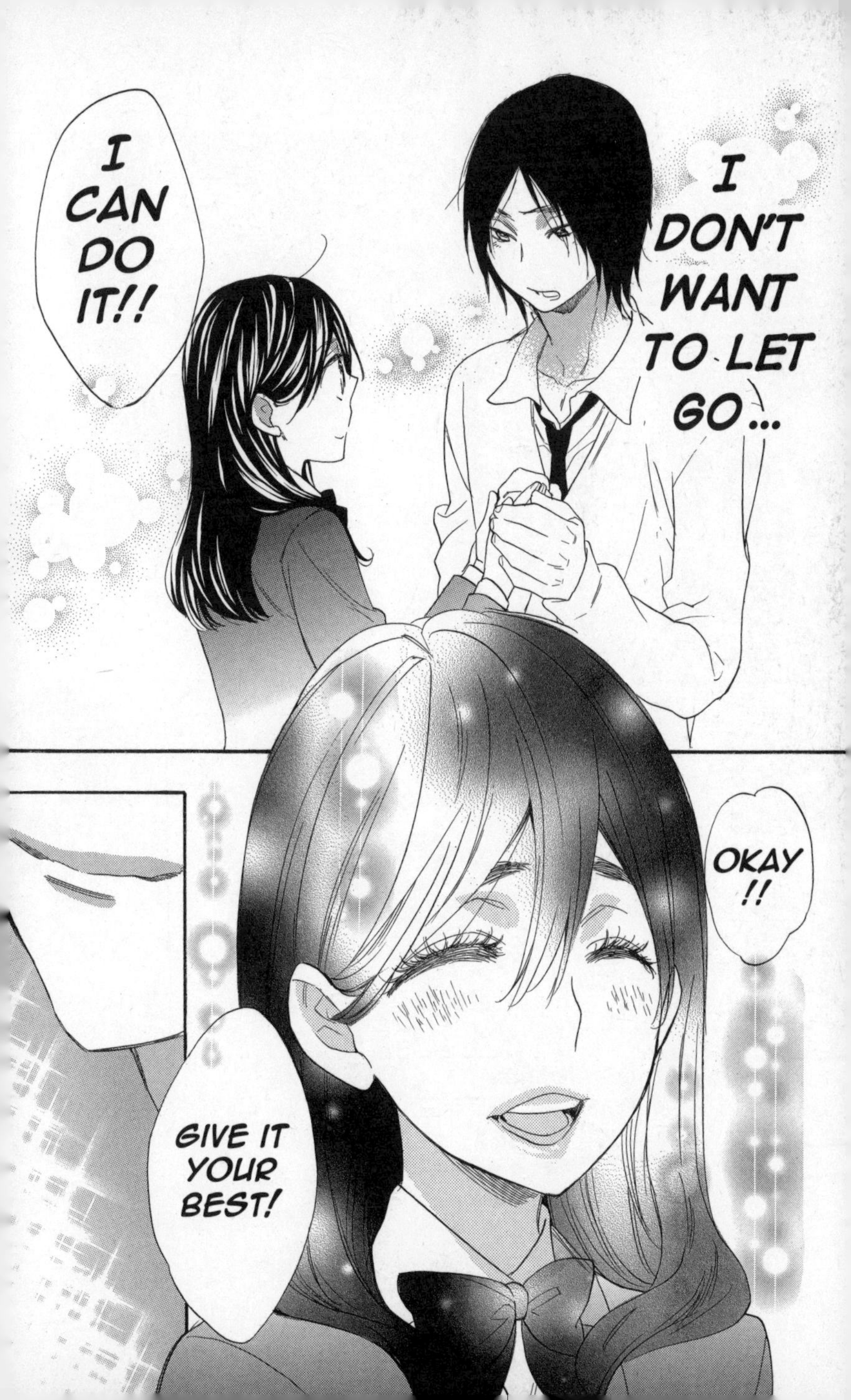
I DON'T WANT TO LET GO...
I CAN DO IT!!
OKAY !!
GIVE IT YOUR BEST!

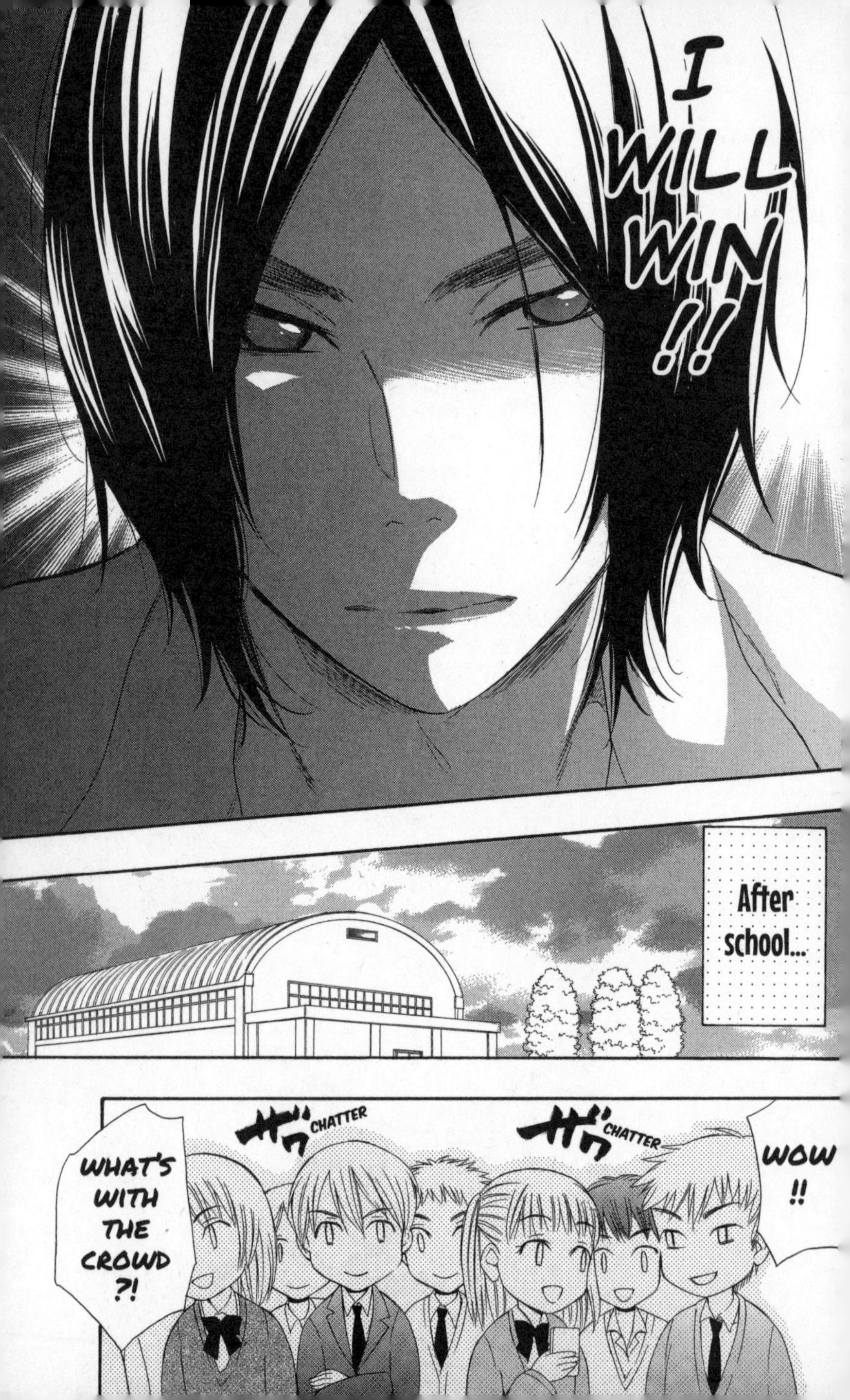
I WILL WIN !!
After school...
WOW !!
ザワ CHATTER
ザワ CHATTER
WHAT'S WITH THE CROWD ?!

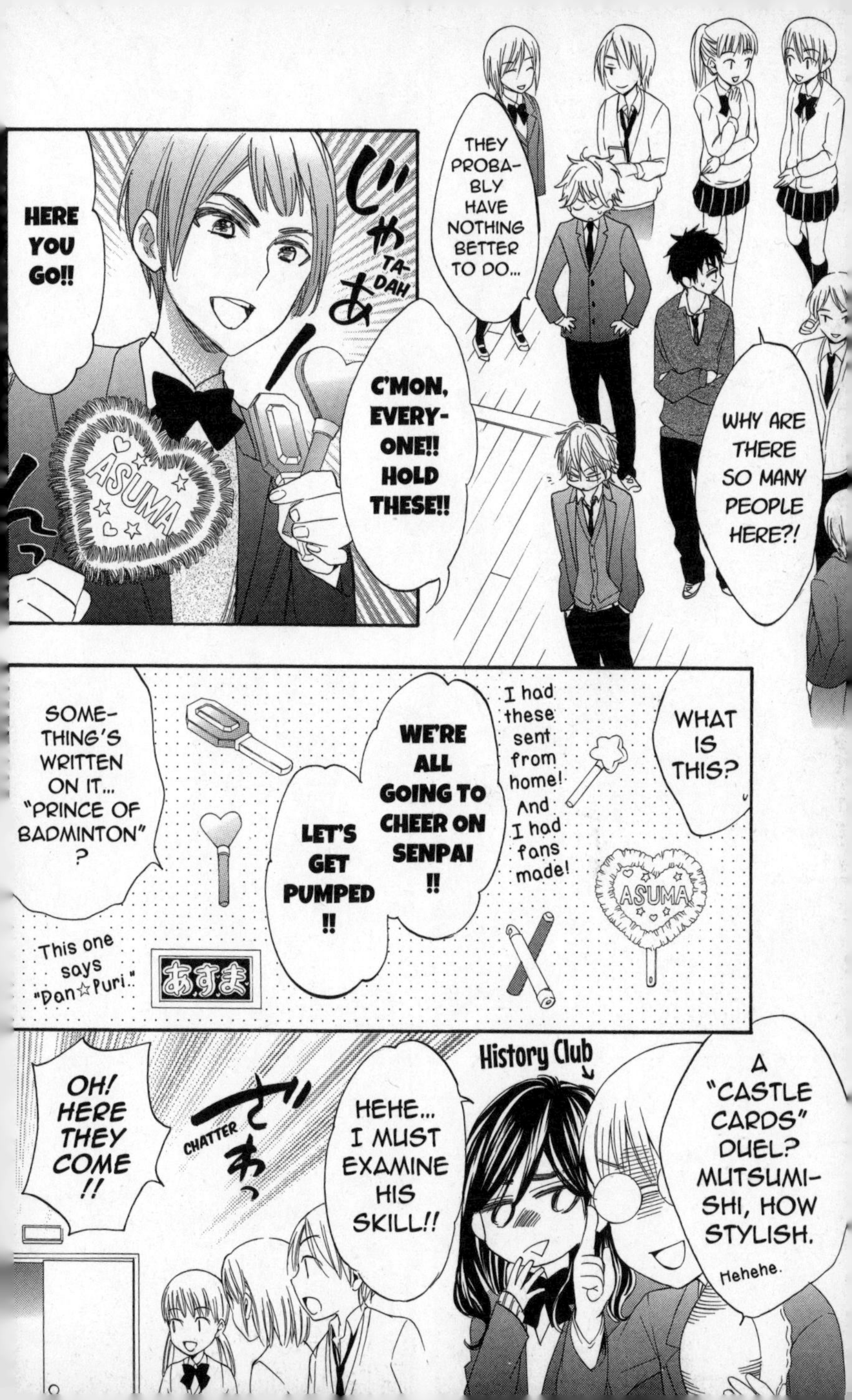
WHY ARE THERE SO MANY PEOPLE HERE?!
THEY PROBABLY HAVE NOTHING BETTER TO DO...
じゃあ TA-DAH
HERE YOU GO!!
C'MON, EVERYONE!! HOLD THESE!!
ASUMA
WHAT IS THIS?
I had these sent from home! And I had fans made!
WE'RE ALL GOING TO CHEER ON SENPAI!!
LET'S GET PUMPED!!
SOMETHING'S WRITTEN ON IT... "PRINCE OF BADMINTON"?
This one says "Dan☆Puri."
あすま
ASUMA
A "CASTLE CARDS" DUEL? MUTSUMI-SHI, HOW STYLISH.
Hehehe.
History Club
HEHE... I MUST EXAMINE HIS SKILL!!
ざわっ CHATTER
OH! HERE THEY COME!!

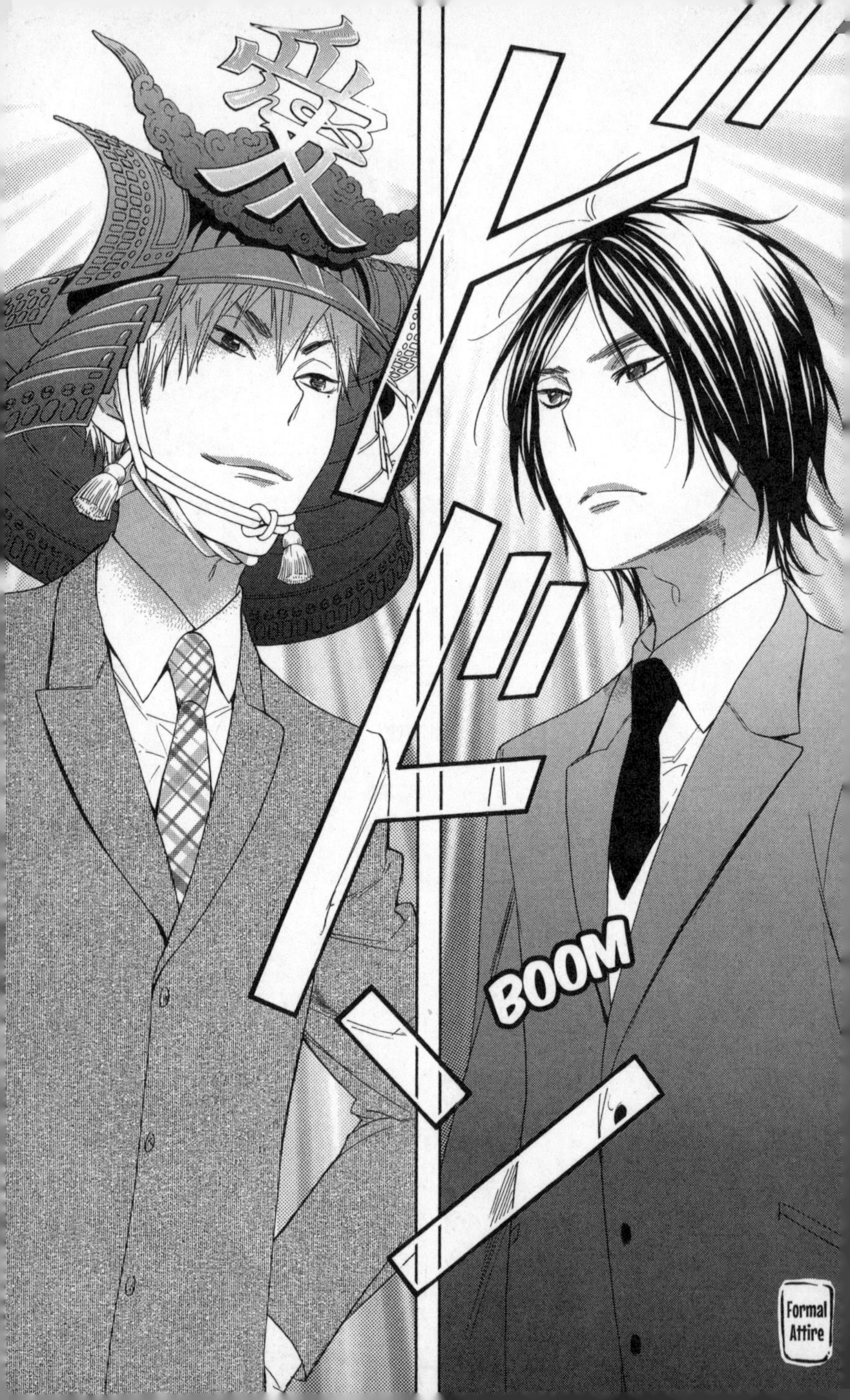
愛
BOOM
Formal Attire

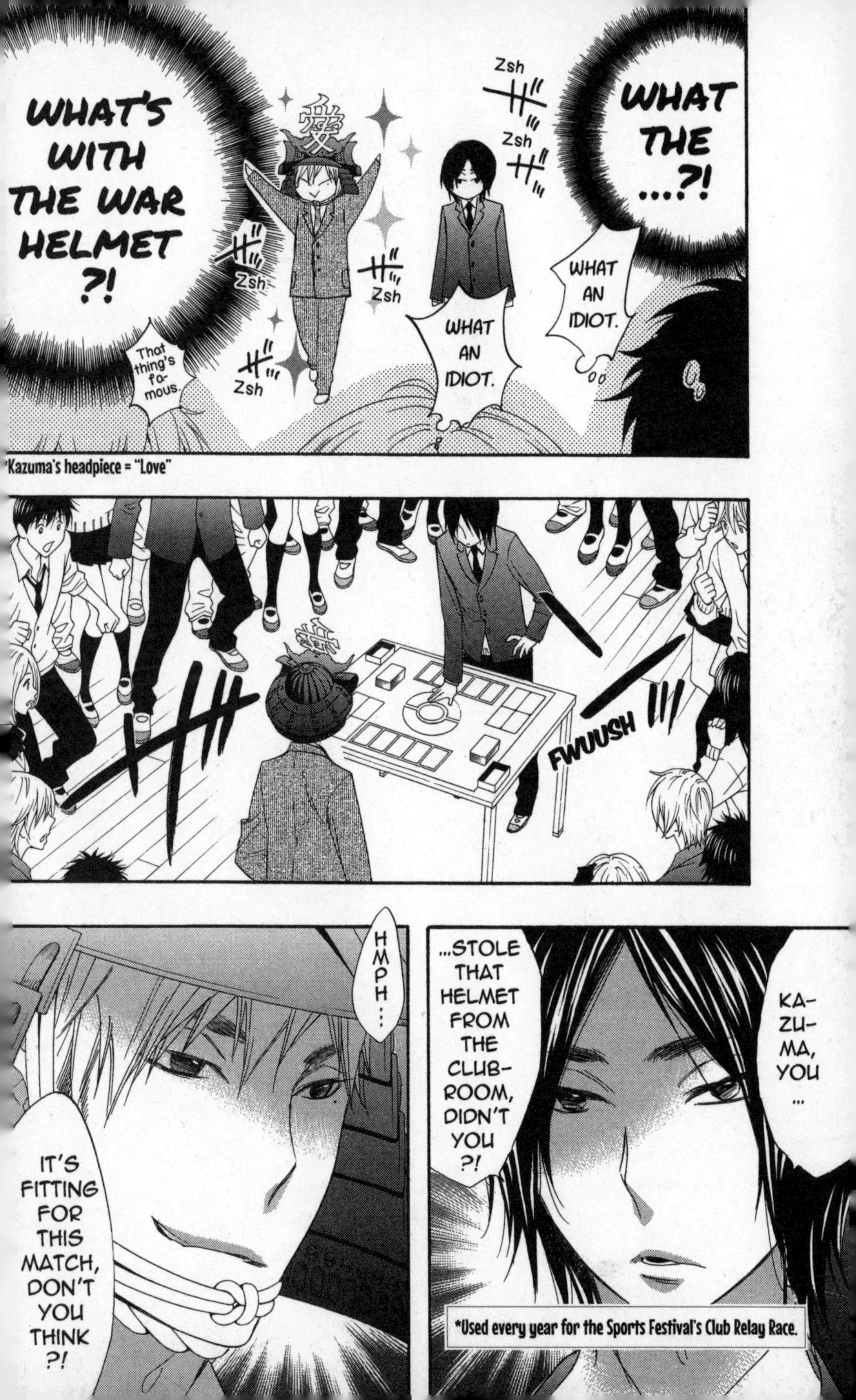
WHAT THE ...?!
Zsh
Zsh
WHAT AN IDIOT.
WHAT AN IDIOT.
愛
WHAT'S WITH THE WAR HELMET ?!
Zsh
Zsh
Zsh
That thing's famous.
*Kazuma's headpiece = "Love"
FWUUSH
KA-ZU-MA, YOU ...
...STOLE THAT HELMET FROM THE CLUB-ROOM, DIDN'T YOU ?!
*Used every year for the Sports Festival's Club Relay Race.
HMPH...
IT'S FITTING FOR THIS MATCH, DON'T YOU THINK ?!

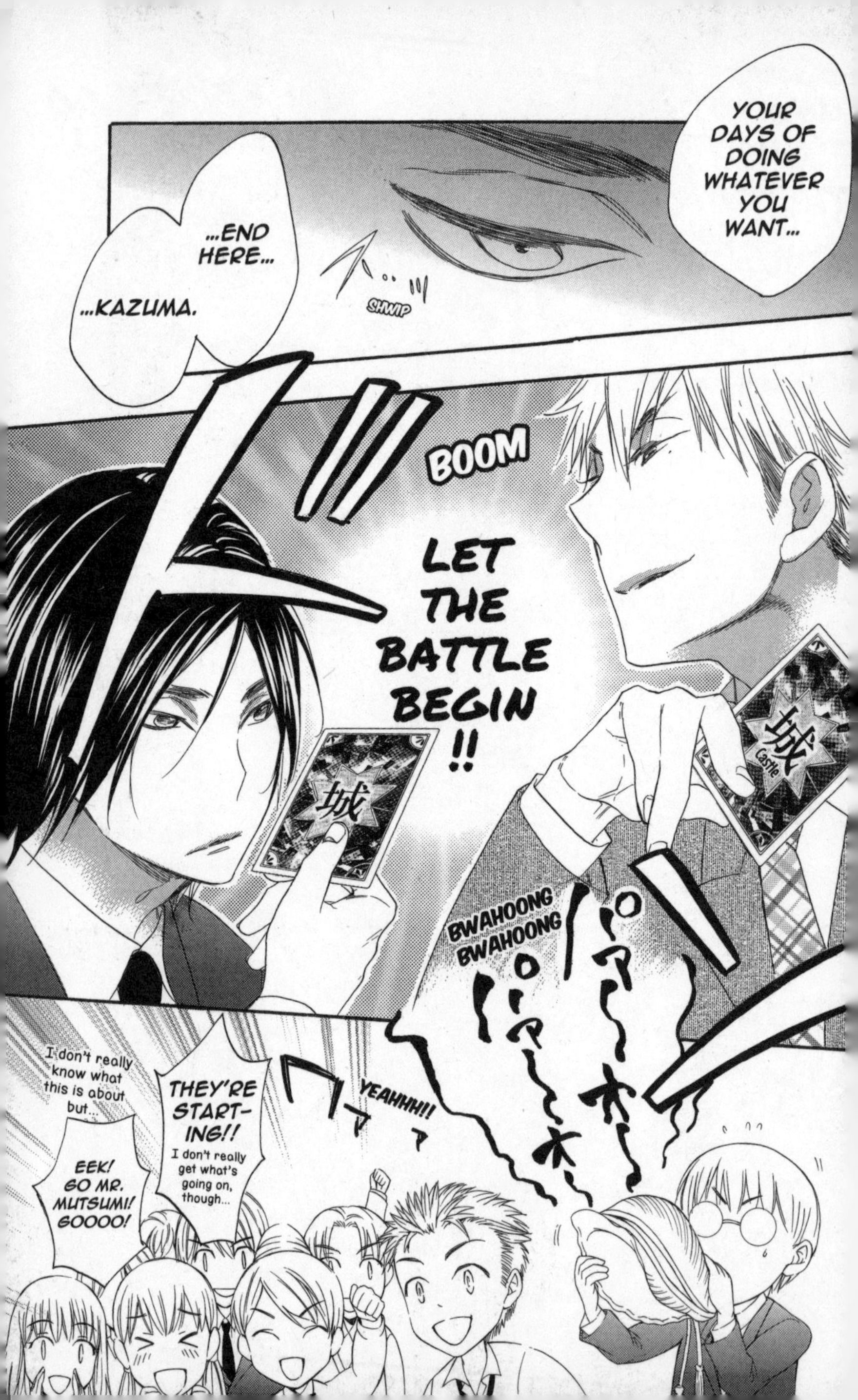

YOUR DAYS OF DOING WHATEVER YOU WANT...
SHWIP
...END HERE...
...KAZUMA.
BOOM
LET THE BATTLE BEGIN!!
Castle
BWAHOONG BWAHOONG
YEAHHH!!
THEY'RE STARTING!!
I don't really get what's going on, though...
I don't really know what this is about but...
EEK! GO MR. MUTSUMI! GOOOO!

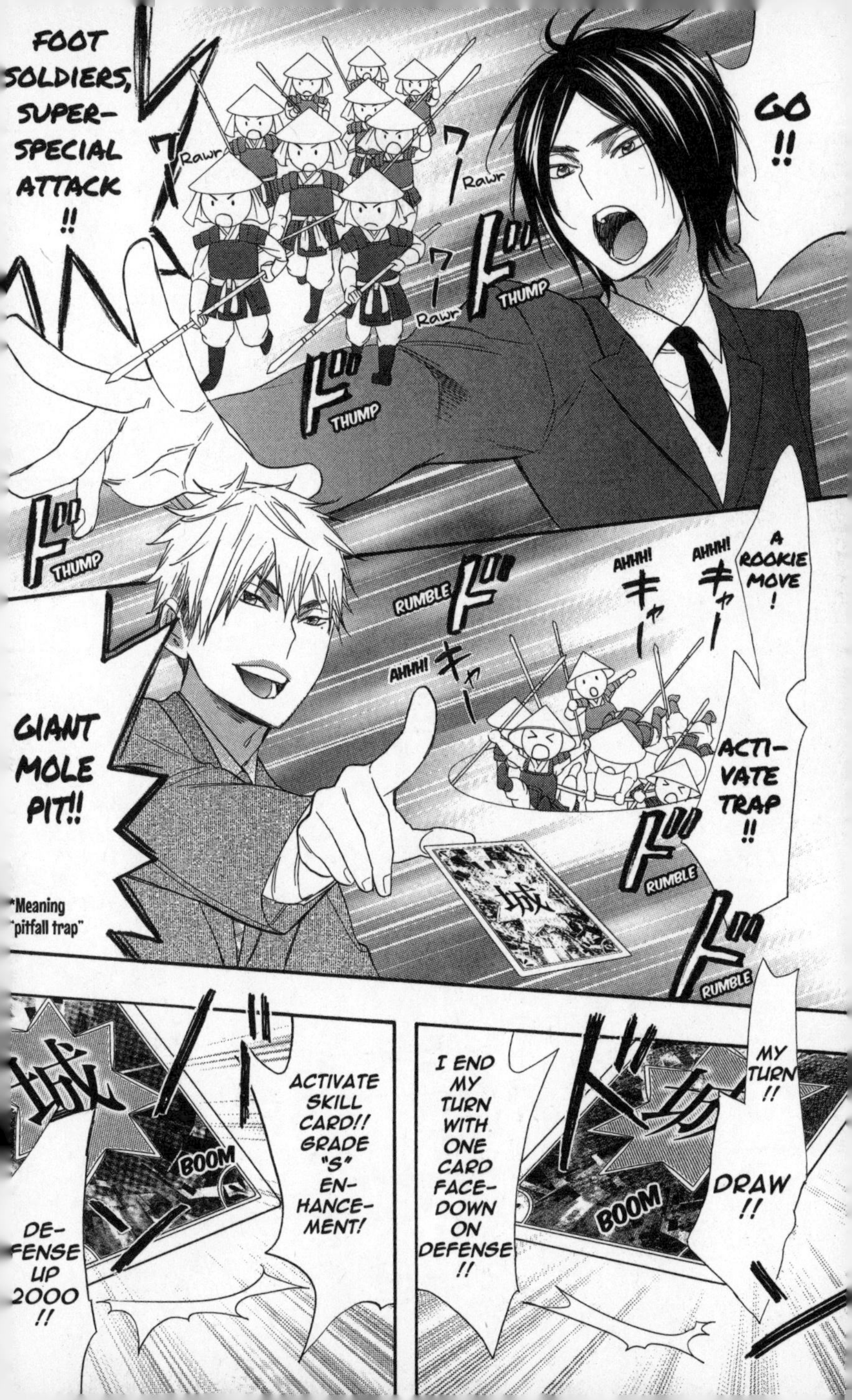
GO!!
FOOT SOLDIERS, SUPER-SPECIAL ATTACK!!
Rawr
Rawr
Rawr
THUMP
THUMP
THUMP
A ROOKIE MOVE!
AHHH!
AHHH!
RUMBLE
AHHH!
ACTI-VATE TRAP!!
RUMBLE
GIANT MOLE PIT!!
城
RUMBLE
*Meaning "pitfall trap"
MY TURN!!
DRAW!!
BOOM
I END MY TURN WITH ONE CARD FACE-DOWN ON DEFENSE!!
ACTIVATE SKILL CARD!! GRADE "S" EN-HANCE-MENT!
城
BOOM
DE-FENSE UP 2000!!

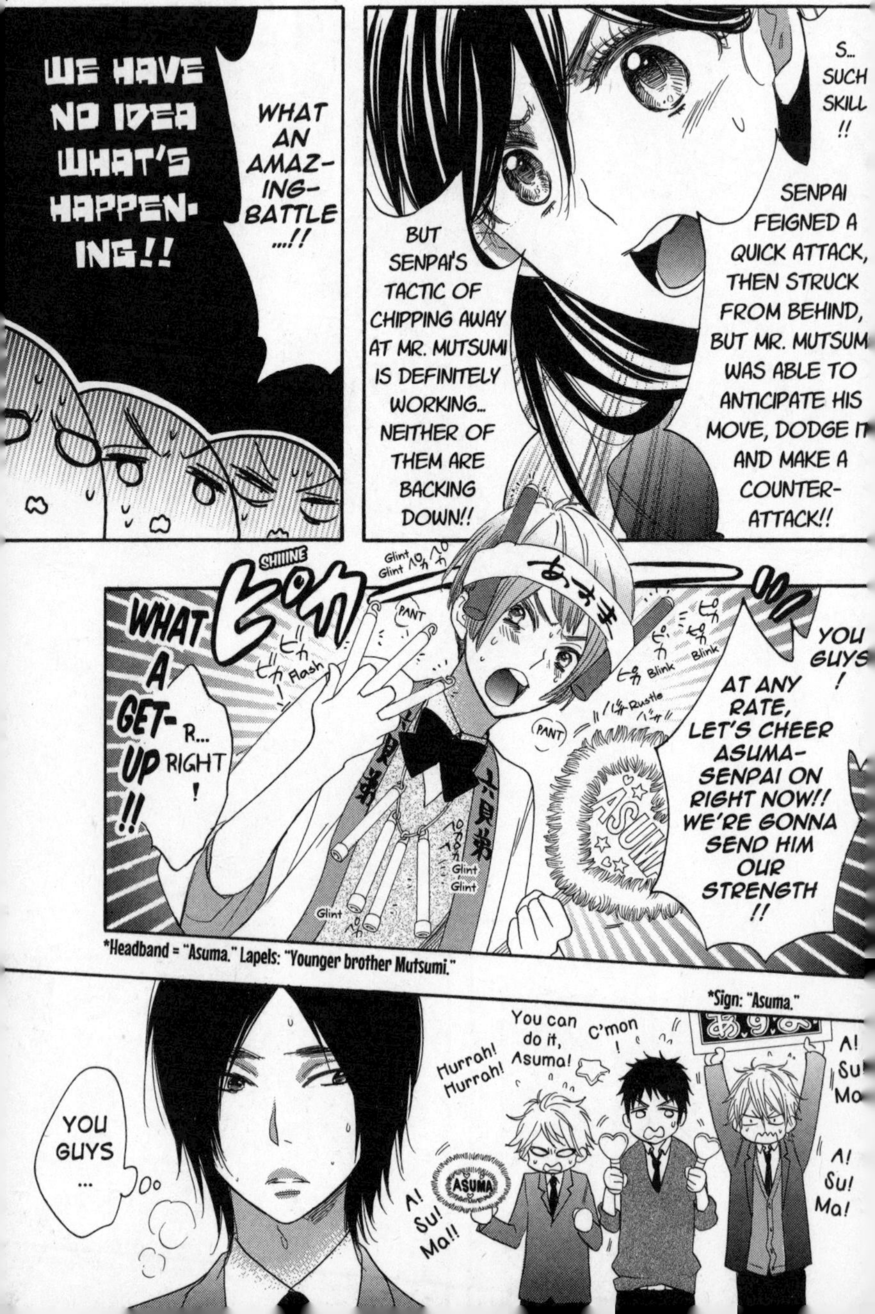
S... SUCH SKILL!!
SENPAI FEIGNED A QUICK ATTACK, THEN STRUCK FROM BEHIND, BUT MR. MUTSUM WAS ABLE TO ANTICIPATE HIS MOVE, DODGE IT AND MAKE A COUNTER-ATTACK!!
BUT SENPAI'S TACTIC OF CHIPPING AWAY AT MR. MUTSUMI IS DEFINITELY WORKING... NEITHER OF THEM ARE BACKING DOWN!!
WHAT AN AMAZING-BATTLE...!!
WE HAVE NO IDEA WHAT'S HAPPENING!!
YOU GUYS!
AT ANY RATE, LET'S CHEER ASUMA-SENPAI ON RIGHT NOW!! WE'RE GONNA SEND HIM OUR STRENGTH!!
Blink Blink
Rustle
PANT
ASUMA
Glint Glint
SHIIINE
PANT
Flash
Glint Glint
Glint
R... RIGHT!
WHAT A GET-UP!!
A! Su! Ma!
A! Su! Ma!
C'mon!
You can do it, Asuma!
Hurrah! Hurrah!
ASUMA
A! Su! Ma!!
YOU GUYS...
*Headband = "Asuma." Lapels: "Younger brother Mutsumi."
*Sign: "Asuma."

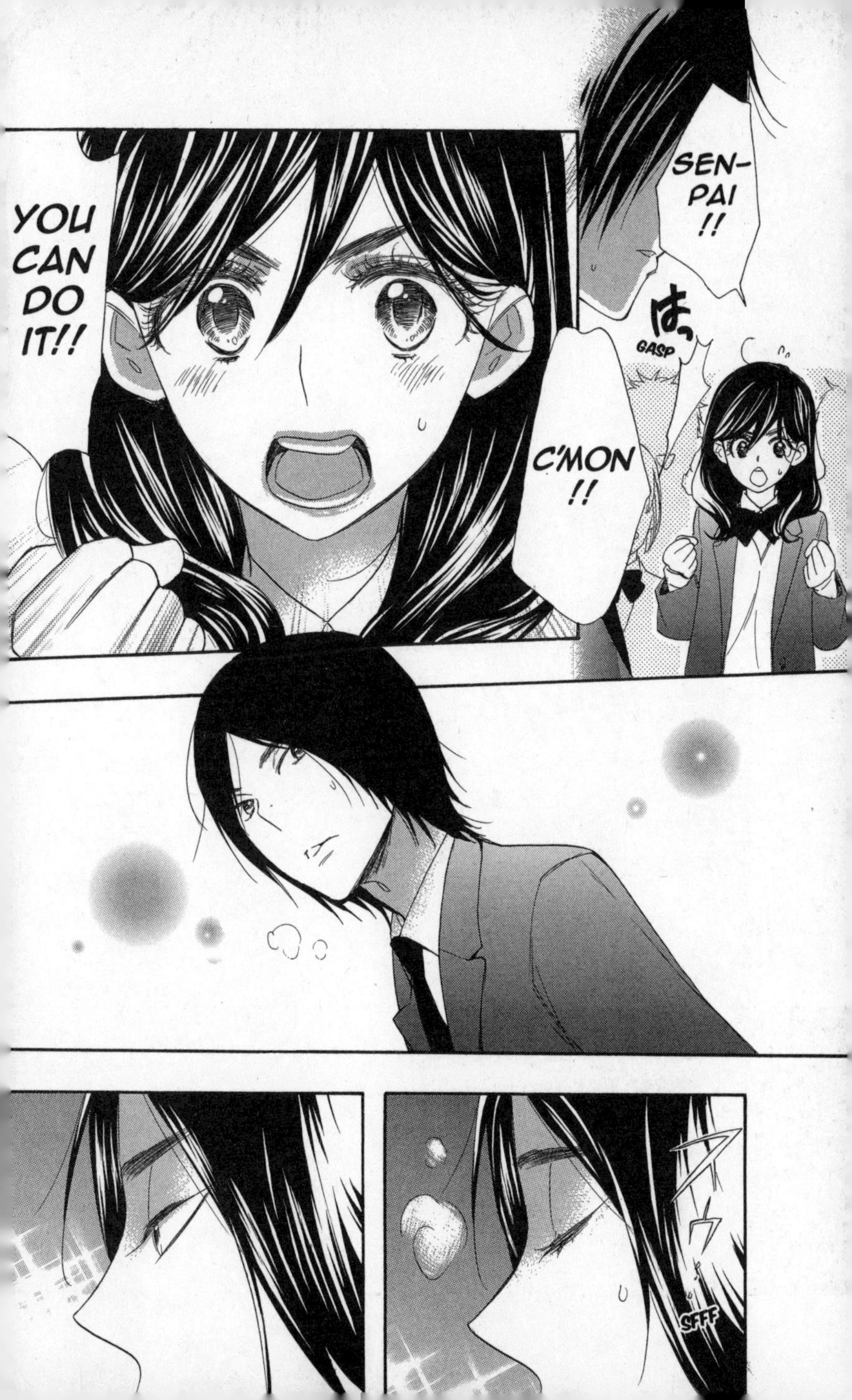
SEN-PAI!!
はっ
GASP
C'MON!!
YOU CAN DO IT!!
SFFF

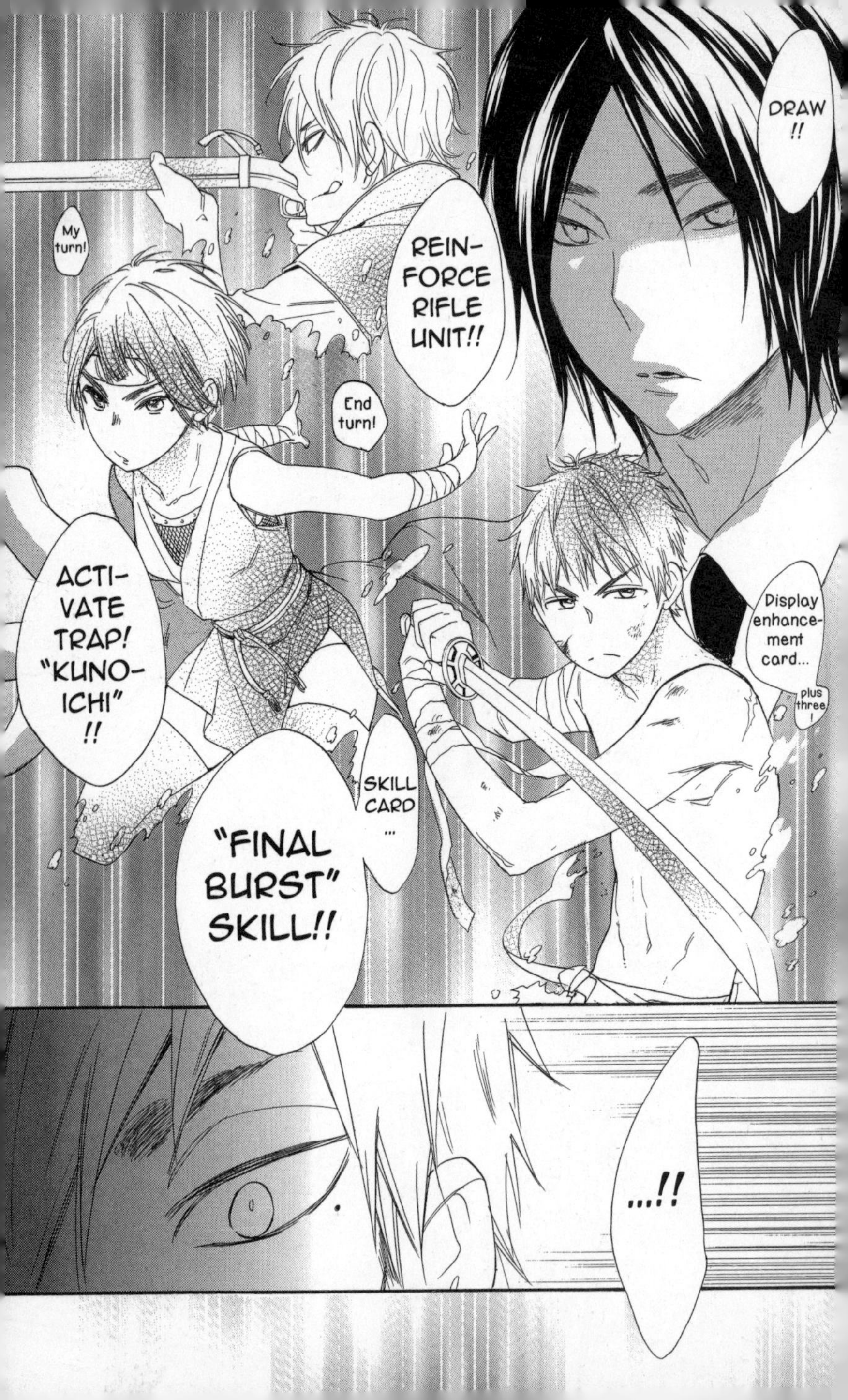
DRAW!!
Display enhancement-ment card...
plus three!
My turn!
REIN-FORCE RIFLE UNIT!!
End turn!
ACTI-VATE TRAP! "KUNO-ICHI"!!
SKILL CARD...
"FINAL BURST" SKILL!!
...!!

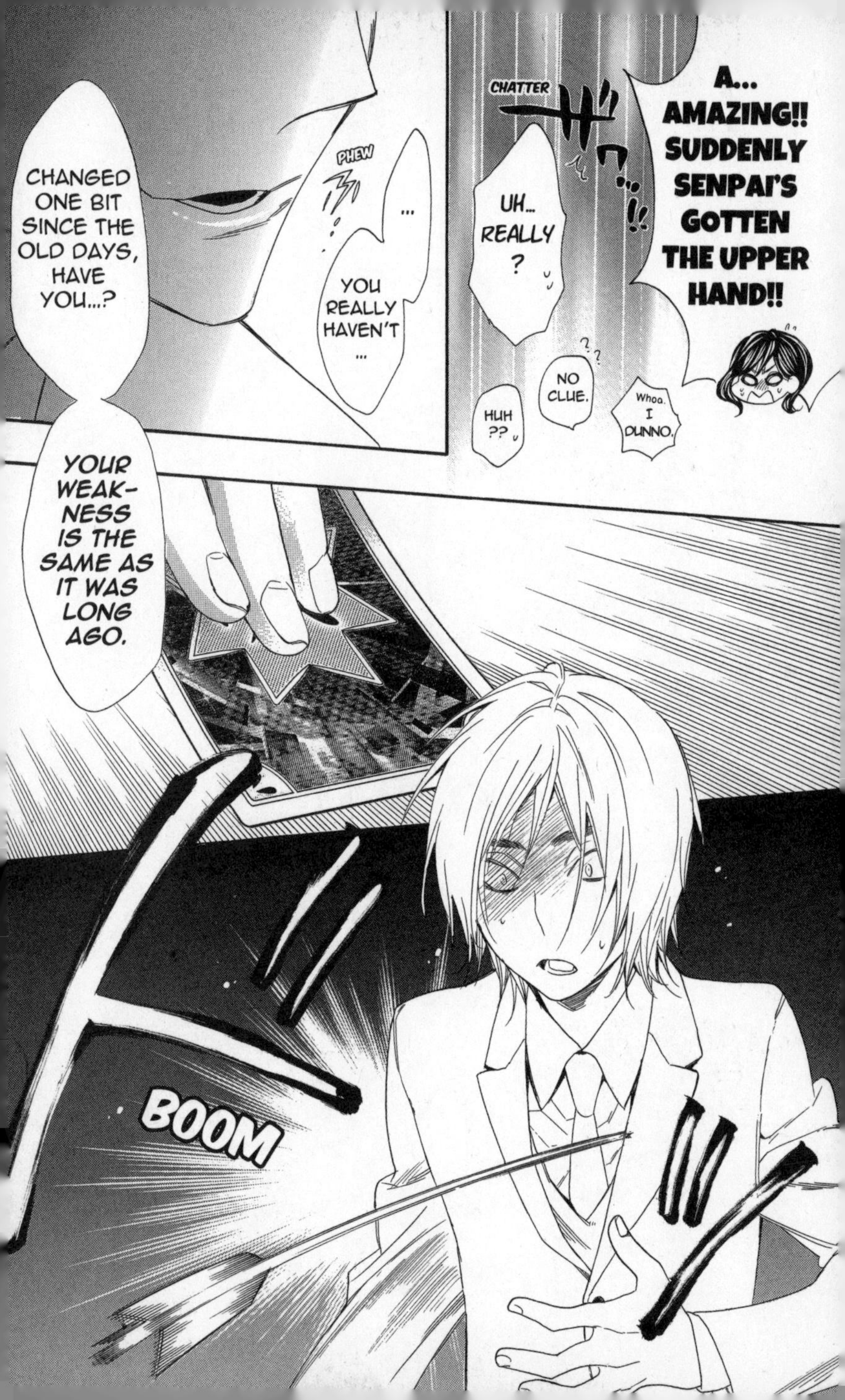
A... AMAZING!! SUDDENLY SENPAI'S GOTTEN THE UPPER HAND!!
CHATTER
UH... REALLY ?
Whoa. I DUNNO.
NO CLUE.
HUH ??
...
PHEW
YOU REALLY HAVEN'T ...
CHANGED ONE BIT SINCE THE OLD DAYS, HAVE YOU...?
YOUR WEAK-NESS IS THE SAME AS IT WAS LONG AGO.
BOOM

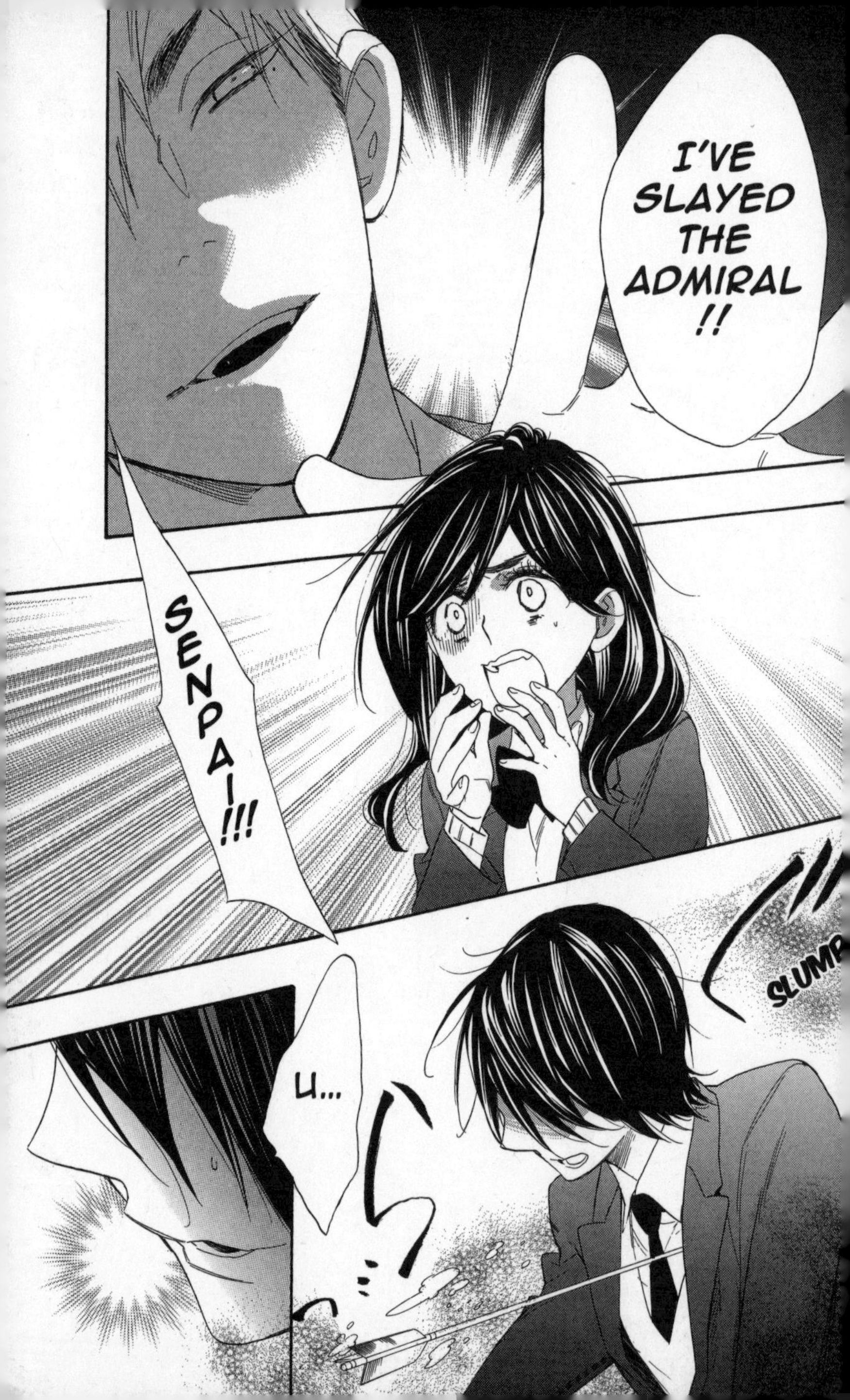
I'VE SLAYED THE ADMIRAL !!
SENPAI!!!
SLUMP
U...

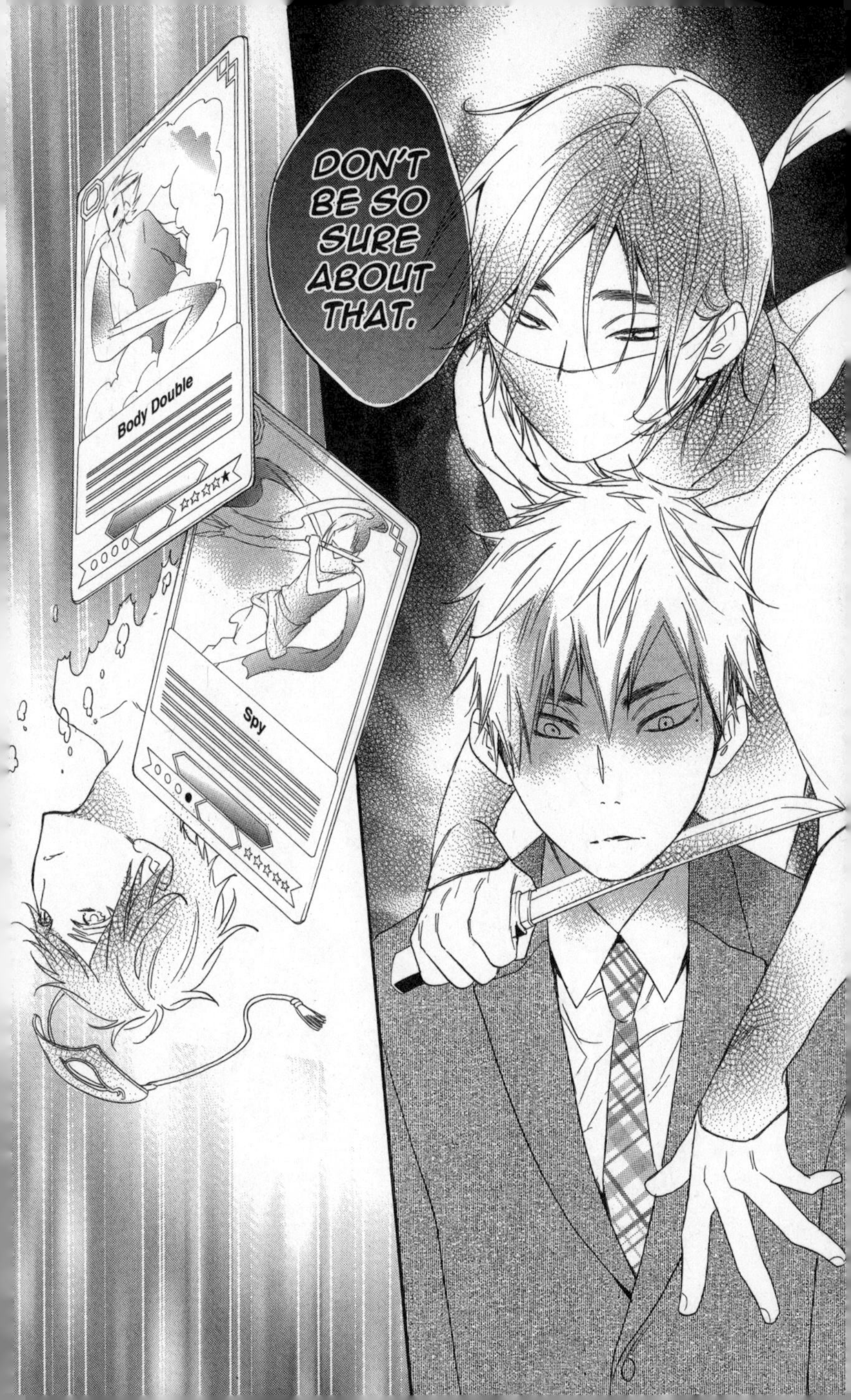
DON'T BE SO SURE ABOUT THAT.
Body Double
Spy

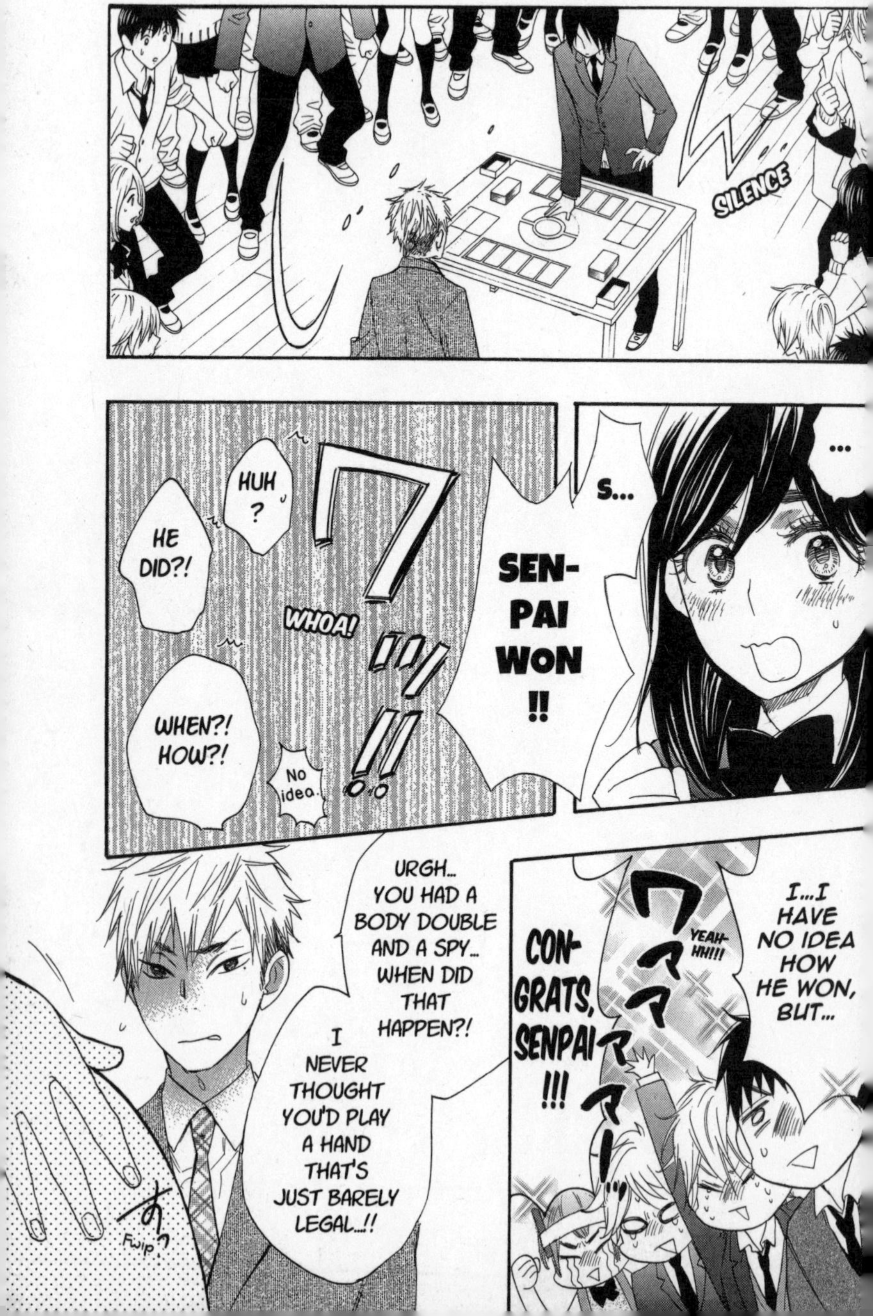
SILENCE
...
S...
SEN-PAI WON!!
WHOA!
HUH?
HE DID?!
WHEN?! HOW?!
No idea..
I...I HAVE NO IDEA HOW HE WON, BUT...
YEAH-HH!!!
CON-GRATS, SENPAI!!!
ワァァァー
URGH... YOU HAD A BODY DOUBLE AND A SPY... WHEN DID THAT HAPPEN?!
I NEVER THOUGHT YOU'D PLAY A HAND THAT'S JUST BARELY LEGAL...!!
Fwip

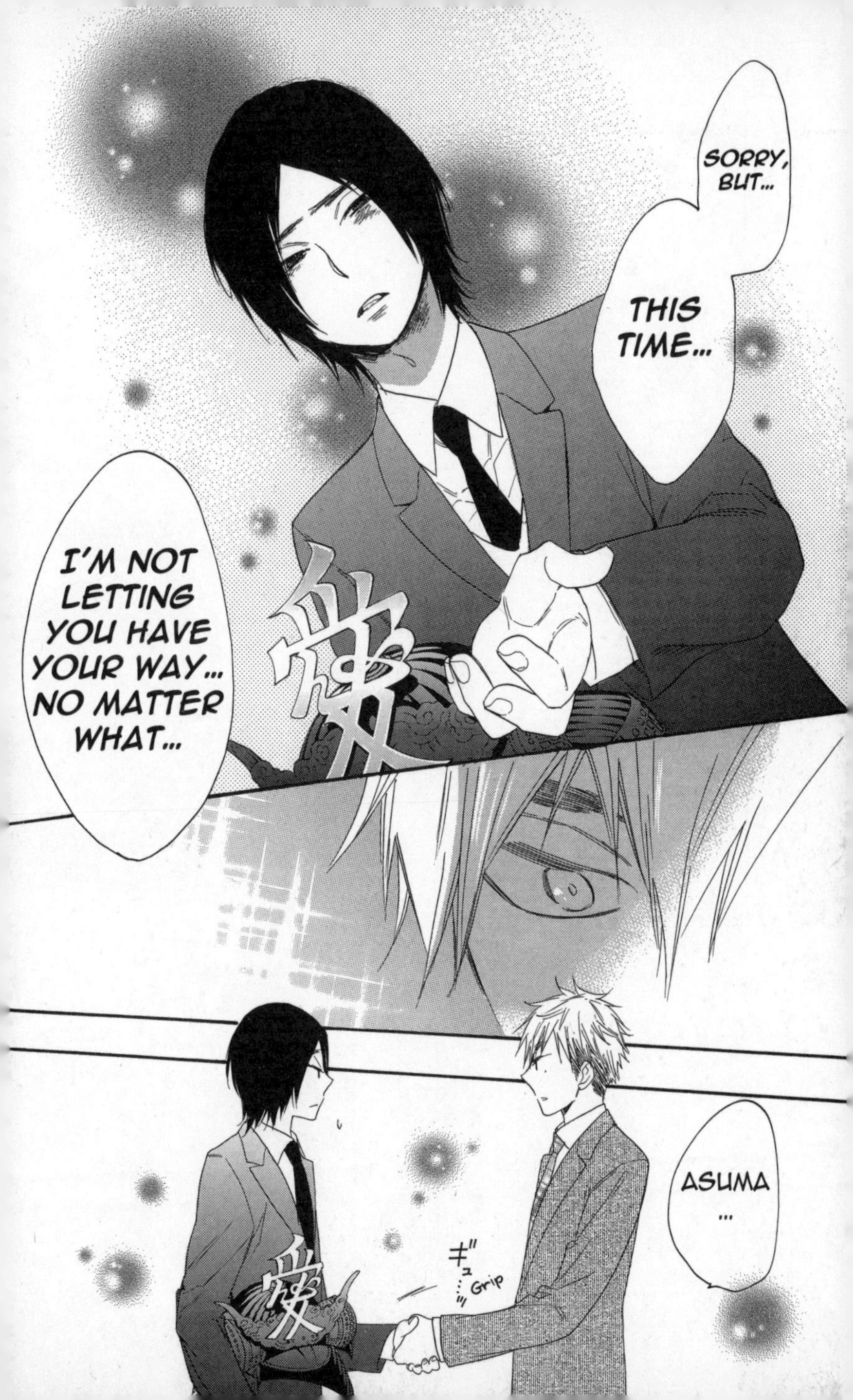
SORRY, BUT...
THIS TIME...
I'M NOT LETTING YOU HAVE YOUR WAY... NO MATTER WHAT...
ASUMA ...
ギュ… Grip

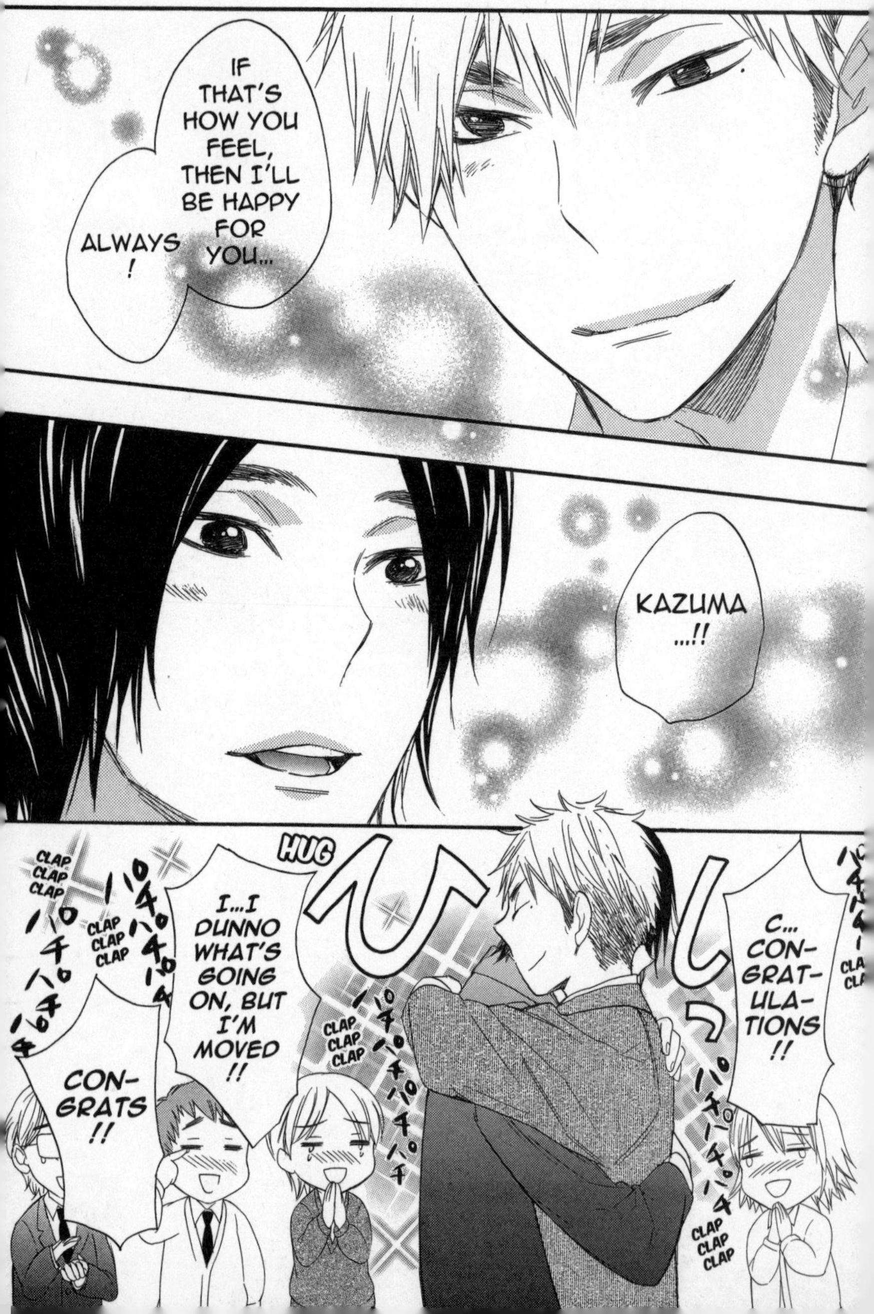
IF THAT'S HOW YOU FEEL, THEN I'LL BE HAPPY FOR YOU...
ALWAYS!
KAZUMA ...!!
C... CONGRATULATIONS!!
パチパチ
CLAP CLAP CLAP
ひしっ
HUG
パチパチパチ
CLAP CLAP CLAP
I...I DUNNO WHAT'S GOING ON, BUT I'M MOVED!!
パチパチパチ
CLAP CLAP CLAP
CLAP CLAP CLAP
パチパチパチ
CONGRATS!!

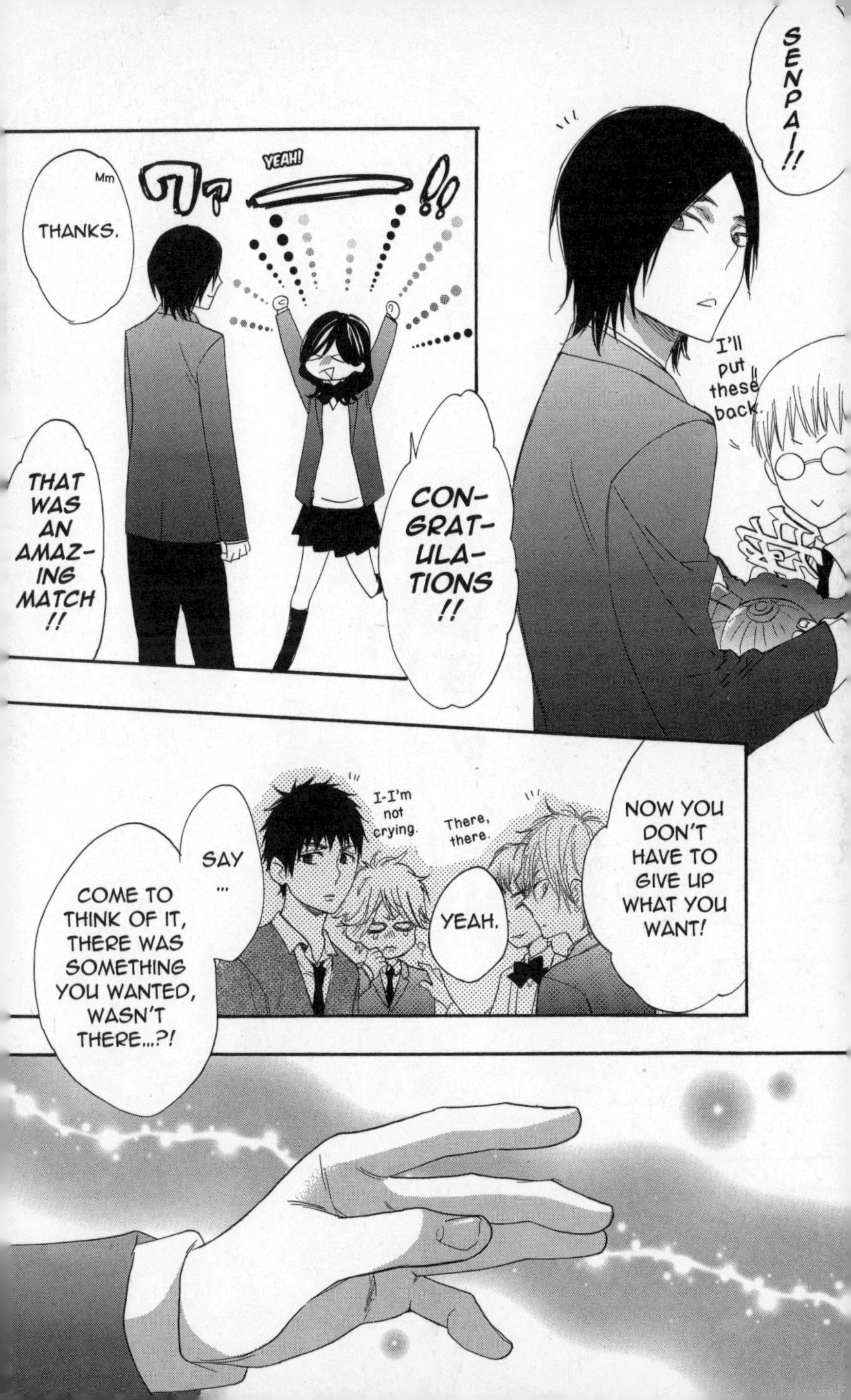
SENPAI!!
I'll put these back.
YEAH!
CONGRATULATIONS!!
THAT WAS AN AMAZING MATCH!!
Mm THANKS.
NOW YOU DON'T HAVE TO GIVE UP WHAT YOU WANT!
There, there.
YEAH.
I-I'm not crying.
SAY...
COME TO THINK OF IT, THERE WAS SOMETHING YOU WANTED, WASN'T THERE...?!

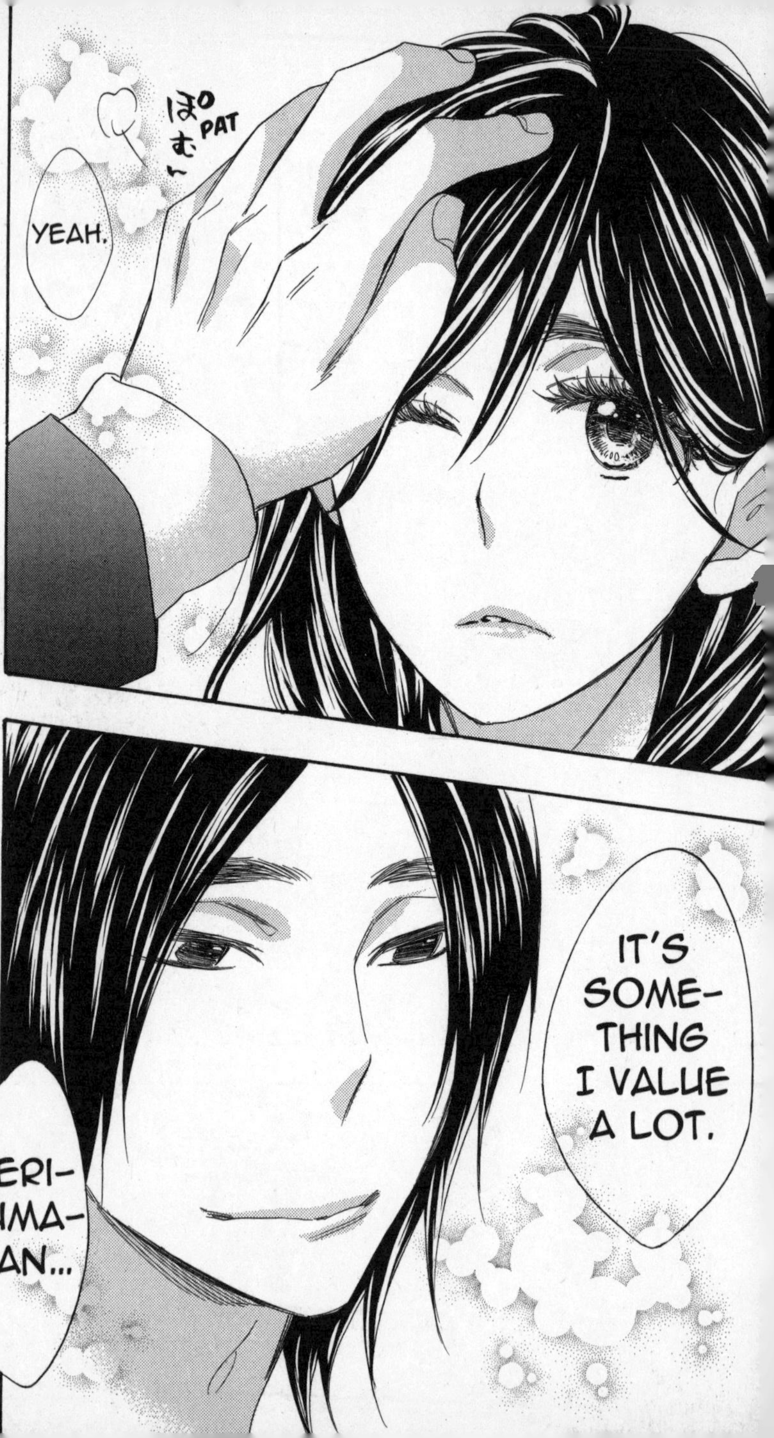
ぽむ〜 PAT
YEAH.
IT'S SOMETHING I VALUE A LOT.
SERI-NUMA-SAN...

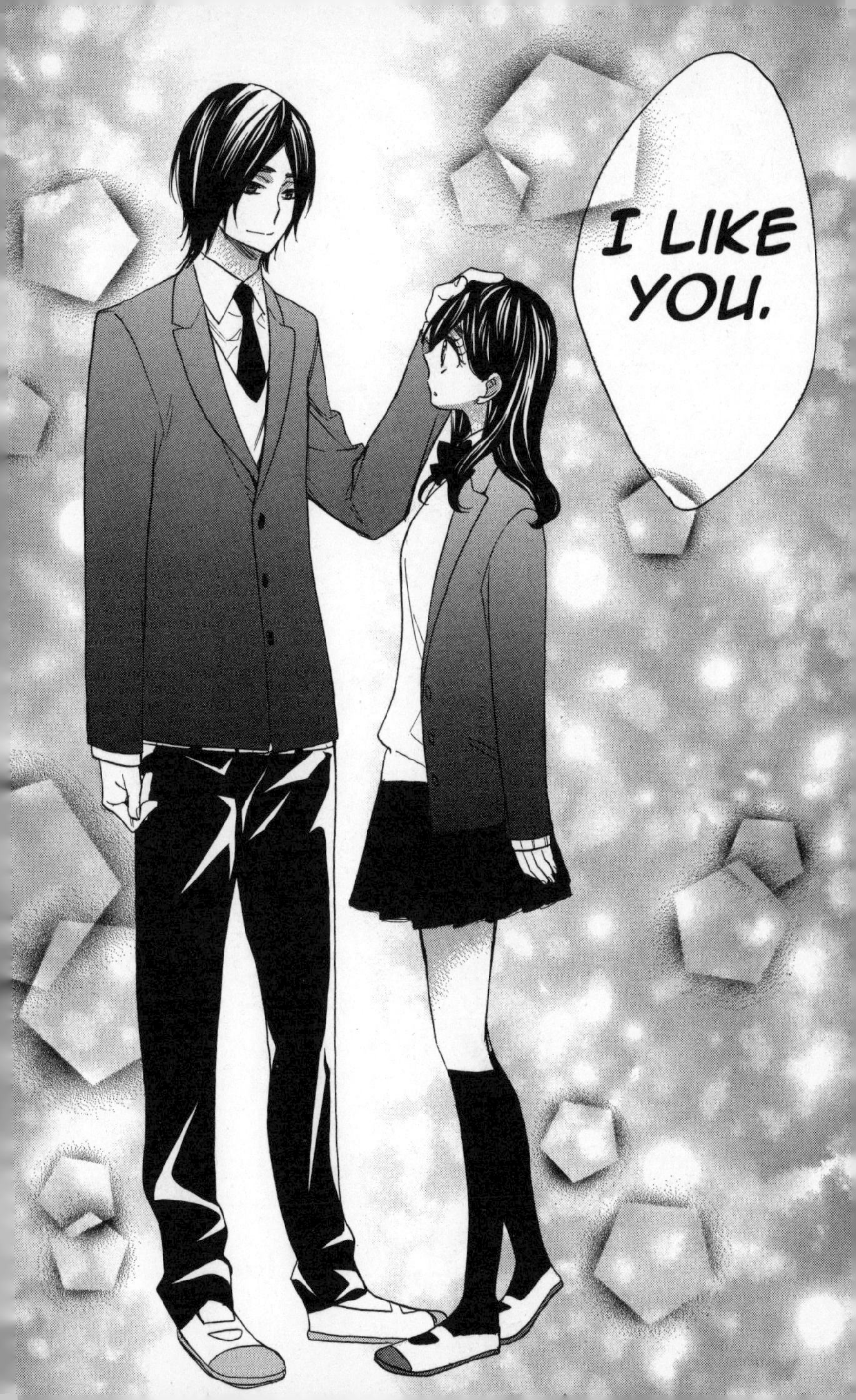
I LIKE YOU.

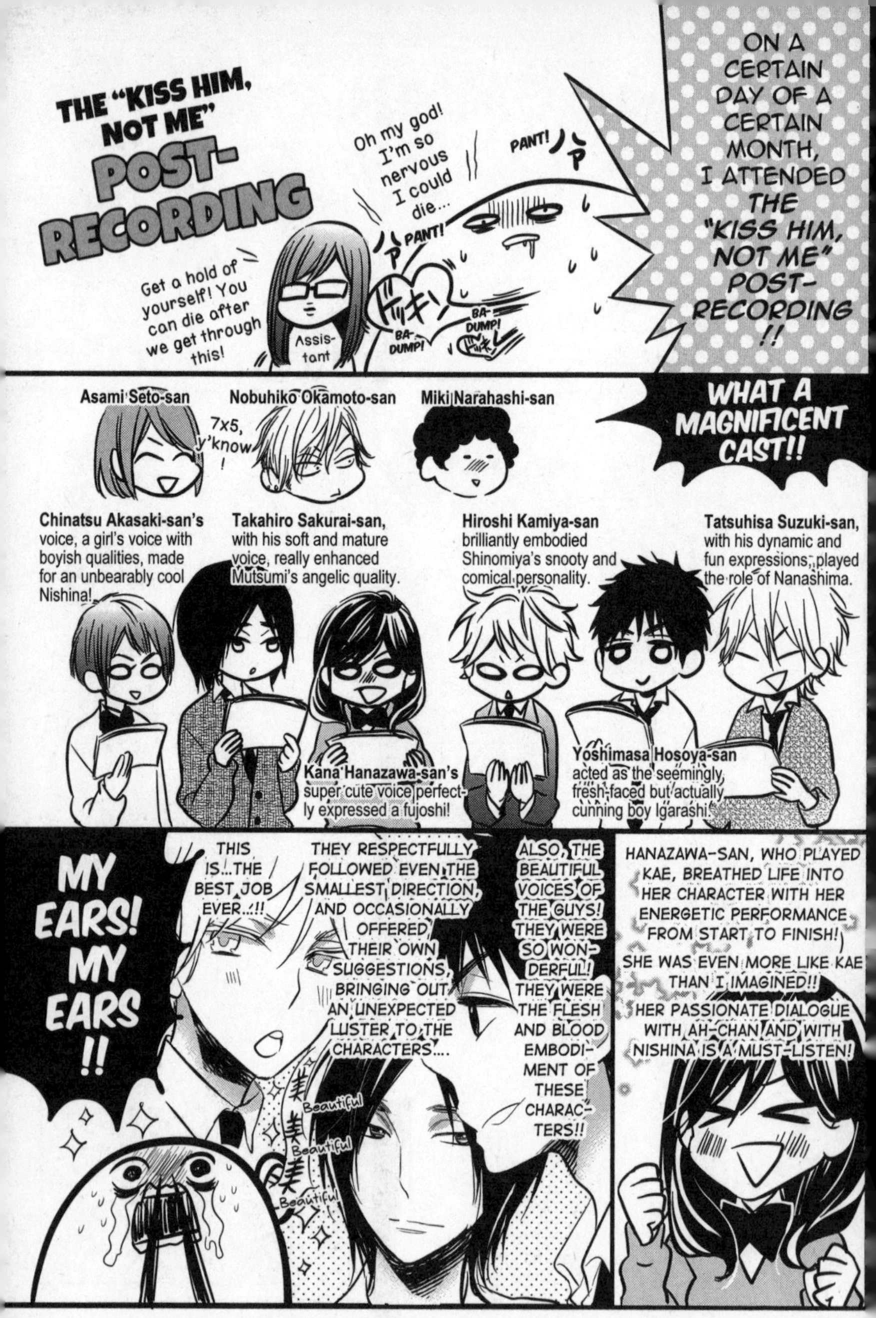
ON A CERTAIN DAY OF A CERTAIN MONTH, I ATTENDED THE "KISS HIM, NOT ME" POST-RECORDING!!
PANT!
Oh my god! I'm so nervous I could die...
PANT!
ドッキ!
BA-DUMP!
BA-DUMP!
Get a hold of yourself! You can die after we get through this!
Assistant
THE "KISS HIM, NOT ME" POST-RECORDING
WHAT A MAGNIFICENT CAST!!
Miki Narahashi-san
Nobuhiko Okamoto-san
7x5, y'know!
Asami Seto-san
Tatsuhisa Suzuki-san, with his dynamic and fun expressions, played the role of Nanashima.
Yoshimasa Hosoya-san acted as the seemingly fresh-faced but actually cunning boy Igarashi!
Hiroshi Kamiya-san brilliantly embodied Shinomiya's snooty and comical personality.
Kana Hanazawa-san's super cute voice perfectly expressed a fujoshi!
Takahiro Sakurai-san, with his soft and mature voice, really enhanced Mutsumi's angelic quality.
Chinatsu Akasaki-san's voice, a girl's voice with boyish qualities, made for an unbearably cool Nishina!
HANAZAWA-SAN, WHO PLAYED KAE, BREATHED LIFE INTO HER CHARACTER WITH HER ENERGETIC PERFORMANCE FROM START TO FINISH!
SHE WAS EVEN MORE LIKE KAE THAN I IMAGINED!!
HER PASSIONATE DIALOGUE WITH AH-CHAN AND WITH NISHINA IS A MUST-LISTEN!
ALSO, THE BEAUTIFUL VOICES OF THE GUYS! THEY WERE SO WONDERFUL! THEY WERE THE FLESH AND BLOOD EMBODIMENT OF THESE CHARACTERS!!
THEY RESPECTFULLY FOLLOWED EVEN THE SMALLEST DIRECTION, AND OCCASIONALLY OFFERED THEIR OWN SUGGESTIONS, BRINGING OUT AN UNEXPECTED LUSTER TO THE CHARACTERS....
THIS IS...THE BEST JOB EVER...!!!
Beautiful
Beautiful
Beautiful
MY EARS! MY EARS!!

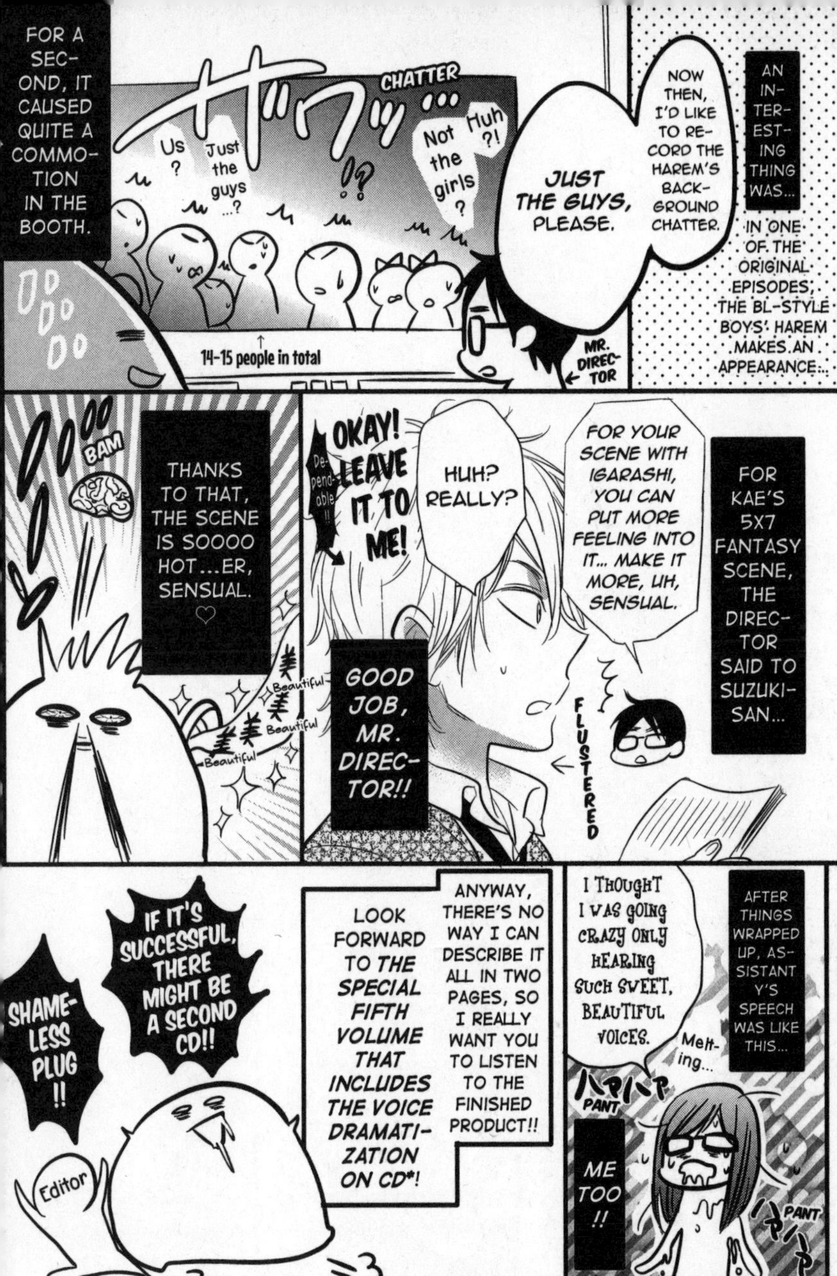
AN INTERESTING THING WAS...
IN ONE OF THE ORIGINAL EPISODES, THE BL-STYLE BOYS' HAREM MAKES AN APPEARANCE...
NOW THEN, I'D LIKE TO RECORD THE HAREM'S BACKGROUND CHATTER.
JUST THE GUYS, PLEASE.
MR. DIRECTOR
FOR A SECOND, IT CAUSED QUITE A COMMOTION IN THE BOOTH.
CHATTER
Huh?!
Not the girls?
Just the guys...?
Us?
14-15 people in total
FOR KAE'S 5X7 FANTASY SCENE, THE DIRECTOR SAID TO SUZUKI-SAN...
FOR YOUR SCENE WITH IGARASHI, YOU CAN PUT MORE FEELING INTO IT... MAKE IT MORE, UH, SENSUAL.
FLUSTERED
HUH? REALLY?
OKAY! LEAVE IT TO ME!
Dependable!!
GOOD JOB, MR. DIRECTOR!!
THANKS TO THAT, THE SCENE IS SOOOO HOT...ER, SENSUAL. ♡
BAM
Beautiful
Beautiful
Beautiful
AFTER THINGS WRAPPED UP, ASSISTANT Y'S SPEECH WAS LIKE THIS...
I THOUGHT I WAS GOING CRAZY ONLY HEARING SUCH SWEET, BEAUTIFUL VOICES.
Melting...
PANT
PANT
ME TOO!!
ANYWAY, THERE'S NO WAY I CAN DESCRIBE IT ALL IN TWO PAGES, SO I REALLY WANT YOU TO LISTEN TO THE FINISHED PRODUCT!!
LOOK FORWARD TO THE SPECIAL FIFTH VOLUME THAT INCLUDES THE VOICE DRAMATIZATION ON CD*!
IF IT'S SUCCESSFUL, THERE MIGHT BE A SECOND CD!!
SHAMELESS PLUG!!
Editor

*UNFORTUNATELY, THE DRAMATIZATION CD IS EXCLUSIVE TO THE JAPANESE VERSION OF *KISS HIM, NOT ME*.

This extra was originally published in the
ecember 2014 issue of Bessatsu Friend magazine.

TO BE CONTINUED
IN VOLUME 6 OF

KISS HIM,
NOT ME!

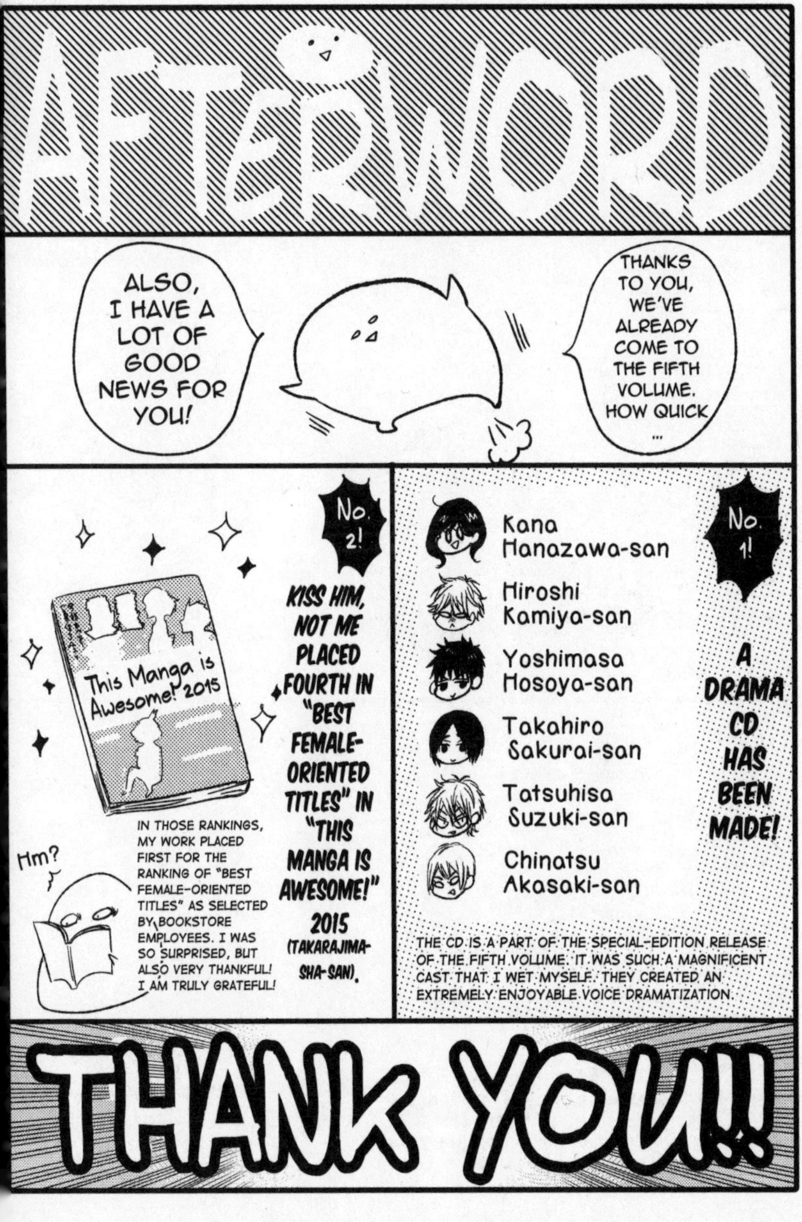
AFTERWORD
THANKS TO YOU, WE'VE ALREADY COME TO THE FIFTH VOLUME. HOW QUICK ...
ALSO, I HAVE A LOT OF GOOD NEWS FOR YOU!
No. 1!
A DRAMA CD HAS BEEN MADE!
Kana Hanazawa-san
Hiroshi Kamiya-san
Yoshimasa Hosoya-san
Takahiro Sakurai-san
Tatsuhisa Suzuki-san
Chinatsu Akasaki-san
THE CD IS A PART OF THE SPECIAL-EDITION RELEASE OF THE FIFTH VOLUME. IT WAS SUCH A MAGNIFICENT CAST THAT I WET MYSELF. THEY CREATED AN EXTREMELY ENJOYABLE VOICE DRAMATIZATION.
No. 2!
KISS HIM, NOT ME PLACED FOURTH IN "BEST FEMALE-ORIENTED TITLES" IN "THIS MANGA IS AWESOME!" 2015 (TAKARAJIMA-SHA-SAN).
This Manga is Awesome! 2015
Hm?
IN THOSE RANKINGS, MY WORK PLACED FIRST FOR THE RANKING OF "BEST FEMALE-ORIENTED TITLES" AS SELECTED BY BOOKSTORE EMPLOYEES. I WAS SO SURPRISED, BUT ALSO VERY THANKFUL! I AM TRULY GRATEFUL!
THANK YOU!!

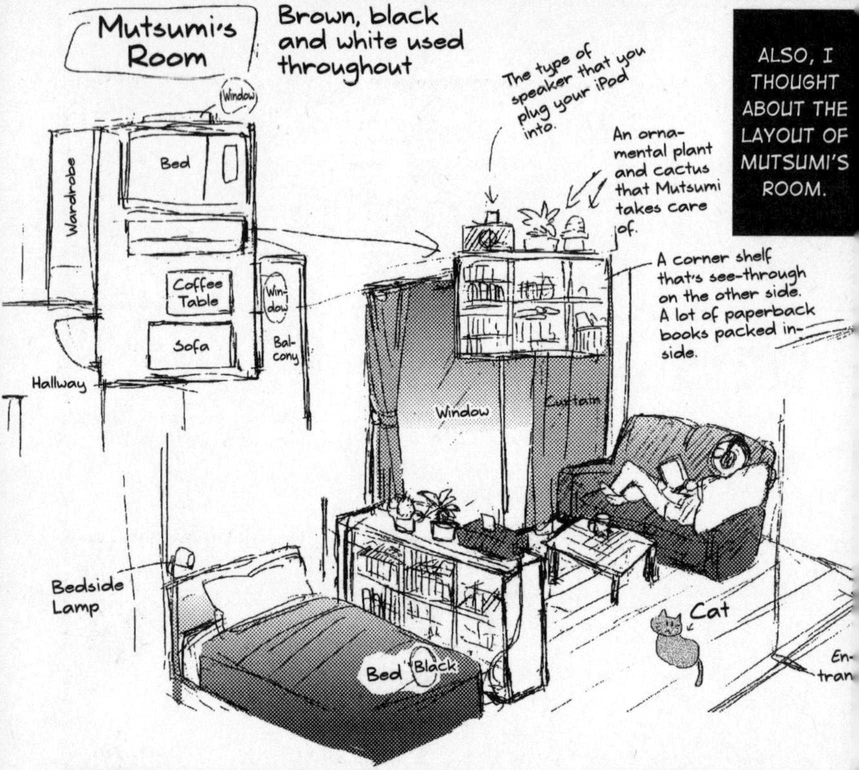
ALSO, I THOUGHT ABOUT THE LAYOUT OF MUTSUMI'S ROOM.
Mutsumi's Room
Brown, black and white used throughout
Window
Bed
Wardrobe
Coffee Table
Win-dow
Sofa
Bal-cony
Hallway
The type of speaker that you plug your iPod into.
An ornamental plant and cactus that Mutsumi takes care of.
A corner shelf that's see-through on the other side. A lot of paperback books packed inside.
Window
Curtain
Bedside Lamp
Cat
Bed
Black
En-tran

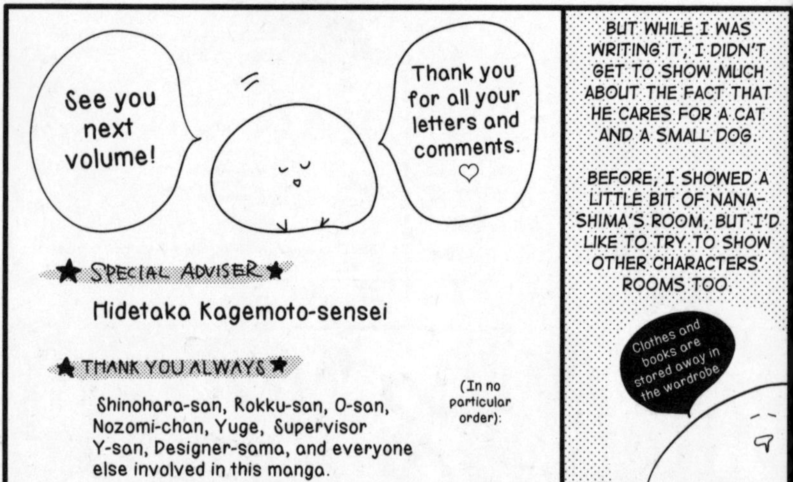
BUT WHILE I WAS WRITING IT, I DIDN'T GET TO SHOW MUCH ABOUT THE FACT THAT HE CARES FOR A CAT AND A SMALL DOG.
BEFORE, I SHOWED A LITTLE BIT OF NANA-SHIMA'S ROOM, BUT I'D LIKE TO TRY TO SHOW OTHER CHARACTERS' ROOMS TOO.
Clothes and books are stored away in the wardrobe.
Thank you for all your letters and comments. ♡
See you next volume!
★ SPECIAL ADVISER ★
Hidetaka Kagemoto-sensei
★ THANK YOU ALWAYS ★
(In no particular order):
Shinohara-san, Rokku-san, O-san, Nozomi-chan, Yuge, Supervisor Y-san, Designer-sama, and everyone else involved in this manga.

AUTHOR'S NOTE

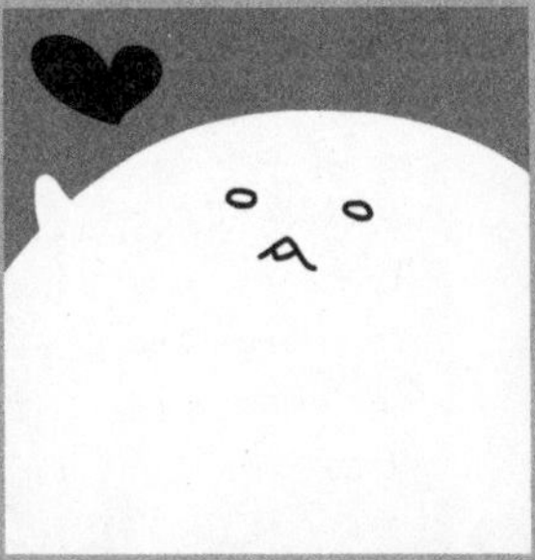

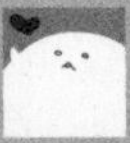

I SAT NEXT TO SOMEONE WHO WAS ABOUT 7 CM TALLER THAN ME AND I ENDED UP BEING ABOUT 10 CM TALLER THAN THEM WHEN SEATED.

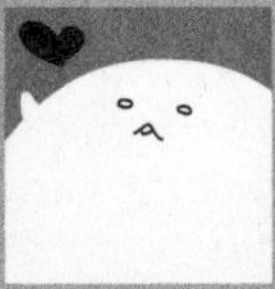

-JUNKO

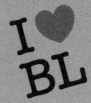

I ♥ BL

Translation Notes

Haniwa, daruma, and kabuto helmets, page 9

Here, Serinuma is talking about several traditional Japanese items located in the club-room. *Haniwa* are clay figures used from about 250 to 538 AD, and would typically be buried with the dead during funerals. *Daruma* are dolls modeled after the founder of the Zen sect of Buddhism, Bodhidharma. They are seen as symbols of good luck and perseverance. *Kabuto* helmets are ancient Japanese helmets that eventually became associated with samurai, and served as an important part of a Japanese warrior's equipment. They were usually comprised of several metal plates, custom-made, and known for their striking designs.

Heisei Year 23, page 39

While the Western calendar is primarily used in Japan, years are also often referred to by the era of the emperor who ruled at the time, followed by the number of years he has reigned. As Japan's current emperor, Emperor Akihito, began his reign in 1989, 2011 would be the 23rd year after that, making it Heisei 23.

Local collaboration, page 72

In Japan, products, but most often delicacies, based on seasons or specific locales, are much more prevalent than they are in America. Cities and towns will often promote themselves with food or items that can only be found in that area and companies will also participate by sponsoring special local-only products. Popular anime and manga also take advantage of such opportunities to produce limited-edition products and advertisements. For example, to commerate the fact that 300 million copies of the manga's bound volumes had been sold, popular series *One Piece* launched an advertisement campaign where they created newspaper ads with characters exclusive to each of the 47 Japanese prefectures. The gift for Kae is an exclusive figure—likely a special prize from a local event, which would make it even rarer than a typical limited-edition item.

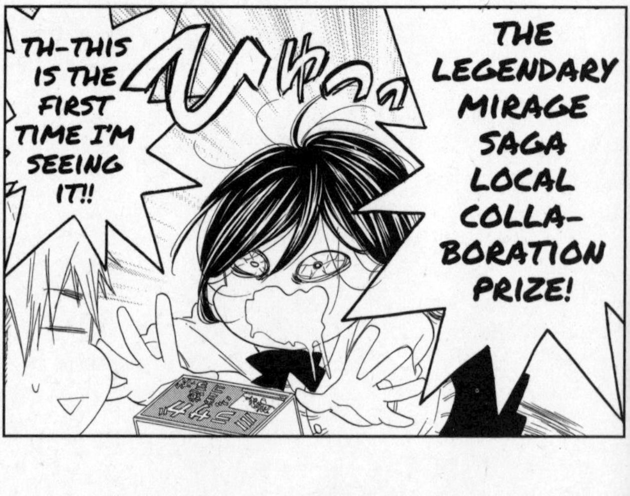
THE LEGENDARY MIRAGE SAGA LOCAL COLLA-BORATION PRIZE!
TH-THIS IS THE FIRST TIME I'M SEEING IT!!

Captain Shinomiya, page 89

Avid *Attack on Titan* readers will recognize the various references on this page, starting with Captain Levi, one of the characters from the series. As Nanashima pushes Shinomiya into action, he calls him "Captain Shinomiya," which prompts Shinomiya to adopt the salute given by soldiers in the Attack on Titan universe and recite a slightly modified version of protagonist Eren Yeager's famous line, "I'm gonna destroy them!!"

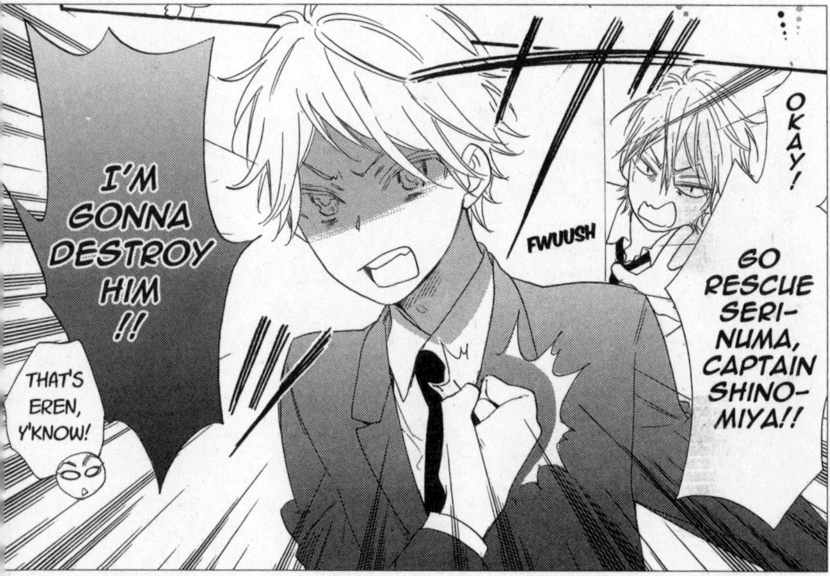
OKAY!
GO RESCUE SERI-NUMA, CAPTAIN SHINO-MIYA!!
FWUUSH
I'M GONNA DESTROY HIM !!
THAT'S EREN, Y'KNOW!

Shachihoko, page 109

Nagoya Castle is famous for its pair of golden statues, known as *shachihoko*. *Shachihoko* are mythical half-tiger, half-fish creatures modeled after killer whales, and can be found on the rooftops of many castles and temples in Japan. Known for their ability to unleash streams of water from their mouths, they were believed to be a charm to protect buildings from fire.

Prince of Badminton, Dan☆Puri, page 134

The names written on these items are references to two series popular among *fujoshi*, namely *Prince of Tennis* and *Uta no Prince-sama* (shortened to *UtaPri*).

War helmet, page 135

This is a replica of a famous helmet worn by Naoe Kanetsugu, a 16th-century samurai who was known for his sharp judgment. The helmet prominently features the character for "love" on its front side.

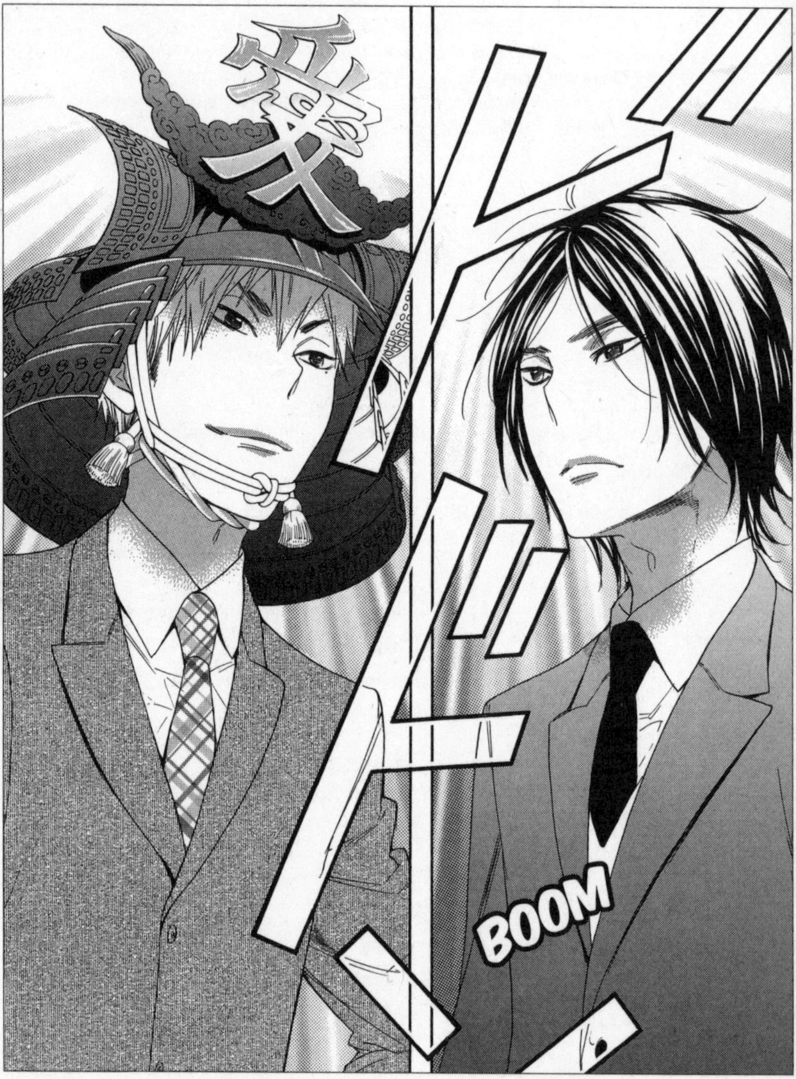
愛
BOOM

Kiss Him, Not Me volume 5 is a work of fiction. Names, characters, places, and incidents are the products of the author's imagination or are used fictitiously. Any resemblance to actual events, locales, or persons, living or dead, is entirely coincidental.

A Kodansha Comics Trade Paperback Original.

Published in the United States by Kodansha Comics, an imprint of Kodansha USA Publishing, LLC, New York.

Publication rights for this English edition arranged through Kodansha Ltd., Tokyo.

First published in Japan in 2015 by Kodansha Ltd., Tokyo, as *Watashi Ga Motete Dousunda* volume 5.

ISBN 978-1-63236-264-3

Printed in the United States of America.

www.kodanshacomics.com

9 8 7 6 5 4 3 2 1

Translation: David Rhie
Lettering: Hiroko Mizuno
Editing: Ajani Oloye
Kodansha Comics Edition Cover Design: Phil Balsman